P9-DBV-648

CHILDREN IN THE BIBLE SCHOOL

CHILDREN
IN THE
BIBLE SCHOOL

The *HOW* of Christian Education

by

LOIS E. LEBAR

Assistant Professor of Christian Education
Wheaton College

FLEMING H. REVELL COMPANY

WESTWOOD, N. J.

Westwood, New Jersey

Printed in the United States of America

1.13

Contents

List of Illustrations

List of Illustrations

For Teachers and Parents Who Use This Book

If there were a Bible teacher for each precious child in our land,
If that Bible teacher were duly qualified by human preparation and divine infilling,
If the power of the risen Saviour were operative in his life,
If the Word of Christ dwelt in him richly in all wisdom,
If he spent time each day praying for the individuals in his class,
If he worked for spiritual changes in the lives of the boys and girls,
If he made every minute of the class session count for eternity,
What would our communities be like?

If Christian parents realized that they are the child's first teachers,
If they realized that they are his most important teachers,
If they knew that his essential character is formed before he enters school,
If they diligently taught the Word of God in daily life situations,
If they helped the child develop inner controls from the beginning,
If the climate of the home were consistently spiritual and joyous,
If Christian precept and example went hand in hand,
What could we expect of our Christian young people?

Here are a few suggestions, teachers and parents, for making effective use of this book as a study guide either for groups in the classroom or for individuals at home.

1. *Take time for the questions at the beginning and end*

of each chapter. These questions are an integral part of the text, to help you relate the experiences of your own boys and girls to the Scriptural principles that are described. General principles are of no value unless you visualize what difference they should make in your teaching of your particular group. Your own Jimmy and Alice should be the focus of this study, but they can be only as you interpret what you read in terms of their needs and activities.

2. *As you read and teach, list all your own questions and problems* under the various topics outlined by the chapters of this book. The best approach to any study is the approach of actual needs. Read with these in mind, and discuss them in study groups or with your personal friends. Every reader will not be able to enjoy the give and take of the ideal small class, but even a mother in a home can invite another mother or two in for tea so that they may together discuss their problems.

3. *After your daily devotional Bible reading each morning* acquire the habit of reviewing that same Scripture portion to discover in it any inferences, direct or indirect, to the place of children and methods of working with them. To the seeking heart God's Word has much to say about ways of dealing with children. Many scattered verses suggest basic principles, such as I Corinthians 13:11; Proverbs 22:6; 29:15; 3:13; Deuteronomy 6:7; Isaiah 28:10.

Many narrative portions of Scripture also yield rich results for the teacher who is child-conscious. As an example of a story from the Old Testament, note what is said about the childhood of Samuel (I Sam. 1-3). Hannah, no doubt, observed diligently the laws of God regarding child training, since she had especially consecrated her son to God as a Nazarite. In keeping her covenant with the Lord, she was not overly zealous, but waited until he was weaned to take him to the temple. In bringing him a new coat each year, she did what she could, and trusted the rest to the Lord.

Don't you suppose that in the training of Samuel, Eli profited by the sad results of the early neglect of his own sons? In the temple young Samuel caught the spiritual atmosphere, and enjoyed physical and mental as well as spiritual activity. Like the Child Jesus, he grew in favor with God and with men. Though he early worshiped God in spirit and in truth, yet when the Lord spoke to him personally in preference to the old priest, he needed interpretation, and the bidding to go directly to God.

4. *Let practice accompany your theory.* This text should be of *some value* to you if you merely read it, of *more value* if you observe good teaching at the same time, and of *most value* if you are actually doing practice teaching. Of course no person should teach until he has a burden for the need and opportunity, and can visualize what he would like to do, but only through his own experience can he adequately analyze and evaluate theory.

5. *Keep a file of all kinds of materials that will be helpful in teaching children.* Children must see and do as well as hear. They need many types of activities and many illustrations from daily life. Teachers should excel in the number of sidelights they can throw on the truth, for if a child misses one aspect, another will meet his particular needs.

If you have an organized place for your materials, you are more likely to be on the alert to collect whatever is valuable, and you will be able to locate at once whatever you want for each occasion. If you hear a good plot for a story or a good illustration from a sermon, jot it down quickly before you forget the interesting details with their local color.

Most teachers even like to clip their magazines; for very few can keep them indexed up to date on cards, with the result that the magazines lie around without being of service. Save all kinds of pictures, large and small, colored and uncolored. Even teachers with the largest collections often want subjects they do not have. Moreover, don't forget to jot down sources for materials, and slip them in the proper place in your file—information regarding books, songs, flannelgraphs, etc. You may not need that material at the moment, nor have money to buy it, but later the data may save you much time.

The following are the subjects which most teachers find practical:

1. The Child—his characteristics and needs
2. Children's Activities—memorization, service activities, etc.
3. The Teacher—his qualifications and training
4. Parents—co-operation, visitation, etc.
5. Organization and Equipment—grading, literature, surroundings, etc.
6. Pictures and Maps—all kinds
7. Object Lessons—ideas and samples
8. Flannelgraph—figures and backgrounds
9. Stories—Bible, worship, character, service, nature, etc.
10. Songs—praise, prayer, Jesus, special days, etc.
11. Poems and Prayers—for children, and about children
12. Handwork—samples and principles of using
13. Missions—information and stories
14. Recreation—games and parties.

As more and more material is collected, these original subjects will need to be subdivided, and whole files made of some, like stories and pictures. When teachers find materials outside their class's age range, they may exchange them with teachers of other departments in the local church.

Acknowledgment is made to Wheaton College for the privilege of submitting this text as a thesis for graduate credit in the Christian Education department. The writer is also grateful for the contributions made by her sister Mary, who wrote Chapters III and XI, and who assisted in innumerable other ways.

A. THE SETTING FOR TEACHING

CHAPTER I

WHY BRING THE GOSPEL TO CHILDREN?

BEFORE YOU READ THIS CHAPTER

1. Did you come to know the Lord in your childhood, youth or adulthood? What difference has that fact made in the past? What difference is it likely to make in your future life? What difference has it made in persons of your acquaintance?
2. What temptations annoy you as a young person or adult? How far back in your life do the roots of these temptations go?
3. At what age should a child's spiritual training be started?

> —though the church is [ever] busy
> Through all the live-long days,
> In stately service lifting
> Her voice of grown-up praise,
> If childhood is neglected,
> And left to stray a-wild,
> Can the church expect the blessing
> Of Him who loves the child?

When Christ Jesus was on earth, He set a little child in the midst of His teaching and preaching (Matt. 18:2). He said to His disciples, "Verily I say unto you, Except ye be converted, and become as little children, ye shall not enter into the kingdom of heaven" (Matt. 18:3). It was as a lowly Babe that God sent into our world His own Son, the Saviour who was the great final revelation of Himself. As the Child Jesus grew "in wisdom and stature, and in favour with God and man" (Luke 2:52), He set the pattern for the growth of the children of all time.

The Creator of heaven and earth has a unique place in His plans for the young of the race. When the church of Christ is ready to follow her Lord and put a child in the midst of her activities, the whole life of that child will be redeemed and the future of the church will be assured.

1. *The Bible clearly teaches that Christ Jesus calls the children to Himself.* All three Synoptic Gospels record Jesus' invitation, "*Let* the little children come unto me, and forbid them not" (Matt. 19:13-15; Mark 10:13-16; Luke 18:15-17). This statement is a contrast to the command which the man who prepared the great supper gave to his servant, "Go out into the highways and hedges, and *compel* them to come in" (Luke 14:23). Whereas many adults must be *compelled* to come to Christ, the children are eager to come if only we adults get out of their way and *let* them come. Much more readily than adults, children feel the need of the Saviour, and gladly come when they hear that He is near, if only parents and teachers are willing to take the time to lead them gently to Him.

Through the ages the church all too often has forbidden the children to come. Like the disciples of old with the best of intentions, thinking they were pleasing Jesus, the church has pushed the children away, because, of course, Jesus was very busy with adults. Students of Scripture today should feel His rebuke if they hinder the children. One of the advantages of the present age is that the church is being forced to acknowledge that a child can truly experience the birth from above, and can begin at once to build on that foundation a sturdy Christian character.

Matthew 18:6 uses very strong language in regard to our treatment of the younger generation. The approach in this scene is the use of a child as an object lesson to teach the disciples humility, but from the need of the disciples Jesus turns in love to the need of the child before them. "Whoso shall offend one of these little ones which believe in me, it were better for him that a millstone were hanged about his neck, and that he were drowned in the depth of the sea." Why should such an awful warning be given, except that it has been the sin of the church to cause believing children to stumble?

The Good Shepherd came to seek and to save the frisky, frolicking lambs that go astray as well as the independent, mature sheep. Since children are born with sinful, Adamic natures, they too need the atonement that Christ came to provide. Such is heaven's concern for children that there their angels always behold the face of the Father (Matt. 18:10).

2. *The most favorable soil for sowing the seed of the Word is the plastic heart of a child.* In Christ's parable of the sower (Matt. 13:1-23) the dry, stony ground which prevents the seed from taking root is a picture of the hearts of most adults, who are increasingly worldly, skeptical, and materialistic. Modern society is interested in becoming smart and sophisticated, not in humbling itself to become childlike—the only attitude acceptable for the kingdom of God.

When the Word is given to adults, moreover, it falls on thorny ground; what is there already—the cares and riches and pleasures of this life—choke the truth. Conceptions so foreign to the old nature penetrate with difficulty into consciousness.

It is easy and joyous work to plow the heart of a child to make furrows as repositories for the seed. Children have never rejected the Saviour's love. They need not turn about face, and learn to love the things they once hated, and hate the things they once loved. The world is not yet so real to them that the spiritual is unreal.

A seven-year-old girl from a worldly home illustrated the reality of heavenly things one day in vacation school when the group was learning Psalm 107:21. One child after another showed by simple gestures and actions why he wished to praise the Lord that morning. A boy made a large circle above his head to represent the sun; another showed the rain falling downward, etc. The other pupils guessed what they were trying to portray, and then together repeated the verse, "O that men would praise the Lord for his goodness, and for his wonderful works to the children of men!"

When Margaret stood to show why she wanted to praise the Lord, she raised her arms and put her fingertips together to form the shape of a roof. The children guessed that she was making a house, a church, a temple, and a dog house, but each time Margaret shook her head, "No." They couldn't think what else she meant. Finally she gave them a cue—it was part of her favorite Bible verses. She had been learning the first verses of John 14, and to her the heavenly mansions were more real than earthly dwellings.

Children are "yearning to be learning anything at all," and they will learn the truth of God from anyone who cares enough to take time to teach them, or they will learn sin through neglect. Teachers who go out after them are thrilled with "children's faces looking up, holding wonder like a cup." Seed sown in the heart of a child brings forth fruit, not thirtyfold, nor sixtyfold, but one hundredfold.

"An Angel paused in his downward flight
With a seed of love and truth and light,

And said, 'Oh, where can this seed be sown
Where 'twill yield most fruit when fully grown?
To whom can this precious seed be given
That it will bear most fruit for earth and heaven?'
The Saviour heard and said, as He smiled,
'Place it at once in the heart of a child.' "

3. *Early childhood's natural faith and dependency are soon outgrown.* Said the prophet of old to his king, "As thy servant was busy here and there, he [my charge] was gone" (I Kings 20:40). Likewise, parents and teachers must often say regretfully to their King, "As Thy servant was busy here and there, my charge, the child, was gone."

Faith is natural to a child, for complete physical dependence is accompanied by absolute emotional confidence. Faith is unnatural to one as soon as he has learned to rely largely on himself and not wholly on others for the supplying of his needs. Yet the whole structure of Christian experience rests on the capacity to believe. A person is saved, not by the ability to repeat a certain number of Bible verses, but by the grasp with which he holds eternal truth, be it only a few verses. Just as children clutch firmly the hand of one who has demonstrated love and understanding, and yield themselves entirely to that person's care, so they yield themselves wholly to the Saviour.

However, children often give evidence of deep spiritual insight, for in the spiritual realm knowing is incumbent on willingness to do (John 7:17). They do not wonder at the simplicity of the gospel and stumble because it is a gift to be received rather than a reward to be earned. They are accustomed to receiving freely from those who love them. They have not yet learned to merit their gifts. The Lord Jesus prayed, "I thank thee, O Father, Lord of heaven and earth, that thou hast hid these things from the wise and prudent, and hast revealed them unto babes" (Luke 10:21).

There is no question about the doctrine of six-year-old Tommy when he expresses in his own words, "Jesus never wasn't, and He's always going to be." When hundreds of boys and girls were asked, "What is the most wonderful thing you can think of?" most of them gave answers which referred to spiritual things. They said in effect, "The Lord, salvation, not sinning, the Bible, heaven, going to church, or worshiping God." One specific answer was, "When my brother took a boy into the bedroom and told him that Jesus can take away his sins, and the boy fell on his knees and asked the Lord to come into his heart, and he really meant it." Others answered more briefly, such as, "That we can be saved and have Jesus for ours."

Several figures illustrating children's natural faith suggest themselves. Childhood is like dawn, the most beautiful time of the day, but so fleeting. The morning of youth is the time when the Sun of Righteousness shines on the soul with the most kindly warmth, the accepted time when the Lord most manifestly works. Though a musical melody may have infinite variations of harmony on base and treble clefs, even a child can appreciate and sing the simple tune. He can enjoy both the high sublime divine notes and the low earthly ones.

Childhood is such a miraculous age that the Biblical miracles present no problem for children—all of life is full of strange, new events which never before happened to them. They have no trouble visualizing Elijah's return to heaven in a chariot of fire, for they have stood on the steps of an escalator and have been delighted with their wonderful ascent to the next floor of a department store.

God has given every person a point of contact with Himself, a meeting place—his conscience. It is the remains of God's image in man, the guardian of God's honor amid the ruin of the fall. Conscience may be compared to the window of a room, through which the light of heaven shines into it. On the walls of that chamber is written the law of God. Even in unbelieving adults it is partly legible, though sadly darkened and defaced. Children come into the world fresh from their Creator with their conscience aiding them in discernment between right and wrong, with a feeling for Someone above and beyond themselves, an almighty God to whom they are responsible. But very soon the Adamic taint is strengthened by actual sin, which stains and defiles the conscience. The window to heaven grows darker and darker, until the light hardly shines through at all, until conscience is to a large extent blinded and without feeling.[1]

As self-consciousness develops, spiritual consciousness recedes. The adolescent glories in a new sense of strength and mastery. If he has been saved in childhood, he will spend his youthful vigor for Christ and not for himself. If he has been saved, his questions and doubts will prove helpful, for Bible proofs will ground him and build him up in the most holy faith. If he has not been saved, these years of storm and stress may prove disastrous. The path to God grows longer and steeper every year past childhood.

4. *Habits of the first seven years are indelibly established.* Educators concur with the Bible that an individual's essential character is formed very early. God says, "Train up a child in the way he should go; and when he is old, he will not depart from it" (Prov. 22:6). If a child does depart from his early teaching, the conclusion must be that he may have been *told* a great deal, but he may not have been *trained* to feel and do according to the truth.

The Roman Catholics have reasons for saying, "Give me a child until he is seven, and I don't care what you do with him." The German National Socialist regime said, "Give me a child of six to educate and he will belong to me for life."[2]

A child first makes his habits, then his habits turn about and make him. Nursery thinking lies at the back of much adult thinking. Many problems in adult life can be explained only by unfortunate occurrences which date far back in childhood.

Formerly the Junior and Junior High departments of the Bible school were considered the ages at which children should decide for Christ. But the many problems that arose with these ages brought the church face to face with the only remedy—begin earlier. The teacher who patiently sows the seed in the Beginners' department may not see the blossom burst into bloom in regeneration till a Primary teacher reaps the harvest, but she may have played a more important part in shaping that life than the Primary teacher. Teachers cannot afford to be weary in well-doing during the habit-forming years.

5. *Less time and effort are necessary to win many children to Christ than one adult.* This is the testimony of Christian workers who know children as well as the Lord and His Word. If the Christian church truly wishes to redeem the time before the Lord returns, she will send many workers where the children are to gather them in. Most of them are not as yet swept into the hurried, feverish, complex activities that absorb their parents. Most of them don't know what to do in all their free play hours.

Will teachers wait until gross sins of adults must be cured, when they might have been prevented? Right formation rather than reformation is the teacher's watchword. The wisdom of economy dictates that the church shall save *from* sin, not *out of* sin—shall use prevention rather than cure.

6. *Children have their whole lives ahead of them for service.* They comprise the church and the leaders of tomorrow.

Returning to his friend's home after conducting meetings in a town in England, D. L. Moody was asked by his host, "How many were converted tonight in the meeting?"

"Two and a half," replied Moody.

"What do you mean?" asked his friend. "Were there two adults and a child?"

"No," said the evangelist, "it was two children and an adult. The children have given their lives to Christ in their youth, while the adult has come with half of his life."

Just as the shoe dealer who led Moody to the Lord will go down in history for that one thing, so many of this generation will be remembered because they led to Christ some boy or girl who will be used mightily by the Spirit of God. One never knows when he has a potential Moody or Hitler in his class.

> Suppose that Paul had been converted at seventy instead of twenty-five. There would have been no Paul in history. There was a Matthew Henry because he was converted at eleven and not at seventy; a Dr. Watts because he was converted at nine and not at sixty; a Jonathan Edwards because he was converted at eight and not eighty; a Richard Baxter because he was converted at six and not at sixty. (Author Unknown.)

Gipsy Smith said, "Save a man and you save a unit; save a boy and you save a multiplication table." There is no larger soul value in the world than children. To impress the boys and girls themselves with the value of giving their whole lives to Jesus, we sometimes ask them if they would keep an apple and not eat it until it has rotted, or an ice-cream cone until it melts, or a new pair of shoes until they are too small, or an automobile until it has rusted.

7. *Children open many homes for personal work.* As part of its extension program a small church enrolled one hundred babies in the Cradle Roll. This provided a powerful entering wedge into each home represented. The mothers were won as they entrusted their darlings to the Nursery teacher, and felt the love of Christ manifested to them.

Though many youths are hardened toward the gospel during adolescence, the first baby who comes into the home of a young couple once again touches chords of tenderness and spirituality. If this second opportunity is neglected, the parents may be lost forever.

Visiting children's homes furnishes a natural approach for conversation about spiritual things. A parent may send his child to Sunday School for the same reason he sends him to dancing class—to round out his education, but when the child has had a vision of Christ, he will help the teacher lift up before his household the crucified and risen Saviour. Only as parents and teachers work together can the enemies of the soul of a child be kept at a distance.

> Sir George Adam Smith in Palestine once saw a shepherd carrying a lamb. He asked if it were tired, or if its leg were broken. "Nothing of the kind," replied the shepherd. Pointing to an old sheep trotting gravely by his side, he said, "That is the mother, and she has a strange habit of wandering. The only way I can keep her with the flock is by taking her lamb and carrying it."

Lloyd George, on his return to England from his first visit to the United States, was asked his outstanding impression of this country. He answered, "The remarkable way in which the parents obey the children." Christians bewail the fact that the children sit on the throne in so many homes. Yet if the children can be reached, the door is opened to the parents also.

The following testimony of Mrs. D. M. Campbell, of the China Inland Mission in Kiangsi, voices the attitude of many missionaries:

> A year and a half ago I opened a kindergarten. It was a struggle for pupils, but I felt that the surest way into the

homes is through little children. When we opened, there were ten enrolled, but only three or four came every day. Sometimes it was hard to see whether it was worth while or not, but I knew in my heart that it was. The people of the church said it couldn't be done in this place, but I felt sure God wanted me to do so, therefore continued.

This year we opened with more than twenty-six on the roll, with an average of at least twenty every day! Now when I go into town there is always a stream of kiddies to follow; the mothers come out and ask me in for tea, and then the door is opened for the message.

8. *A teacher's own life is matured as he sees himself as God's child learning His higher ways.* The disciples of old were amazed to discover not only that Christ gave children preference over adults, but also that adults had something to learn from children. A young teacher recently remarked, "God let me have a Sunday School class not because I know so much, but because I need to learn so much." And another, "Outside the Word itself, no other single factor has helped me grow spiritually as has work with children."

God desires for us as His children all that we desire for the boys and girls we teach, only infinitely more. He expects of us all that we expect of them, and more. Even after we explain to children the reason for certain commands, they cannot comprehend all that is involved; God expects us to obey implicitly although we may not always understand the reason why. How willfully children act to gain some momentary pleasure without considering future implications! God teaches His older children not to sacrifice the permanent on the altar of the immediate. He disciplines us, and we should discipline the children, but, as He does, always in love.

In your mind single out the child in your class who is most

tractable, most responsive, most eager to learn. Are you as God's child *that* tractable, *that* responsive, *that* eager to learn?

A noted doctor examined from all angles the famous statue of Christ at Johns Hopkins, and was frankly disappointed. As he turned to walk away, a little girl said to him, "Mister, you didn't look at it right." "How should I have looked at it?" asked the man. "I will show you," she replied. Kneeling at the foot of the statue, she looked up into the face. In that humble position, so natural to the child, even the great man would be in an attitude to see Jesus and to accept Him as Saviour and Lord.

AFTER YOU HAVE READ THIS CHAPTER

1. Have you heard any objections to bringing the gospel to children and inviting them to accept Christ? Are you at present able to answer these objections?
2. In what ways do the disciples of Christ today hinder the children from coming to Him? (Such as lack of trained and consecrated teachers.)
3. Make a list of ways in which it is easy for an adult to limit the faith of a child.
4. How do the similar verses of Matthew 18:11 and Luke 19:10 differ? In the light of the context, how can you account for the difference?
5. Paraphrase Christ's parable of the sower in terms of the good soil of a receptive child and the poor soil of a hardened adult.

CHAPTER II

THE TEACHER FOR CHILDREN

BEFORE YOU READ THIS CHAPTER

1. Recall the teacher who has meant the most to you. Analyze his strong points and his influence on you. Did he have any weak points?
2. Are teachers "born" or "made"? What advice would you give to the teacher who claimed to be a born teacher? To one who claimed he was not a born teacher?
3. Do you have any real friends among boys and girls? Of what value is that friendship to you? Of what value to them?
4. Do you think it requires more patience to teach a child or an older person? Why?
5. Do you agree with the statement, "You will never know too much to teach children a little"? Why, or why not?

A Sunday School teacher planned her week's work so that she could often walk past the near-by elementary school building at the hour in the afternoon when the children were being dismissed. In a casual, friendly way she usually got into conversation with one or more of the boys and girls—with those of her own class, as well as with those who did not go to Bible school.

One afternoon she finally found the propitious time to talk with a bashful child whom she had watched for weeks. She showed the child a picture card of Jesus, and talked about the Saviour. She asked her if she went to any Sunday School.

The girl said, "Nope." The teacher asked her if she wouldn't like to come and hear more about Jesus. The child answered, "Nope." The teacher went on to tell about the songs the children sang. She sang one of their favorites, but the child shook her head. The teacher then described other activities and interesting things connected with Bible school. But the girl still said, "Nope."

With a prayer to the Lover of little children, the teacher was about to turn away disappointed, when the child suddenly tugged at her coat and asked, "Will *you* be there?"

You yourself, teacher, are the voice through whom God speaks the name of a child as He spoke the name of Samuel long ago; and the day will come when the child will recognize the voice as the Lord's, and will answer, "Speak, for thy servant heareth." It is your hand holding the child's which leads him gently in the paths of righteousness, until he recognizes that over your hand is the hand of Christ, which was wounded for him.

Christ gave to the church for its edification some to be apostles, some prophets, some evangelists, and some, pastors and teachers (Eph. 4:11). *To some He gave teachers.*

The eloquent Chrysostom said, "Higher than every painter, higher than every sculptor, and than all other artists, do I regard him who is skilled in the art of forming the soul life of children."

The Lord gives some the ability of working with Him to fashion from crude human nature staunch Christian characters who will teach others also, and thereby shine as the brightness of the firmament forever (Dan. 12:3). With what other talent does this compare? Lifeless pictures on canvas compared with a child's living faith, cold gray marble statues compared with a hero of the cross, evanescent melodies compared with the prayer of a believing heart, idealistic poems compared with the saint who embodies the words in his daily walk!

With such an exalted opportunity, O teacher of children, what are your qualifications?

1. *Represent Christ aright*. No thought is more humbling than that children cannot conceive of love or sacrifice greater than they see in their teachers. At best they have to stretch their thoughts to apprehend God, and naturally think of Him in terms of the most wonderful human person they have ever known, only far superior. If they love not the teacher whom they have seen, how can they love God whom they have not seen (see I John 4:20)? How can they think of One altogether lovely if the teacher does not adorn the doctrine of Christ and make herself or himself as attractive as possible with the inner ornament of a meek and quiet spirit (I Pet. 3:4)?

You are fit to be a Bible teacher if you know God's Word, and can look it, and talk it, and act it, and love it, and are willing to sacrifice for it.

Teachers have distinct advantages over parents, the latter being connected in the children's minds with the mundane routine of eating and sleeping and cleaning, while Bible teachers are associated with the holy things of God, with the Lord's day and Sunday clothes, with God's house and its worshipful atmosphere, with God's Book representing the highest authority.

A mother one day told the teacher of her young son, "John was playing on the floor this afternoon, when all at once he stopped and watched me and then said, 'Mamma, I wish you were as much like Jesus as my teacher is.' "[3]

Parents, however, may leave more lasting impressions on the child than teachers, since they are with them more than one hundred hours a week instead of one hour, and their lives are inextricably interwoven. An older child recalled, "I always had a feeling that Jesus and God were such particular friends of Mother."

2. *Remember that force of example is stronger than precept.* "The unconscious influence of any person is greater than the conscious." How can teachers assure children that the Lord is concerned about every part of their lives, knowing even the number of hairs on their heads, if the teachers themselves stay out late Saturday night, sleep late, and arrive late on Sunday morning? Children possess that rare gift of penetration which enables them to discern the heart despite any kind of mask on the outside. From their earliest days they learn to read smiles and frowns and postures long before they comprehend words. Certainty of firm convictions and practices rings out in looks, tones, and mannerisms.

A child who attended a dead, formal church with her family liked also to go after that session to a warm, orthodox Sunday School. A casual comment regarding the contrast between the two churches was most discerning. She noted, "My sister teaches in that church, and she swears. They just *talk* about things over there."

Said Archbishop Tillotson, "To give children good instruction and a bad example is but beckoning to them with the head to show them the way to heaven, while we take them by the hand and lead them in the way to hell."

Mrs. Stella Daleburn's group of Beginners were talking one Sunday about heaven. She told them that it was wonderful and not sad to die if one loved Jesus. Three weeks later this teacher's own little daughter went to be with the Lord. The Beginners knew the child and had prayed for her when she was sick.

The other teachers in the department were amazed to hear

that Mrs. Daleburn intended to teach Sunday School as usual the next Sunday. That day heaven was much more real to the Beginners than it had been previously. Said one boy to his father when he reached home, "Mrs. Daleburn told us all about her little girl in heaven. And she even smiled when she told us!"

No wonder the orphans in George Mueller's home had a clear, unmistakable vision of their heavenly Father after seeing in that man of faith such a daily portrayal of power and love. No wonder little Abbie (Sister Abigail) who frequently visited the orphanage grew to be such a mighty woman of faith. Early one morning little Abbie saw Mr. Mueller going past her house, and asked if she might go with him to see the orphans eat breakfast. Although Mr. Mueller did not know where food for his children was coming from, he gladly took Abbie along to see how a faithful Father would supply. Would *we* have had *that* faith, to take a child with us, when no prospects were in sight? After grace had been said over empty bowls, a knock at the door revealed a milkman whose wagon had broken down, and whose milk would sour before it reached its destination. As the milk was being poured into cups, a second tap at the door admitted a baker, whom God had wakened in the night and instructed to make a fresh batch of bread for the orphans.

3. *Develop a calm, confident, radiant, outgoing, humble disposition.* One dear woman who loved children, who had taken teacher training courses and longed to teach, humbly protested when she was asked to take a class because she said she lacked the essential personality traits enumerated in the teacher's manual. That is a wholesome, natural response, for children deserve the best, and all of us fall short of what we strive to be. Yet the wise superintendent gave that teacher a class, advising that since she had love and training, actual teaching was the quickest way to develop the qualities she sought.

The great teacher never ceases to be a humble learner. "Thou which teachest another, teachest thou not thyself" (Rom. 2:21)? Unless a teacher is himself continually growing, he will serve his class cold spiritual food. But if the food is always served hot and tasty, the pupils will return for more with keen appetites.

If children ever mention a color which they like to see a teacher wear, it is usually red. This is indicative of the type of personality they prefer under the clothing. Why should a Bible teacher be drab and not sparkling, gray when he might be colorful, burdened when he should be buoyant? Christ Jesus was burdened about many things and may have been talking very seriously with the disciples on that day of old when the mothers brought their children to Him. But we cannot think of Him looking sorrowful in their presence.

Childhood is a period of sincerity and joyousness. Its vitality requires corresponding enthusiasm and courage on the part of leaders. A playful spirit of humor in the teacher shows children that she is one of them and has faith in them. Its delicate, light touch often relieves tensions and offsets mistakes in trying situations.

The personal qualities of a teacher might be multiplied endlessly. Some of the characteristics which the children themselves mention are: one who is jolly, one who laughs, does not lose her temper, never hollers at us, not crabby, not cross, friendly, a good sport, gives us another chance when bad, gets the point, and talks plainly. One boy said, "I like a teacher with a kind spirit like Jesus." A girl said, "One who loves and understands children." Socrates once sent a boy home, saying, "I can teach him nothing. He does not love me."

The teacher should be tactful, impartial, co-operative, resourceful, faithful, well adjusted, and cheerful. A spirit of diligence and perseverance cannot be expected from the pupils unless they see it continually demonstrated by the teacher. The pupils should feel that their teacher would rather teach them than do anything else in the world.

4. *Give yourself wholly to prayer, preparation, and leadership.* "This sacred work demands not lukewarm, selfish, slack souls, but hearts more finely tempered than steel, wills purer and harder than the diamond," said Père Didon. It is given to teachers to travail in soul until Christ be formed in their pupils (Gal. 4:19). In the figure of Oswald Chambers, we must be willing to be "broken bread and poured out wine" until the children can take spiritual nourishment for themselves.

Any curriculum is 90 per cent teacher. No program can rise above the level of its leaders. A good teacher will transform a poor curriculum, a poor teacher will spoil a good one. "To my pupils a heart of love, to my God a heart of flame, to myself a heart of steel." God allows children to try our patience to see if our love is genuine, our preparation to see if it is thorough, our methods to see if they can be trusted.

A Primary department which met during the second hour of the morning once lacked teachers so badly that one of the teachers from the Senior department volunteered to teach Primaries after her regular class during the first hour. Though the class which she was given was considered one of the easiest in the department, she seemed to have very little control over the girls. At the end of the hour they were crawling under the table and disturbing others. The teacher could not understand why, for, "of course," she told the Primary superintendent, "I know the Bible very well."

The superintendent suggested that she try spending as much time on her Primary lesson as she did on her Senior lesson; that she study the girls, their needs and interests, and the best methods of teaching that age.

The next week those girls were fascinated with their class

session, for the teacher was teaching *them* rather than discharging a given Bible portion. The teacher too went home thrilled with the response.

Teaching can be a dutiful chore, or it can be an exciting adventure. What it means to a person depends on how much *he* is willing to put into it. Teaching is an art and a science and a philosophy to those who are ready to pay the price of the artist and the scientist and the philosopher, but hours of research and experiment and devotion are required.

Only when a teacher knows what may naturally be expected of children on the human plane can he contrast the working of God on the supernatural level. Only when he has made a study of his pupils will he know the joy of analyzing their progress. Only when he studies the effective methods of teaching will he appreciate every response the pupils make and be able to predict what measures should next be taken. When he knows what he is doing and why, he will be able to lead with a sure step and a firm tread. Each life will then become a great experiment in which he and the Supreme Teacher join hands to shape a destiny for all eternity.

5. *"Enjoy the very tone and temper of childhood in close comradeship."* For an adult to be *childish* is shameful, but to be *childlike* is admirable. One child expressed her fondness for a teacher by calling her a "girl—woman." Another was heard to whisper to her playmate as her teacher passed them on the street, "She isn't really a teacher. She's just a girl grown up."

Is more patience required to teach children than older pupils? Those reply "No" who feel a kinship with young life. Does the teacher really enjoy their games with them? They perceive when an adult merely condescends to mingle with them. When he asks them about their interests, is he truly interested? Affected tones and condescending manners close every avenue of approach to their real selves. Children are people, and worthy of respect.

The children's favorite teacher has retained enough imagination to visualize all truth through their eyes, and to perceive how it relates to their home and play and school. One Sunday when the pastor of a church visited the Beginner department of his Sunday School, a new member of the group went home and told his mother that a man had talked to them. When the mother asked what he said, the boy replied, "I don't know what he said, but he didn't talk *baby* to us." Adults can come down to the level of boys and girls without a patronizing attitude.

The problem of getting into the inner lives of boys and girls is very similar to that of understanding the heathen on the foreign fields. In Africa the missionary has to learn not only the anthropology, sociology, and psychology of those people, but also to "think black." Among the children the teacher has to learn to "think young." The missionary on a new field begins by gaining the confidence of the natives and cultivating their friendship. He gets right down alongside them rather than standing on a pedestal to give them something good. He does not try to make Americans of the Africans, but to show them how Christ will make them the best Africans. Teachers do not try to make adults of children, but to let Christ meet their needs today.

6. *Sympathize with their limitations and yet hold them up to high standards.* It is the exceptional adult who appreciates the delicate balance between childhood's limitations and potentialities. If too much is expected of children, they grow discouraged; if too little is expected of them, they grow

lazy and delinquent. Most of them are very eager to please, if only they know what is expected and are humanly able to comply.

When students of the Moody Bible Institute asked hundreds of boys and girls in the Chicago area what kind of teacher they liked best, Beginners and Primaries gave answers which implied "easy" and "strict," in the same proportion. Three times as many Juniors preferred the strict teacher. These are their own words:

> One that teaches me the most.
>
> One that makes us behave.
>
> We have to do as she says and be quiet.
>
> One that knows how to scold.
>
> Snappy, because she does not let me jump around and talk.
>
> One that laughs once in a while, but gets down to business lots of times.
>
> Grouchy ones. You know why? When you're nice to them, they're better, and they "learn" you how to behave.

Two Juniors put these characteristics together in the right combination: "not too easy or too hard," "makes us work and like it." Is not that the best teacher, one who makes the pupils work and like it? If they work but do not like it, they will put down the Bible when left to their own choices. If they do not put forth effort to work, no growth will result.

We cannot know too much to teach children a little, but we may give them more than they can at present assimilate. Christ said to His disciples, "I have yet many things to say unto you, but ye cannot bear them now (John 16:12). Only from a broad background can a teacher comprehend all phases of truth sufficiently to express it in simple terms and to select what is needed for each child.

The following is a young woman's testimony to the influence of a teacher in her life:

> "I wanna be like her." That's what I told my mother one Sunday noon after church. I was talking about my Sunday School teacher, who not only portrayed Christ to us in the words of truth, but even more than that impressed us by her way of speaking, her actions, and her deep love for each member of our class.
>
> Then came the day when she said good-by to us and left for Bible school to prepare for the Lord's service. We hated to see her go, but she explained to us that it was God who was calling her and she had to go.
>
> I waited eagerly for her to come home for holidays, vacations, and week ends. I remember very distinctly watching her enter church, and noticed that she prayed as she sat down. With the exception of our pastor, I had never seen anyone else do that.
>
> Years went by swiftly. I was often in a rebellious state of mind. Yes, I wanted to be like her some day, but not now. I wanted some day to go away to a Bible school, but not now. No, I didn't want to give my life to Christ. One day—and what a happy day it was—I yielded my heart to the Saviour! I wished I could tell my old teacher, but I did not forget her or her love for me.
>
> Instead of coming back to us when she finished Bible school, my girl friends and I learned what was to us the sad news that we would have to give her up again, this time to the African girls. Yes, she loved us, but again she said, "God has called. I must go." My heart was heavy, but to my amazement when she left on that memorable afternoon, she was smiling and not crying. I understand now why she left us to go to Bible school, and in that respect I have followed in her steps. God only knows whether my life will continue to be molded like hers, but that happy smile as she left all to follow Him has influenced my life more than she ever realized or than I even realized at the time.

1. Work out a service of dedication for teachers, including such elements as a song, a short message based on Scripture, covenant questions to be answered by the phrase, "With God's help I will," and perhaps concluding with prayer.
2. Why does a mother often ask a teacher to help her solve a problem with her child, though the teacher has the child for the short period of only one hour a week?
3. "The unconscious influence of any teacher is greater than the conscious." Name five unconscious acts of teachers which indirectly teach some helpful lesson, and five unconscious acts which indirectly teach some negative lesson.
4. What are some "childlike" activities which a teacher can truly enjoy without being "childish"? What "childish" things should a teacher put away?
5. What is likely to be the weakness of the typical young teacher? The typical old teacher? The teacher who is a mother? The unmarried teacher?

CHAPTER III

PHYSICAL SURROUNDINGS

1. Do you recall a time when the physical environment in which you found yourself turned your heart to God? What elements in the situation led to worship?
2. Why do the more exclusive dress shops display only a few models in their show windows, while cheaper shops sometimes crowd samples of all their merchandise into their display?
3. When you step into an empty public school room, what tells you the grade of that room? When you step into an empty Bible school room, what should tell you the grade of that room?
4. What factors in the room in which you teach are conducive to worship and work? What factors hinder?

We walk into the woods, and step into a narrow opening among the trees where tall branches form a leafy arch over our heads. The sunshine comes sifting through the green in soft patches of gold, lighting up flowers and picking out ferns of exquisite tracery. Because we are sensitive to the beckonings of the Almighty, we involuntarily lift our hearts in worship. And again on Sunday morning we step into a church building, of similar proportions, with tall arching timbers over our heads, sunshine through colored glass giving a subdued light and picking out bits of beauty in carving and color. Again we lift our hearts in worship.

Though a person's inner spiritual condition is of course more important than external factors, yet physical surroundings either help or hinder spiritual teaching. The child, even more than the adult, is keenly susceptible to external environment. His thinking is concrete; he learns of the invisible realities from the visible. A dark, drab Sunday School room does not teach him that God is a God of truth and beauty, a God of joy and gladness.

"I don't like Sunday School," said one child. "It always looks as if it's going to rain."

He does not learn reverence in a confused, cluttered place, or thankfulness in an oppressive, dismal room. The little child is extremely sensitive and impressionable. He will catch the attitude toward the house of God which the teachers and the physical surroundings set for him. Therefore every room where God's Word is taught speaks a message; it should say, "Worship the Lord in the beauty of holiness." "In his temple every thing saith, Glory."

Sunday School rooms often suffer by comparison with the church sanctuary. "Why isn't our room soft and pretty like the big church?" was a child's expression of it. Many children cannot but feel a vast difference between their attractive homes and the barn-like church school room. They naturally compare their public school room with the church school. How do the two "schools" compare? What message is the church room giving the child as to the importance of spiritual training, compared with secular education?

LOCATION OF DEPARTMENT ROOMS

A small church was bursting its walls with Sunday School pupils. The young people succeeded in getting a room built behind the platform to house their new teacher training class—a clean, light, new room. But the Beginners were meeting in the basement kitchen on a cold cement floor, where every outward suggestion combined to prevent their room from eliciting worship.

"The little children should have the best room. Young people could work better in the kitchen than they," came the suggestion.

"A revolutionary thought! Impossible! The young people have worked hard and long for their new room; they would not give it up."

But in their teacher training class the young people began to study the characteristics and needs of the little child. It wasn't long before they recognized the importance of the Beginners and voluntarily furnished the new room for them, while the young people themselves met in the basement.

In new or old buildings, the little children should be given the best rooms, not the leftover ones. Rooms should be allocated on the basis of age, beginning with the babies whose sensitive nervous systems and delicate physiques cause them to suffer most from poor environment.

The Nursery class of three-year-old children will ideally be situated on the first floor of the building, with large windows on south and east to catch the morning sun. It should be near the entrance so that small children may not have far to go to find their room, and so they may easily go outside for a walk of discovery or other activity. A drinking fountain and toilet should be located near the room if not included as adjoining features. (See drawing of the Nursery room plan on page 47.)

A very helpful arrangement is to have a classroom for the mothers next to the Nursery classroom. Often mothers who wish to start their young children in Sunday School prolong their visits until they become a problem to the Nursery class teacher, whose work is hindered by their presence. Mothers may be more easily drawn into an adult class and out of the Nursery classroom if their own classroom is very near. Children may be shown where their mothers are to be, and not have long to wait for them at the close of the hour.

The Primary and Junior departments, rather than the younger children, might better occupy a second floor room. If divided departmentally, a room primarily for group worship, and classrooms sufficient to care for the total number, will be needed for each department.

The room for worship may be in the nature of a chapel where the reverent atmosphere of the church sanctuary is maintained, and the classrooms become the real workshops and study rooms for instruction of smaller class groups. Or, if there is division by grades in the manner of public schools, each grade will require an adequate room in which to worship, study, and carry on activities for spiritual growth. Entrance always should be from the rear to avoid interruptions.

HEALTH PROVISIONS

Since little children use more oxygen proportionately than adults use, they require ample space and good ventilation. Cradle Roll and Nursery class children should have twenty to thirty square feet per child; Beginners, eighteen to twenty-five; Primaries and Juniors, fifteen to eighteen in their classrooms, and six to eight if a separate assembly room is used for worship.[4]

But even if the requisite number of square feet is provided, thirty-five three-year-olds should not be placed together in one large room. The smaller the child, the more stimulating and confusing is the strain of a large number of people. He is used to home life, where comparatively few people, all familiar,

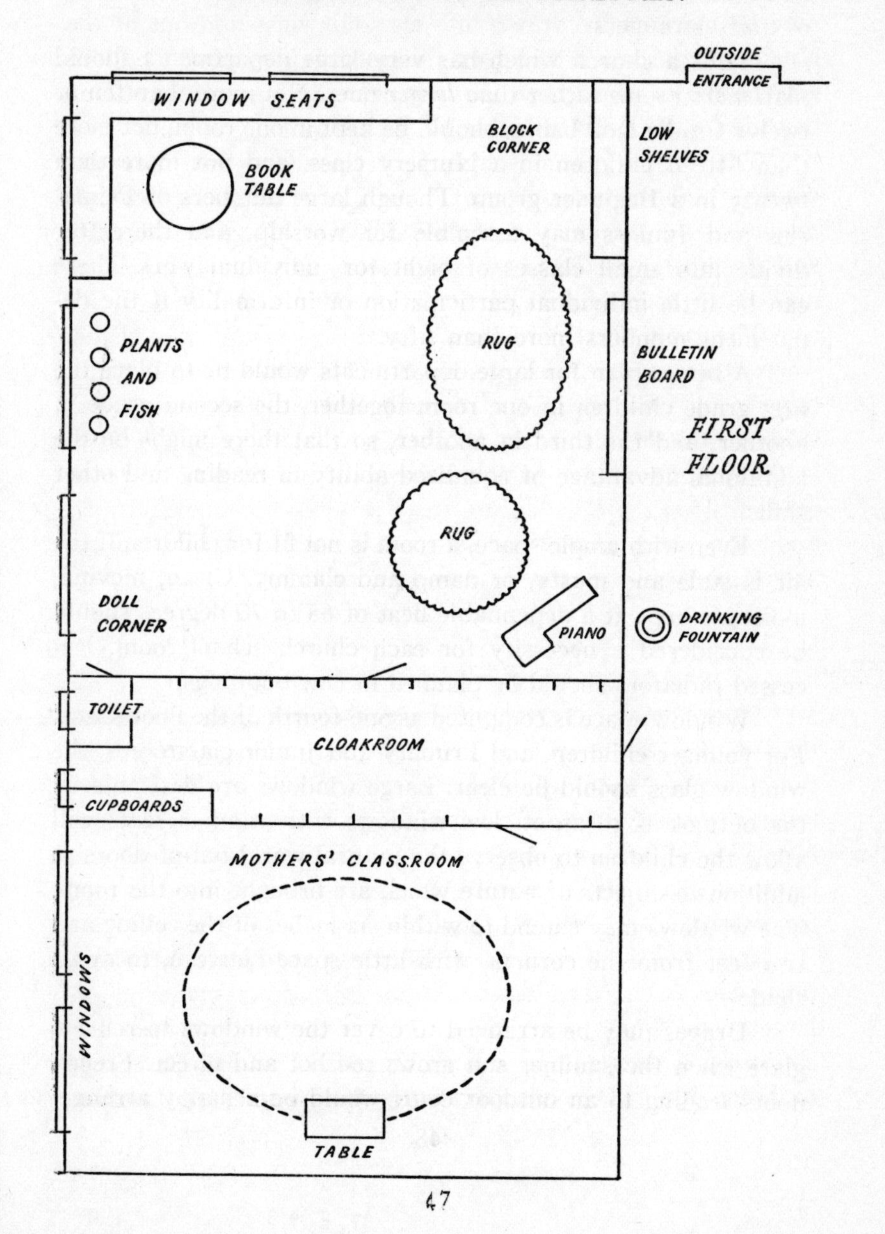
NURSERY FOR 10-15 CHILDREN
OUTSIDE
ENTRANCE
WINDOW SEATS
BLOCK
CORNER
LOW
SHELVES
BOOK
TABLE
PLANTS
AND
FISH
RUG
BULLETIN
BOARD
FIRST
FLOOR
RUG
DOLL
CORNER
PIANO
DRINKING
FOUNTAIN
TOILET
CLOAKROOM
CUPBOARDS
MOTHERS' CLASSROOM
WINDOWS
TABLE

surround him. His nervous system is very sensitive to a crowd of noisy strangers.

Thus a church which has very large departments should plan *more* rooms rather than *larger* ones. Not more than ten or twelve Cradle Roll babies should be kept in one room, not more than fifteen children in a Nursery class, and not more than twenty in a Beginner group. Though large numbers of Primaries and Juniors may assemble for worship, and thereafter divide into small classes of eight for individual work, there can be little individual participation or informality if the department numbers more than fifty.

A better plan for large departments would be to place the first grade children in one room together, the second grade in another, and the third in another, so that there might be the additional advantage of equalized ability in reading and other skills.

Even with ample space, a room is not fit for children if the air is stale and musty, or damp and clammy. Clean, moving, moist air kept at a dependable heat of 65 to 70 degrees should be considered a necessity for each church school room. Recessed radiators should be planned in new buildings.

Window space is computed as one-fourth of the floor space. For younger children, and Primary and Junior classrooms, the window glass should be clear. Large windows are desirable. If the outlook is pleasant, low windows with window seats will allow the children to observe the natural world out-of-doors in addition to objects of nature which are brought into the room. The windows may extend to within six inches of the ceiling and two feet from the corners, with little space between, to avoid shadows.

Drapes may be arranged to cover the windows to remove glare when the summer sun grows too hot and direct. French doors leading to an outdoor court would be a happy arrangement for the Nursery class and the Beginner department. Light should fall on seated children from the left rear, and they should never face the windows or sit in a glare of light.

FURNISHINGS

Floors. Perhaps the carpeted floor is most desirable for little children, providing a warm, homelike atmosphere, and serving to deaden noise. However, carpeting which is constantly in use, and not kept clean, will in a short time be unfit for children's play. Since few department rooms are reserved exclusively for the use of the children, and since such space is expensive, many churches use linoleum as a floor covering. Battleship linoleum may be glued to the floor, is warmer than many floor coverings, comparatively noiseless, and easily cleaned. It comes in a variety of colors which enable selection to accord with the color harmony of the room.

For babies and small children washable rugs should be provided for activities on the floor. There seems little excuse for allowing small children to gather on cold, noisy concrete.

Walls and Ceilings. Walls and ceilings should provide soft, mellow backgrounds for pictures, drapes, and decorations. Subdued colors give the effect of space better than bright ones. The colors selected will depend on the decorative scheme for the room, which should be carefully planned as a whole.

In the Nursery light enamel will probably be chosen for woodwork and furniture so that it may be washed and kept sanitary. In other department rooms which are bright the natural wood of furniture and woodwork may be stained. Some prefer this to light colored paint, which chips and wears off.

If the room is very bright, the walls may be pale green or blue; if not very bright, soft tones of yellow or buff may be chosen. Calcimine is soft in appearance and permits frequent renewal of surface because of its inexpensiveness.

Tables and Chairs. Usually furniture should match the woodwork. Sometimes attractive and unusual combinations of colors are worked out, but such planning should be done under the guidance of a person with an artistic eye.

Chairs should be chosen with attention to their construction and comfort. A sturdy style, with rounded edges, is necessary. Folding chairs should never be used by children. A proper seat and back will make erect posture the most comfortable one to assume. The back should be form fitting; the seat should slope backward, and be short. If chairs must be either high or low for some in a group, it is better to keep them low, for it is possible to sit comfortably in a chair lower than is needed, whereas dangling feet are not conducive to concentration. Having two sizes of chairs in children's departments does not work very well, for small children delight to sit in the larger chairs, or there is confusion in placing the taller children in the larger chairs whenever informal groups gather.

Nursery chairs should be eight to ten inches high, sturdy but not heavy in build. Beginner chairs should be ten inches high; Primary, eleven and twelve inches for first and second grades, if there are separate rooms or classrooms; fourteen inches for third grade. Fourth and fifth grade Juniors will probably need fourteen-inch chairs, while the sixth grade may use sixteen-inch. All tables should be approximately ten inches higher than the chairs with which they will be used.

Sunday School furniture usually must last for years and survive severe usage. Therefore it should be well made, and carry its share in the room's message of refinement. Rubber tips on chair and table legs will help to lessen noise on hard floors.

Folding tables will be found useful in many situations, if they are of such solid construction that they do not wobble or collapse. Each department may like to have a round table for a library or browsing table, but work tables will be more practical if they are of oblong shape, since the group sit closer together without wasting the space taken by a round table. The matter of handling and storage is facilitated by oblong tables, and the space taken in the room is considerably less.

The secretary will need a desk or table also, and the Primary and Junior superintendents will doubtless want a table, to use for centering worship or for displaying materials. Where space is cramped, the secretary may have a small table outside the door, or fold up her table during the class session. The various departments may also wish to have small tables as offering centers, as display space for objects of interest, nature objects, a bowl of fish, and a vase of flowers. Such tables should be chosen for solid construction as well as harmony with the prevailing color scheme.

Decorative Features. The homelike, lived-in, attractive appearance of many church rooms is due to the drapes, pictures, rugs, and flowers which bring beauty and color to what might otherwise be an uninteresting place. Curtains or drapes present many and varied possibilities for delighting the eye and cheering the room for children. Sheer, bright curtains will help greatly in a dark room. Dirty, drab, drooping curtains will speak of neglect and indifference. Real flowers are always a delightful addition to any room. Rugs, too, will be chosen for their contribution to the atmosphere as well as for their usefulness.

The number of permanent pictures depends on the size of the room and the amount of wall space. They should be chosen for the enduring message they give the children, not solely for decorative purposes. Therefore they must hang at eye level, be large enough and clear enough for the children easily to see their content.

If the standards used in decorating a home are kept in mind, the teacher will be preserved from the common error of cluttering the room with too many pictures. Where one worthy picture might carry a definite message, ten would give only a confused blur.

Temporary pictures may represent seasonal changes and current interests, and be changed often. Also, care must be exercised not to overcrowd the space on the bulletin board.

Display Space. Every room should have a place to display temporary pictures. A picture rail or bulletin board may be used. The picture rail or ledge has the advantage of enabling little children to put pictures up and take them down without the difficulty of thumbtacks.

Beginner, Primary and Junior departments should have a blackboard. A portable one is quite possible, especially if it would not be used often enough to merit permanent wall space. Built-in blackboards have the advantage of stability for writing, especially if children are to use them.

However, if blackboards tend to disfigure the appearance of the room by their large black expanses, drapes may cover them. In new buildings, the boards may be set into the wall, and a hinged section of wall cover them when not in use, so that they are not visible.

Departments above Nursery will also want a sturdy easel for flannelgraph pictures, and for drawing by the children. Easels will vary in height according to the department.

Storage Space. Work with children requires materials, which, in turn, require space for proper care and storage. Every department room should have its own cupboard space under lock and key to protect it from the ravages of other groups in the church who may fail to appreciate the worth of its carefully garnered materials. Of course, the young people may only borrow the scissors for an evening's project, but the scissors may be missing, wholly or in part, when the Primary children are ready to use them next Sunday.

Many unused bits of space in crowded churches could be utilized for cupboards by means of a little carpentry work. Other cupboards might be made more serviceable if compartments were built in them, or labels attached to them, or boxes of similar color and size were collected to hold materials. There should be a definite place for each type of material, and the cupboard should be kept meticulously in order so that a glance will locate what is needed, or enable the superintendent to compute quantities that need to be ordered.

Since pictures are such an important item in teaching children, a cabinet will be needed for the picture collection in each department. The cabinet may be a part of the cupboard space. A workable arrangement is to have a shelf at a convenient height divided into narrow, vertical compartments in which pictures are classified and labeled. Then if a rainy Sunday morning arrives, the superintendent may go to the compartment marked "Nature" and select pictures of growing gardens or flowers or falling rain to direct the conversation of those who arrive early into profitable channels.

It is well also to have a large, thin cabinet made for large posters and pictures which get soiled if they are rolled up or left lying around. Such a flat cabinet may occupy unused space, as the wall in a cloakroom. Cabinet space must also make provision for care of flannel and figures used in flannelgraph pictures. The flannel should always be carefully folded and neatly piled in a box or compartment; the figures may be placed in folders and filed alphabetically according to the subject.

The leadership education of children begins very early when they assume responsibility for the use and care of church property and materials. Even the tiniest tots who come to church may learn to put their toys away in provided receptacles. Nursery children may select from low shelves their choice of the materials the teacher has placed there for them to use;

Beginners and older children may select books and other materials from the shelves, put away materials, and keep the shelves in order. The older children may even learn to use a picture cabinet to choose pictures which will fit the lesson or the subject they are discussing.

> John and Jerry had shown great interest in the outside stairs of a model of an Oriental house. They quickly responded to the teacher's suggestion that they find pictures of outside stairs in the picture file under the classification "Bible Scenes." The boys made a display for the class and from their own observation pointed out features in the various pictures which made oriental life real to the group.

Primaries and Juniors will need display shelves for curios and models, and Juniors also space for their hymnbooks. They will need a special section in the cupboard for maps. The Junior department probably will want a bookcase in which to keep Christian literature and reference works for their study. Primaries and Juniors should have a Bible school library with a simple filing system which the children themselves can operate.

Care of Wraps. Probably the ideal arrangement for the care of wraps is the cloakroom which adjoins the department room, so that the children may remove their wraps before entering the room. They hang their coats on hooks placed one foot apart, at a height they can easily reach. A shelf over the hooks provides a place for hat and gloves. A compartment on the floor below each hook provides space where rubbers or boots may be placed directly below the owner's coat and kept separate from all others.

Sometimes hooks for wraps can be placed in the hall outside the room. If they must be placed in the room itself, they should be kept at the back, and a screen placed around the section where latecomers enter, so that they will not disturb the group after work has begun. In some cases movable racks may be prepared for each class, and at the end of the session may be rolled noiselessly to the class to avoid congestion in the section where the racks are kept during the hour.

Piano. A piano is least necessary in the Nursery class, where all singing should be done by following the teacher's voice. A piano drowns the light voices of small children. But a piano is helpful in the Nursery class for rhythmic activity. It should be of small size, and be enameled a light color to correspond with the woodwork.

The other departments will want to have a piano kept in good tune for singing, quiet music, preludes, marching, and such activities as story interpretation. Some Juniors and even an occasional Primary will be able to contribute some hymn or meaningful piece of music they have learned to play.

Interest Centers. Attractive centers of interest will help to create atmosphere, to stimulate thinking and questions, and to recall past experiences. The background for a missionary worship service may be an open Bible surrounded by pictures of foreign children, foreign dolls, foreign curios, or foreign flags. A Junior unit of work on the subject of the Bible may be launched by the questions called forth by a display of the various kinds of translations and versions. A collection of toy boats and pictures of boats will help Primary boys and girls recall their own past experience with boats in readiness for stories of Bible boats.

An offering center near the door encourages the children to deposit their money at once, and also makes giving a meaningful act. A plate or suggestive receptacle may be used for each type of work which the group has been led to support. A poster, picture, or table screen behind the receptacle will help make giving an act of worship.

EQUIPMENT

Cradle Roll

Cribs and cots
Adult chairs; rockers with blunt edges
Washable rugs and blankets
A chest of blocks
A chest of toys
A few pictures and picture books

Beds should be made up with fresh linen each week. Washable blankets or rugs may be used for babies who wish to play on the floor. Toys should be durable and washable. Shelves and boxes should be provided for toys so that the children may help to put them away. Great precaution should be taken to avoid anything dangerous in the way of contagion, sharp toys, or babies harming each other because of insufficient supervision. Competent attendants might well include a nurse.

For two-year-olds who show an interest in books and pictures, the helpers should have a few simple, clear pictures and picture books prepared for children of this age. One or two carefully chosen permanent pictures may be hung low on the walls. Sometimes a Nursery song will be enjoyed. Pictures of flowers, birds, trees, or animals, might be enumerated, each accompanied with the phrase, "God made . . ." Other simple activities may be introduced as individuals are ready for them, but teaching should not be forced at this age.

Nursery Class and Beginner

Pictures and picture books
Toys with spiritual implications
Nature objects
Models; objects
Piano; toy instruments
A Bible
Offering receptacles
Large crayons and paper; paste
Dustpan and brush; dustcloth
Wastebasket

Pictures for the Nursery class should be mounted on heavy cardboard or bristol board, and shellacked so that the children can freely handle them. When so prepared, pictures may be wiped with a damp cloth if they get soiled. Those frequently used by Beginners should be similarly mounted and shellacked. Otherwise, Beginner pictures may be mounted on construction paper. A magazine rack or assigned place on a low shelf should be provided so that the children may get pictures and put them away. The teacher guides the use of pictures and other materials by placing on the children's shelves such materials as have seasonal interest or contribute to the theme of the day.

Books should be carefully selected to fit mental and spiritual maturity. A Bible for little children who cannot read should be selected for its outward appearance and pictures. (Take care that there are no pictures depicting Abraham with uplifted knife about to slay Isaac.) Gold letters on the outside, divinity edges, and durable leather will help to make this book a very special one requiring special care. A pretty bookmark may be placed at some particular story or picture. The Bible should be kept in a special place; the children will enjoy getting it for the teacher before the Bible story is told, and then putting it away afterward. They like to pretend to read the Bible words, or tell something the Bible says.

In general, offering receptacles should have a small opening for the money, though a narrow slit may be too difficult for little children to put money through. But an open basket tempts them to pick up the money and play with it. The receptacle may well be of metal or glass so that the money makes a delightful noise when it falls. Beginners may have two receptacles, one for their own church and one for the faraway boys and girls.

All toys and equipment should be carefully selected, first

with regard to their purpose, which should be more than entertainment in both Nursery and Beginner departments. Dolls are introduced as Bible children. Animals are those from Noah's ark, which tell of God's care. Toy instruments are used in imitation of David's praise to God. Blocks, dolls, and balls, all may be useful in giving opportunities for sharing, playing together happily, or imitating helpful actions.

In addition to the purpose for which the toy is selected, it should be durable, hygienic, and safe in construction. Toys which break easily are likely to lead to habits of carelessness. Toys which call for co-ordination beyond the child's ability will either be broken in his attempts to manage them, or give him a sense of failure. Crayons and paper should be of larger sizes than those used by older children.

Primary and Junior

Boxes of materials for each group	A department Bible
Pictures	Offering receptacles
Visual-aid board	An interest center
Cases of models; curios; nature objects	Piano
Lending library, or bookcase of books	Hymnbooks for Juniors

Unless each class has its own room where materials are kept, it is well to have class boxes prepared by the secretary. If these boxes are uniform in size and color, and labeled, they will make a much better appearance than a motley collection. They may contain scissors, pencils, crayons, and paste, with such additional materials and paper as are required for the particular activities.

Often, models, curios, and nature objects will be brought into a discussion for illustration or instruction. Missionary curios stimulate interest and prayer. Models give understanding of Oriental life. These objects may have a permanent case for exhibition, or a small case may hold whatever is of present interest, and be changed with a change in activity.

DEPARTMENTALIZATION

One of the first projects of the small church should be the division of its pupils into departments, in which the needs of each age group may be met on its own level of development. As in the realm of nature, so it is in the Bible school that the rule is "multiplication by division"—pupils multiply as they are divided into homogeneous groups.

Dividing space is an easier problem than getting space where there is none. The large room may be made into an ideal arrangement, if it is large enough. Whenever possible, partitions should be permanent and soundproof. For the two or three special programs a year many a church endures difficult conditions every week in the year.

However, for those rooms where permanent partitions are impossible a number of temporary types have been worked out. Curtains or sliding doors are possible, but less desirable than portable solid partitions. Rigid plaster board screens on rollers may be placed around classes to cut off others from view, and partially eliminate sounds. Such screens may be tinted to harmonize with the walls of the room. A blackboard may be placed in the middle, with other space used for a bulletin board for pictures.

When there is one chapel or attractive room for worship, different departments should rotate in using it. Thus, although classes might be located in odd corners, the department could have a reverent service of praise and prayer in the larger room.

BETTERING POOR SURROUNDINGS

Though good teaching can be done under very poor physical surroundings, the wise teacher is alert to make the

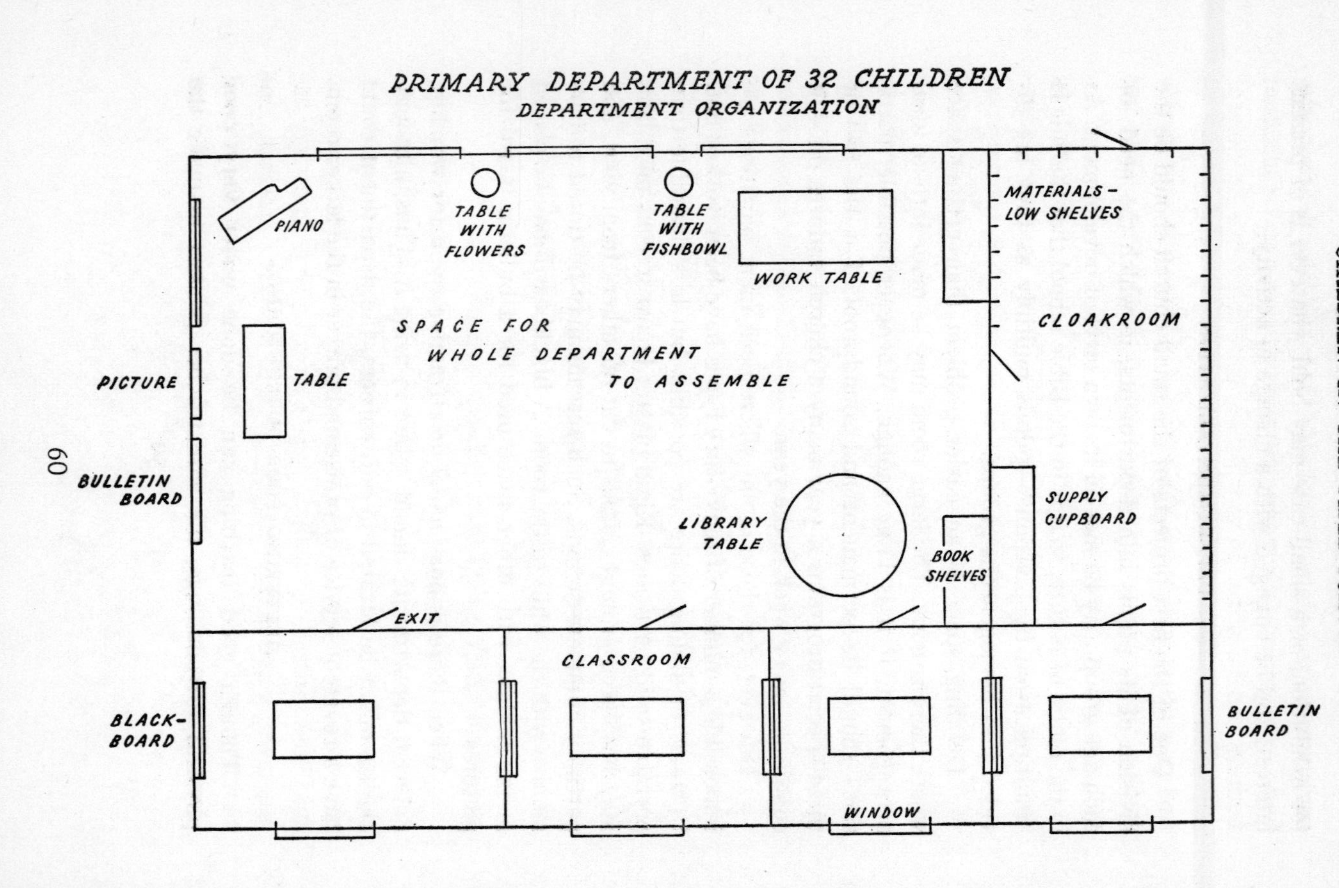
PRIMARY DEPARTMENT OF 32 CHILDREN
DEPARTMENT ORGANIZATION
PIANO
TABLE WITH FLOWERS
TABLE WITH FISHBOWL
WORK TABLE
MATERIALS – LOW SHELVES
CLOAKROOM
SPACE FOR WHOLE DEPARTMENT TO ASSEMBLE
PICTURE
TABLE
BULLETIN BOARD
LIBRARY TABLE
SUPPLY CUPBOARD
BOOK SHELVES
EXIT
CLASSROOM
BLACK-BOARD
BULLETIN BOARD
WINDOW

environment as helpful as possible. It is the poor teacher who finds excuses for failures in the surroundings, and sighs that nothing can be done. In most cases something can be done if a positive attitude is assumed and ingenuity is exercised to find new ways and means. Thoughtful teachers are continually finding clever ways of getting around obstacles; no ceiling has yet been set on originality.

The first step is to eliminate the attitude, "We can't do anything about it." The outsider who comes into such situations often sees something that can be done. The continuation of that hopeless cry usually means, "It isn't worth our time and effort to improve conditions."

Where the true and living Word is being preached in power, the commonest difficulty is overcrowding. This condition is healthy spiritually, but not physically. Probably the first attack on the problem should be training in stewardship. Even children should be taught the necessity of sowing bountifully in order to reap bountifully from doing their part in buying bricks for an addition to the present church building.

Once the educational building has been envisioned and future plans begun, the need is for immediate relief from bulging classrooms. Sometimes temporary buildings may be set up on adjoining tracts of land. Some classes can meet in near-by homes. Sometimes churches find it practical to buy a near-by home and adapt its rooms to church needs.

Sometimes crowded conditions are solved by having two Sunday School sessions. Some churches have an early Sunday School before church for those who wish to come at that hour, and another Sunday School session after church for those who find that time more satisfactory. Other schools find that the Beginner department can be divided into two sessions, one meeting at the regular Sunday School hour, and the second during the church service. One church solved part of its problem by having the whole Primary department meet for its Sunday School session during the church service.

Needed equipment and materials also are in the realm of attainment for the ingenious worker. Rugs for Cradle Roll and Nursery are suitable projects for the women's groups; they might be braided from materials donated by the whole church. The best blocks are not the fancy ones which cost so much, but unpainted ones which may be made from odd pieces of lumber and carefully planed and sandpapered to avoid the danger of splinters. Under guidance, the men's fellowship could have a jolly time doing this work, as well as satisfaction from knowing their service has been so valuable.

The whole church can contribute pictures and magazines for the children's departments. An interesting demonstration of the use of pictures among little children, either before or after the contribution has been made, will be ample return to the donors.

Poor teaching blamed on physical environment usually can be traced to spiritual needs of the teachers. In few cases can a church group of workers say, "We have done everything that can be done in the way of using what we have and providing what is possible." Until that can be said, opportunity holds out its arms in the name of Christ.

1. List what is favorable in the surroundings in which you teach. What is unfavorable? Plan what can be done to remedy each of the latter difficulties.
2. Visit the public school room which most of your pupils attend. Observe the physical features of the room, mentioned in this chapter, as well as the teaching methods. Is the attitude of the pupils the same as their attitude in church? If not, can you explain why?

3. Plan the color scheme you would like to see worked out in your room the next time it is redecorated. Include floor, walls, ceiling, woodwork, furniture, drapes, permanent pictures, and any other items of interest.

CHAPTER IV

ADMINISTRATION OF THE CHILDREN'S DIVISION

1. Why is a house divided into separate rooms for different purposes? Why is a business enterprise organized into departments and committees? Why did the early Christian church appoint elders and deacons? Why is a Bible school organized into departments and agencies?
2. As Creator and Preserver of the universe, in what ways does God show that He is a God of order? What evidences can you find in Scripture?
3. If every teacher in a Bible school should teach any lesson he wished each week, what kind of curriculum would be provided for the pupils? What would be the probable result?

The Lord is a God of order, of method, of system, of law. The perfect harmony of nature and the universe from the smallest flower to the largest planet reveals our Maker's ways of working. Consider the remarkable organization of our own human bodies and immaterial souls, to behold His wondrous efficiency of operation. When one member of the body gets "out of kilter," the malady is felt by every other member. Certainly in the Bible school, the school of God's Book, should "all things be done decently and in order."

A MEANS TO AN END

Organization in the Bible school is simply good management, or the creating of teaching situations in which the Spirit of God is free to work through the Word and through the Christian teacher. Confusion, not efficiency, is the natural result of each person's going his own way, thinking only of his own welfare. An organizing mind or corporate mind is always behind smooth procedure, relating each member and his activities to the total program.

There must be a part for all, and all doing their part; a place for everything, and everything in its place. "To every man his work" (Mark 13:34). One individual is responsible for each part of the program. His work is clear and specific. Only as each person has a clear conception of his own function and that of others on the staff can waste and duplication be avoided. Only as every ounce of energy and every minute of time are conserved, can adequate returns in spiritual power be realized.

Because organization is not an end in itself, but a means to an end, we shall not be disturbed when exceptional adjustments need to be made.

Discuss as a staff and decide on the policies best suited to the majority of teachers and pupils. Then keep on the alert for places in the organization where the general system does not meet particular needs. Remember that teachers as well as pupils are individuals, and that the purpose is not regimentation, but provision of an atmosphere in which the Bible may be taught most happily for all concerned.

THE PRINCIPLES OF ORGANIZATION

Increasing the number of organizations may hinder rather than promote organization, though of course a school of one thousand might need more organizations than a school of one hundred. On the surface, the school which is *best* organized may appear to be *least* organized, for everything seems to be running smoothly with no one fussing about his child or that record. Yet smooth procedure is always sure evidence that there has been careful and prayerful planning behind the scenes. Organization will be first of all just as *simple* as possible.

In the second place, organization will be *flexible,* since it is based on definite requirements and need never remain static unless a school is dead. The vacation school of rural community may have to meet in the evening because the only available teachers are working in the fields or home during the daytime. Periodically, organization should be evaluated anew in light of changing conditions lest procedures once useful but now defunct are allowed to stifle enthusiasm for fresh purposes and activities. A varied program exciting expectancy and challenge requires flexibility.

In the third place, organization will be *democratic,* including as many persons as possible, for everyone in it should feel responsible for its administration, and will grow spiritually as he attends his duties. Though some offices requiring specialists have comparatively long terms, some of them may be rotated so that many people may share the responsibility and get the viewpoint of the administrator.

RELATION TO THE REST OF THE CHURCH

In one school where children's work was appreciated and where earnest workers gave generously of their time and energies, a group of Juniors still failed to show interest and gratitude for all that was being done for them. An investigation revealed the fact that in Sunday School these Juniors were studying the book of Exodus, in Week Day Church School they were studying the book of Exodus, and in Pioneer Girls also they were studying the book of Exodus.

No matter how excellent a piece of work any teacher is doing, he cannot make his efforts count if he goes his merry way regardless of what else is being done for his pupils. His work must fit into the total program for those children without duplication or omission of the essential elements of instruction, worship, service, and fellowship. He or his representative must plan and visualize the whole of which he is a part.

This comprehensive view is in the hands of the standing committee on children's work, which is composed of a representative of each agency—Sunday School, Junior Church, Junior Choir, Week Day Church School, Vacation Bible School, Pioneer Girls, Boys' Brigade—plus two impartial members. The leaders of each agency naturally promote their own interests even though they be broad-minded, while the two others should be vitally interested in children in general, without preferring one agency to another.

This over-all committee educates the church on the importance of early training, outlines general policies and the total program, correlates the work of the various agencies, helps each one appreciate what the others are contributing to the children's spiritual growth, and relates children's work to the other phases of the work of the church. In turn, one or two members of this committee meet with the committees on young people, adults, leadership education, finance, and equipment, to discuss questions which affect all of them.

Seldom does one find a church in which the departments co-operate with each other as they might, in spite of the fact that one family often has members in three or more groups. If materials such as Biblical models and visual aids and library books of interest to all were supervised by a general committee and received contributions from all, the school could build up

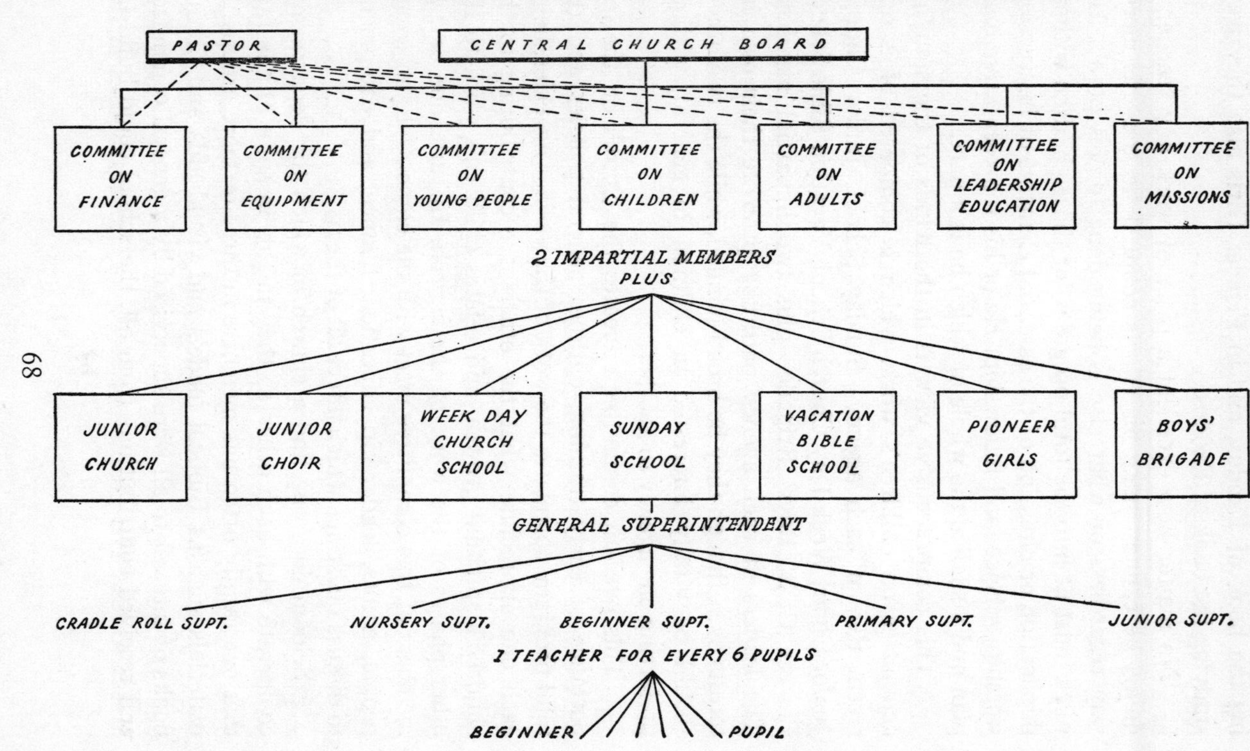
ADMINISTRATION OF THE CHILDREN'S DIVISION
PASTOR
CENTRAL CHURCH BOARD
COMMITTEE ON FINANCE
COMMITTEE ON EQUIPMENT
COMMITTEE ON YOUNG PEOPLE
COMMITTEE ON CHILDREN
COMMITTEE ON ADULTS
COMMITTEE ON LEADERSHIP EDUCATION
COMMITTEE ON MISSIONS
2 IMPARTIAL MEMBERS PLUS
JUNIOR CHURCH
JUNIOR CHOIR
WEEK DAY CHURCH SCHOOL
SUNDAY SCHOOL
VACATION BIBLE SCHOOL
PIONEER GIRLS
BOYS' BRIGADE
GENERAL SUPERINTENDENT
CRADLE ROLL SUPT.
NURSERY SUPT.
BEGINNER SUPT.
PRIMARY SUPT.
JUNIOR SUPT.
1 TEACHER FOR EVERY 6 PUPILS
BEGINNER
PUPIL

valuable collections available to all. Older pupils would assume more service projects for the younger children and get the benefit of the activity which they need but which busy teachers do not need.

GROUPING CHILDREN

Each Bible school's space, equipment, and leadership condition its method of grouping children. The aim is maximum growth for each individual, both teachers and pupils. A natural situation provides for small interest groups which may often regroup as interests change, yet affords occasional times when larger groups meet together for a common purpose. When children are kept in large groups, the individual is lost sight of, he cannot fully participate, and emotional tension is likely to result in a distracting atmosphere which makes worship difficult.

Organization by Department or Grade? At present the most common type of organization for Primaries and Juniors is the department in which the whole group assembles for a worship service, usually at the beginning of the hour, then divides into small classes for Bible study. The advantages of this plan are that for part of the hour all the children enjoy the leadership of the superintendent, who is the best qualified leader in the department; the teachers have the benefit of observing his expert methods; each teacher has definite responsibility for his own class, and works intimately with these few individuals.

There is a decided disadvantage, however, in the departmental plan. The schedule must be so rigid that all the classes worship at the same time and go to their classes at the same time. The hour is cut up into unnatural divisions, which may hinder an absorbing problem from being carried to its completion. If Juniors are working on the question of why God chose Moses to lead His people out of Egypt, or why houses in the

Holy Land at the time of Christ were built differently from ours today, they would very likely worship informally during the study and at the end rather than at the beginning of the hour.

If a department is not dismissed from the worship service at the right moment, the teachers may feel that the superintendent is encroaching on their time, for which they have carefully prepared. A strong superintendent may feel that he should keep the children as long as possible, since he can spend the time more profitably than the teachers; capable teachers may feel that "opening exercises" (instead of a worship service) are a waste of time, and it is very true that often they are.

Younger children of Nursery and Beginner age are usually organized as one group with a great deal of individual work. Since dividing into classes is detrimental for young children, why not use the same principle of flexible organization for older children? If they remain in one group, they can set up a problem and carry it through to a satisfying conclusion by worshiping and working with paper whenever the need arises instead of artificially awaiting the period when that activity is scheduled. The session can be made an informal real-life situation, with the progress of the group regulating the time schedule instead of its being fixed arbitrarily. Some weeks a larger proportion of time might be spent in worship, while other sessions might be occupied almost wholly with the study of the lesson. The leader would see to it that over a period of months both worship and study received their proper emphasis.

Organization by grade is similar to public school organization. Each grade works together for a whole period under the supervision of one leader and several teachers or associates. The children worship as an entire group, and break up into smaller interest groups when working on different problem and project activities. Occasionally they assemble with others in the same department, for instance the first grade with the second and third grades of the Primary department. In a small school the Primary department would be composed of first, second, and third grades. Each group of twenty-five or thirty Primaries and Juniors needs a separate room, with an able leader in charge of each, and an associate for every eight pupils.

Since the teachers in the grade plan are associates of an expert leader rather than conducting a class on their own responsibility, they need not be as well trained as those in the departmental system. They have opportunity to observe good teaching and to practice good principles under supervision. Vacation schools often are organized by grade when teachers are scarce. Because the children frequently regroup themselves according to the interest at hand, the teachers do not try to concentrate on a certain few pupils, as do those in a department plan.

As soon as a group grows larger than the following, it should be divided, if possible:

Grade Plan

Nursery	15 pupils	
Beginner	20 pupils	For each,
Primary	25 pupils	1 superintendent
Junior	30 pupils	and 3 teachers

Department Plan

Primary	40 pupils:	1 superintendent and 5 teachers
Junior	50 pupils:	1 superintendent and 6 teachers

Nursery and Beginner children should not be divided into classes. Younger children require more teachers per pupil because they need more individual attention than do older boys and girls. In the department plan, the number of Primary and

Junior pupils in a unit may be somewhat larger for the reason that each teacher is personally responsible for a small group.

Age or School Grade? When a Primary or Junior group exceeds the above quota, there is a question whether the children can best work together when they are graded according to age or school grade. Although the criterion for Bible school teaching is spiritual progress, yet grading on that basis is impossible, since no human being can set himself up as an accurate judge of spiritual maturity.

Grouping by school grade seems to be nearly as simple and natural as age, with certain other advantages. Even a slow child expects to work with those of his own ability, and eventually will enjoy himself more than if he were put with others who leave him far behind mentally. There will be sufficient individual differences for breadth and richness of experience if the pupils are similar in one respect. A real school can be conducted with dignity and standards of achievement if the pupils are all in the same grade, and can read and write on the same level. Proud parents may try to push their child ahead in Bible school even if he is backward in public school, but most of them comprehend the explanation that the individual child can make more progress with those of his own ability.

This question is not so serious as it might seem, for most children in the same grade at public school are also the same age. If retarded children, or more likely their parents, are offended, they can be put with those of their own age. Since organization is a means to an end, rigid rules defeat their own purpose. A group graded according to school grade is usually satisfactory, with a few exceptional adjustments. If a child insists on being with his best friend, it is possible that he will work better there than in a grade higher or lower.

The following seems to be the best practical grouping:

Nursery	2, 3 years of age
Beginner	4, 5 years of age
Primary	grades 1, 2, 3
Junior	grades 4, 5, 6

Even if the Nursery and Beginner groups are small, the children two years of age should be separated from those of three if possible; and the four-year-old Beginners from those who are five. Each year at these early ages makes a great difference in interests and attention span.

Promotion. What should be the criteria for advancement from one group to the next? This is a very difficult question. A real school should have standards; the Bible school should have standards of Christian growth, but these are not easy to set up and maintain.

Mechanical requirements such as attendance and memorization are certainly inadequate. A child from a worldly home may have advanced remarkably through the year, may have been saved and established wholesome spiritual habits; yet his record of attendance and factual information may fall below that of a child from a Christian home who is merely marking time though he is in church regularly and easily repeats words without much meaning.

What would be the effect on a child if he were to be kept back from promotion? What would happen to those new pupils who are reached during the year and who have missed a part of the course? If good teaching is being done, there will be continual growth on the part of all children, and failures will be remedied immediately, without waiting for promotion season.

Probably the most satisfactory basis is to advance all pupils with a promotion service which looks back at past achievements and forward to new goals. There can be recognition of work done and spiritual victories won. The emphasis should be on coming to know the Lord and growing in grace in order to be of service to Him. Each step ahead signified greater possibilities for usefulness.

Although promotion time is naturally in the fall after summer vacation, and the school year and most lesson manuals are built on fall promotion, it occasionally happens that an individual pupil is ready for a change in the middle of the year. This will be an exception, and he will miss the promotion service. But, for instance, if a Beginner feels too mature for the young children and begins first grade in the middle of the year, he may be quietly moved into a Primary group where the work will meet his needs.

PERSONNEL

Since the qualifications of teachers have been discussed in the second chapter, and the pianist will be discussed in the fourteenth chapter, only the superintendent and secretary will be considered in this section.

The Grade or Department Superintendent. Capable superintendents are usually the key to the success of any school, for they stand in the gap between the executive committee with its objectives and the individual teachers with their pupils. The superintendent is responsible for seeing that the objectives are actually carried out in each life. He is both an executive and a teacher. He is entrusted with detail and planning, and must have a burden for winning the lost as well as time to spend on a program of reaching and teaching. He must have every good qualification or the work of the department will be seriously hampered.

The department superintendent is responsible for organizing and supervising the department, selecting and training teachers, relating them to the rest of the church, and leading worship services when all assemble. The superintendent of a grade plays even a larger rôle, for he directs all the activities for the whole grade. In a sense all is dependent on him. If a superintendent is a genuine leader with ability and vision, he can inspire others to follow his lead to great heights of spiritual experience. If he lacks leadership qualities, though teachers and pupils have the best of intentions, they will succumb to the weakness of the flesh and follow the line of least resistance.

His first duty, therefore, is to show by consistent example what can be done. He knows biblical message and method, how to adapt them to his own situation, and uses them to demonstrate the power of the Lord. His sacrificial attitude toward the school in general and the pupils in particular raises the whole department to a lofty spiritual plane. This exalted example wins confidence. Teachers feel privileged to get their training under a person like this. He doesn't need to boss or "snoopervise" them, for they know he is deeply concerned, and they voluntarily come to him with their joys and sorrows.

One of the superintendent's best methods of stimulating growth on the part of the teachers in his department is to keep reading material before their minds. A few standard references dealing with his own departmental specialization might be suggested to every new teacher. When the superintendent is approached with a problem or discovers a weakness in any teacher's leadership, he not only gives advice from his own experience, but also refers the teacher to certain chapters in certain books for further discussion on the subject. He watches everything new which is published in his field and arouses the teachers' interest and curiosity in timely books and articles. He realizes that teachers are inclined to get into ruts unless they are continually evaluating anew their procedures in the light of the principles of good teaching. The bibliography at the end of this book suggests a list of books from which to select.

Even if a church does not have in its membership those who fully measure up to the requirements, at least we can keep our standards high, retain the vision, and strive toward it. In some kinds of enterprise this would not be possible, but "all things are possible to him that believeth." If a worker has ability and foresight, but cannot be depended on to be faithful, the leaders can pray that he may see the dreadful losses caused by ups and downs, and working by spurts and starts. In almost every church a great deal of latent talent lies dormant, waiting to be aroused.

When the name of Mrs. Wagner was suggested as a teacher in the Beginner department, her friend shook her head. She was ill most of the time, and she made such a ritual of her home duties that she was free for nothing else. But someone was sorely needed, and prayer was made in her behalf. She was tactfully approached, presented with the challenge of reaching children, and reminded that salvation had come to her home through the regeneration of her own young daughter in the Sunday School. She replied that she could at least help the Beginners take off their wraps.

Today Mrs. Wagner is one of the best of Beginner teachers. She is seldom ill. She gets into the homes of the children and knows all about each one. If she wants the shirt off your back for her department, she easily convinces you that the children need it more than you do.

One of the chief hindrances in the Bible school today is the leader who is in a rut, doing exactly what he did twenty years ago. No doubt he does love the children, and his paternal needs are being met, but the children's needs are not being met. How is new life to be injected into him, or a new leader given the department?

Perhaps the most natural way is for a new leader to emerge from the ranks of the teachers. If a teacher is qualified for leadership, the church will soon know it. If that teacher is doing an outstanding piece of work, others will hear about it and will come to find out the reasons. He will be asked to speak to other teachers, they will come to observe his methods, parents will pass along the word as to what has been done for their children, and soon he will be leading in actuality if not in name. When the old leader feels the expulsive power of a new force, he will drop out of the picture if prayer has been made to that end. The new leader must not run ahead of the Lord, but like David of old must wait for the Lord to depose Saul.

The Secretary. Let not this officer in any department either say or feel, "I'm only the secretary." Let no one else belittle the work of the secretary in protecting and promoting the teaching ministry. Bible schools need secretaries and librarians and custodians of materials as well as department superintendents.

The type of personality who enjoys working with details as well as with people has a large office only if he or she is willing to make it so. His attributes are efficiency and humility. Though he is the spirit of organization, he does his work behind the scenes, to be seen of God rather than men, though he is sure to be approved of men also.

Whereas one concern of the secretary should be to prevent interruptions, he himself is sometimes the chief interruption. He makes such a stir about his duties that it might be better if they were not performed. It is he who should cause the machinery of organization set up by the executives to run smoothly, with as little evidence as possible that there is any machinery.

His chief duty is to keep accurate and adequate records—any information which will help the teachers teach more effectively. He will often confer with the superintendent on which facts are being used, will discard any which are no longer needed, and add any items which the teachers would like to know. Upward and downward trends will be analyzed and weaknesses remedied.

The department secretary also can have a legitimate intimate touch with the boys and girls. He can stand at the door to care for latecomers who arrive after group activities are already in progress; discuss with them their reasons for being late and what they miss thereby; help them remove their wraps and slip in quietly. He can help solve individual difficulties by seeing that a cap left on the floor is not lost, and that money and materials are not a temptation to anyone. He leaves little tasks for the children to perform in the church—errands, sorting and distributing materials, arranging furniture.

A Primary superintendent contrasts two secretaries:

> Miss Marshall wanted to help in the church, but being a secretary was not her particular niche. Whenever I turned around, there was Miss Marshall, very much in evidence, doing something for the department by disturbing someone else. She is the human interest type of personality, and now is making an excellent church caller.
>
> Miss Perkins, on the other hand, has magnified the office until I would feel as if my right hand were cut off should she have to leave. I seldom see her, but everywhere I turn I see the results of her forethought. Whenever I need colored chalk or thumb tacks, I go to her desk and there they are, neatly arranged and labeled. Her figures are *vital* statistics, they really speak, for they are listed in connection with our present interests. Not only is she orderly and systematic in caring for details, but she is always ready to make a poster or arrange a bulletin board, or help a child find a picture or a book. I don't know how I ever managed to teach when I had to bother about all these trifles which used to frustrate and annoy just at the wrong moment.

LEADERSHIP EDUCATION

Though there are few born leaders, the majority of any church group can be trained to be leaders. It is not the right of any believer in the Lord Jesus Christ to underestimate the inherent talent with which he has been endowed; he is to offer it gladly to the Master of the harvest for Him to use as He chooses. It is a mistake for Christians to get the idea that a few in the church with particular ability should hold all the offices because others are not competent. These few persons spread their energies so thin that they are not doing justice to any office, while the rest of the members sit placidly drinking in the Word, but stagnate spiritually because they have no outlet for service. Adults in a church need the Bible school for their own growth quite as much as the pupils need them for guidance.

An Indigenous Program. The time to begin leadership education is at the age of three rather than twenty-three. Training for service in the church should begin as soon as a child comes to church. "I can't remember a time when I didn't want to be a teacher," remarked one young woman.

The ideal is steady growth on the part of each individual in the church, from the youngest to the oldest—healthy metabolism from taking in and giving out. Why wait until the formative age is past before challenging a child with his responsibility to the work of the Lord? Everything that he can do to help is a learning situation, and should be an essential part of the total program.

The Nursery child is beginning his leadership training when he learns to hang up his hat and coat and to put away the materials with which he works. Beginners and Primaries can take responsibility for keeping their own rooms neat and attractive, for making a few simple regulations for group procedure, and can understand how they are a part of the whole church. Juniors often change the membership on their various committees so that all may share responsibility; they often discuss and plan their own programs and carry them out, and perform many deeds of service, such as stamping and folding and mailing letters, cleaning rooms and materials, and arranging bulletin boards.

Courses on teaching methods as well as Bible surveys should have a place in the program for all young people, whether they plan to be parents or teachers or secretaries. All need study of the age groups and methods and administration of the Bible school to be intelligent participants of the work of the church. Then those who feel called to teach can take intensive specialization in work with children or youth or administration.

Teacher's Meetings. Teachers, when do you feel the need of meeting with other teachers in your department? How can you help them? How can they help you? What kinds of programs are most valuable to you when you come together?

The purpose of teachers' meetings is primarily for inspiration and education, only secondarily for business and fellowship. If teachers take their valuable time to come to a meeting where a few people discuss whether to buy Christmas candy for 10¢ or 15¢ a pound, or to have the Sunday School picnic at Thatcher's Woods or Lone Rock, they cannot be expected to put forth much effort to be present next month. If trifles of this kind are relegated to committees, the regular teachers' meeting can be devoted to matters of genuine concern to all who come.

The superintendent should plan a teachers' meeting on the same principles as a children's session—it must proceed along the line of the teachers' needs, interest, and abilities, and provide variety, participation, and new experiences. As soon as subjects of concern to all are cared for, the teachers adjourn to departmental meetings where they can get down to business regarding their own problems.

The following are suggestions for making teachers' meetings vital:

1. Share teaching victories, questions, and problems.
2. Discuss specifically the next unit of lessons.
3. Discuss suggestions for improvements—why they are needed, what can be done.
4. Discuss special projects, such as a new educational building, a department library, etc.
5. Discuss the adjustment of aims and methods to changing conditions.
6. Report on current books and articles of timely interest.
7. Report on conventions, and visits and observations in the public schools and other Bible schools.

ABSENTEES AND NEW MEMBERS

No Bible school is working to capacity unless it is reaching all in the community who are not connected with other churches, and unless it holds all that it reaches. Of course, effort is wasted if workers with more zeal than wisdom make spasmodic attempts to enlist new members without adequate facilities for taking care of them when they come. Few churches have ideal arrangements, and yet if the Lord's people do what they can, He will do what they cannot do.

A Follow-Up System. Each school needs a routine system for absentees, not because Miss Judson does not care what happens to her Johnny who is sick, but because when she has caught a vision of the opportunities for Christian service she has so many other concerns. She leaves church with the best of intentions to call at Johnny's home and take him a picture book. But other activities crowd in on her week until it is Sunday morning before she thinks about it again.

One of the most practical methods of follow-up for absentees is:

The first week—the secretary sends a card or telephones.
The second week—the teacher makes a personal call.
The third week—the department superintendent calls.
The fourth week—the general superintendent calls.

Reaching the Constituency. After a school is strong enough to take care of those already enrolled, the next step is to reach out for others who should be attending. Perhaps there are fewer people in this day and age who feel that "no one cares for my soul," and more who want to be let alone to go their own way. Yet the Lord's people are as responsible for the latter as for those who already feel the need of something more satisfying than material things.

The first means of approach is the example of Christians who show forth the power as well as the humility of Christ, whose daily lives prove that the joy of the Lord and the way of the Lord are strength to the upright. The regularity of church attendance, the carrying of Bibles, the tone of voice used in casual conversation, the harmonious working together for spiritual enterprises, all are necessary before direct words of invitation will carry weight.

Then each school has to decide which systematic approach is best suited to its own situation. For a teacher or church member to pray and work among his own neighbors who watch his life is much more potent than for an outsider to come in appearing like a solicitor. To canvass a district with factual questions will secure information, but it often fails to secure friendly response in terms of spiritual need.

Much more effective is the indirect acquisition of information, then a personal call by the third-year Junior teacher on eleven-year-old Ronald. His would-be teacher tells him about the other boys and what fun they are having finding out why God chose Palestine to be the land of the Bible. Usually, both Ronald and his parents are impressed with the fact that he is missing a part of his rightful heritage when he is not attending Bible school.

The Cradle Roll Department. "But Ronald already has spent eleven years outside the church, and is maturing quite nicely without Bible training, thank you," the parents may answer.

If a young parent, however, is approached about the new baby, very few will refuse to have his name placed on the Cradle Roll of the church. Unless more antagonistic than most parents, the new parents want to start the child with every possible advantage. They realize in a measure the temptations rampant in the world, and desire to give him more training than they had.

The Cradle Roll superintendent has a key position in the church for real soul-winning. She has more favorable circumstances for reaching new prospects than any other officer, than even the pastor, perhaps. Preferably, she should be a mother with a burden for the souls and homes of other parents; with a radiant, tactful, resourceful, hopeful personality, and, preeminently, with time to call. Her position being such a strategic one, a church may well hire someone to come into her home to do her routine housework rather than curtail her time when she might be out adventuring in friendship for Christ.

Many are the avenues by which this mother will detect the arrival of new babies. She seems to have a sixth sense for tracking them. She quickly spots newcomers in the church and community. She watches the birth list in newspapers, observes clotheslines and moving vans for signs, and receives reports from a "spy ring" of secretaries and friends and Girl Scouts.

Placing a white flower in the pulpit of the church for each new baby serves to tie that home to the church. After the church service the Cradle Roll worker takes the flower to the hospital, and the mother is delighted to know that the church cares that much about the new life. The worker then can explain the worth of a soul, how it is born with Adamic nature, which needs redirection, but with possibilities for receiving the new life of Christ and His great salvation.

Once a year, preferably in May, the church should celebrate Cradle Roll Day, in which all the Sunday School departments assemble for twenty minutes to honor its youngest members. All the babies enrolled during the year may be brought to the altar for blessing in the name of Christ. The Cradle Roll superintendent introduces each one in turn, perhaps with some personal comment. A short worship service may include an appropriate song by children, a short message on child training by the pastor, and, if the weather permits, a church school parade.

Visitation. Teachers need to visit the homes of their pupils as much for their own sakes as for the sake of the children and parents. They can properly teach a child only in the light of his background and home training, in terms of his everyday needs and interests. In the second place, a teacher needs to know how the Bible school is affecting the child's daily life. If the Bible is being truly taught, parents are glad to meet and talk with the teacher who has made a difference in their darling's conduct, and who cares that much about a child who is "only a Sunday School pupil."

Four-year-old Joan came to vacation school with a very difficult, negative attitude. She stood just inside the door, sulky and obstinate, refusing to remove her wraps. Attempts to induce her to participate in the activities which absorbed the other Beginners only increased her resistance. Calling in the home, her teacher soon learned the reason for her negativism. She felt entirely different toward the child when she realized what the home was doing to make her that way.

Her mother, father, grandmother and older sister all nagged at the child continually. They quarreled with each other, disagreed as to what they wanted her to do, slapped her and she slapped them back, until the poor child was torn in pieces emotionally.

At church the teacher emphasized the opposite extreme in her treatment of Joan. She made no demand or suggestions, showed consistent love, and let Joan take her own time about entering activities. Joan began to blossom an entirely different personality in church. "It's so different here," she confided.

A visitor cultivates the art of being unobtrusively helpful to parents. She finds the most convenient time to call in each home instead of intruding at a moment when parents appear at their worst and are cross for making a poor impression. She realizes that it is as important to know when to leave as when to come. Without taking too much of their time, she has a leisurely attitude, making friends with them as far as they wish to go. She makes their interests her own, taking pains to bring them a favorite recipe or article or book. She prays and waits for natural opportunities to speak for Christ, without a "holier than thou" attitude.

The visitor also has brought a paper or picture or story for the child, and talks with him about his pet or his tent or his train, but not about him to the parents in his presence. She approaches a shy baby gradually, a reticent father tactfully, an older brother along the line of current world events. If her whole attitude is like a breath of spring fragrance, people will be sincere, not just polite, when they ask her to return.

1. What factors in your Bible school organization hinder effective teaching? What would be the *best* ways to remedy the situations? As you are praying and working to those ends, what can be done in the meantime to help *temporarily* at least?
2. Work out a Promotion Day service in which each department will feel approved of the Lord for its past accomplishments and challenged to attempt greater things in the strength of the Lord for the future.

Lead each department in evaluating some of the aspects of Christian growth which have been apparent in their lives during the past two or three years. For instance, the Primaries and Juniors may want to testify as to their salvation and how they *show* that they are Christians. The smaller children may sing one of their songs which they carry home and live with during the week.

What kind of brief message would be most helpful by the pastor? What feature might well tie all the contributions together into a unified whole?
3. What kinds of committees are valuable for children of Primary and Junior age to help them assume responsibility and leadership?
4. Plan an inspirational and educational teachers' meeting around a need which you feel in your school, or a need of a child or certain children. What parts of the meeting would require special prayer and preparation?
5. What illustrations can you give of the benefits of visitation, both to the home and to the Bible school?

B. ASPECTS OF CHILD DEVELOPMENT

CHAPTER V

INDIVIDUALITY

1. In your opinion, how does the average Bible school teacher measure up to the standard set in Chapter II? Rate from one to ten your estimate of the average teacher's spiritual consecration, his burden for the lost, his experimental knowledge of the Bible, his concern about the children's everyday lives, his knowledge of the age group he teaches, and his efficiency in teaching methods. In which of this list of characteristics do you consider yourself to be average, in which above average, and in which below average?
2. In the group of children with which you are most familiar, can you select any one who is average in all respects? What is the outstanding characteristic of each individual? How far can you analyze the factors which have formed each distinct personality?
3. Can you remember an occasion in your own childhood when someone did not understand you? What effect did that treatment have upon you? Do you know any child who is not understood? How does that fact affect his reactions?

In the study of childhood from infancy to adolescence it is necessary to speak of the Nursery child, the Beginner child, the Primary child, and the Junior child, implying typical characteristics for the various age levels. While there are typical characteristics, there are probably no children who are typical in all respects; the average child is a phantom child. Yet when all the characteristics of all the children of an age group are combined, these form a composite child for purposes of analysis and comparison with other ages.

At first glimpse of Elizabeth, it was hard to refrain from joining all the thoughtless adults in commenting aloud, "Isn't she darling!" With prim complacency she sat, neatly starched and curled, weighted with the accumulated poise gained by reigning for four years as queen of the home. Noisy little boys should have felt rebuked by her glance. She did not take part in the activities until a hard question gave the rest of the group pause. But when all the restless little boys and girls became donkeys to prepare them for the story of the Good Samaritan, Elizabeth sat aloof—so aloof that even the teacher felt foolish "trotting" before her condescending gaze. . . . Elizabeth has already a very self-righteous air, which is inclined to exalt her to an altitude where she looks down on other sinful people, but never dreaming that it was for her that Jesus died, as well as for the rambunctious Pete who sometimes manages to sit beside her despite her disapproval.

During the long week Pete has been anticipating with pleasure the flurry of Sunday morning, when Father and Mother and he bustle to get to church on time. He comes bouncing into the Beginner room, his eyes dancing at the prospect of playmates. Before the teacher arrives, he has already organized the chairs into a train and has prevailed upon several timid souls to ride. The teacher's arrival ruins the game, and her rebuke sets him busy arranging the chairs in the required manner. He wants to please the teacher, so he sits on his chair—for three seconds. At the mention of prayer, he is down on his knees and has mumbled his genuine love to God. By the time the other children understand what the teacher has in mind, he is again a train, pushing his chair merrily around the room. . . . Pete already has a firm sense of his own sinfulness, for he cannot please all the adults although he truly tries, and tries hard. When he is told that he can ask Jesus to be his Saviour, and that Jesus will help him do these things that he cannot do by himself, he clings to that promise of hope and is already acknowledging his own helplessness and hopelessness, and his constant need of a power greater than himself.

What is the teacher's point of view in regard to these individual differences? Will he seek to mold or drill them all into a uniform pattern? God has put in each life latent capacities and talents which He hopes to use for His glory, and Christ in the life will strengthen weaknesses and develop abilities, enabling each one to reflect the Saviour in his own unique way. How fascinating to deal with such diverse human reactions! Teaching is never monotonous, since no two people are alike and no person can be absolutely depended on to react twice the same way.

WHY KNOW CHILDREN AS INDIVIDUALS?

If in our prayer and in our study we visualize a class and not individuals we may as well deliver a message to a circle of chairs and call our work done. The criterion in all our teaching is not how smoothly or orderly an hour we conduct, or how fluently we tell a story, or how much the children enjoy it, although these are necessary objections—the criterion is the degree to which the individual child is making spiritual progress. If he has not yet bowed at the foot of the Cross we must perhaps go afar off to the place where he is spiritually and lead him on from there. After the foundation of personal acceptance of Christ has been laid, he should begin at once to build a worthy life on that foundation, that he may grow up into Him in all things.

Progress should be measured, not by the place where a child is at the present moment in his spiritual development, but by the distance we have helped him come. How can we hope to meet a child's need until we have discovered how much or how little background he brings with him to class? Yet many a teacher begins blithely with a new class without finding out about the children's homes and parents, or their past Sunday School experience from former teachers. In the event of an epidemic or stormy weather, when our classes number one or two, do we make the most of the opportunity of personal discussion about individual problems, or do we double up small classes lest any teacher's time be "wasted"?

We must know the children as well as the Lord and His Word if we are to lead the children to the Lord through His Word.

If we are ready to enjoy the boys' ball games with them they will be ready to enjoy the Bible with us. If we show genuine interest in the girls' dolls they will show interest in our Bible verses. If we are eager to "by all means save some" we shall study each child until we find the point of contact to his interest and his heart.

Nothing is unimportant in the trifles of their lives. No mortal is so hard, no child is so shy, that we cannot discover some avenue of approach to his inner being if we will spare no pains. It may be the singing, or the handwork, or the Christmas party, that first draws a child to the Bible school—and then to the teacher, and then to the Saviour.

A mother visits a Primary department, and cannot understand why a teacher insists that one boy repeat his Bible passage until it is letter perfect, and the next minute approves another for saying the same passage haltingly, with help on several words. The mother does not know, as does the teacher, that the second boy has expended much more effort than the first without half the visible results. The first, being mentally superior, is tempted to relax into bad habits of laziness because he grasps new ideas so quickly. The second has several handicaps, and becomes discouraged unless he feels that he is succeeding. The first boy rattles off Bible verses with little meaning and little personal application. The second does not get every word in its place in the sentences, but he is saved and allows the truth to operate in his daily life. Head knowledge is more natural for one, heart knowledge more natural for the other.

METHODS OF STUDYING INDIVIDUALS

A teacher is expected, of course, to be constantly availing himself of various means of studying the typical reactions of average children. But much more stimulating than book theory is the study of real, live boys and girls. Teaching may be a chore if it is regarded as the discharging of a lesson, or it may be a thrill and a science if it is regarded as working with God to produce eternal changes in young lives.

Observation of Individuals. Where shall the teacher observe children? He will observe them everywhere he finds them and under all circumstances. He will observe them at play when they are free from restraint, to discover their natural tendencies; observe them at home, where they form part of their first social unit; observe them at school under supervision, and observe them in church.

A few words of warning may prevent injury to the child as we seek to promote his welfare. We must observe without stirring his self-consciousness, and without discussing him in his presence. A friendly interest in whatever he is doing, and natural conversation on his level about that activity, will disclose more to us than will any other method. Questions innumerable may be profitably asked of parents and teachers, but not in his hearing.

As we observe, we shall avoid jumping at conclusions and hastily labeling a child superior, stupid, dull, or lazy. The stupid may only lack confidence, or physical care, or a familiar environment. We may soon tire of the garrulous and audacious child who at first seems readiest to respond. Many children develop slowly at one stage and then spurt ahead at the next. The poet Wordsworth is an example of a famous character who as a child was easily distracted and had no ability to concentrate. Moreover, those who realize that they have no strength in themselves often mature into the great men of faith who trust an all-powerful God to use the weak things of the world to confound the mighty.

Most children are better students of human nature than are their teachers; they do not always study their lessons, but they study their teachers to find out how much they can "get away with."

Bible School Records. When a teacher receives a new class in the Bible school, what information would he like to have about those pupils? It is not necessary for more than one teacher to make a case history of each pupil or to ask the parents and children for the same information. The new teacher can start with this background and get acquainted by using more interesting methods, such as working and playing with them and going to places with them.

While a few schools keep case histories of their pupils, at least of those who present difficulties, most Bible school records are not complete or up to date. Most of them are superficial, giving the number of years of attendance, the number of Sundays of attendance in each year, the degree of punctuality, and the number of times an offering and Bible were brought. More vital matters as to the individual's personality and spirituality are not recorded. Why cannot a permanent record card be kept which also notes his interests, his abilities, his home conditions, his health, and the major spiritual victories and weaknesses for each year? Would not this type of information be more valuable and more often referred to because it probes to the roots of the problems?

THE BASIC NEEDS OF EACH CHILD

Although the outward symptoms of behavior problems are many, yet the basic needs of all children are few. Failure to satisfy these needs constitutes the real cause of difficulties. The needs, to be discussed later, are:

A. Spiritual
1. Faith and dependence on the Lord
2. Genuine experience of salvation
3. Daily growth in grace
4. Worship of the high and holy One
5. Growing independence in overcoming temptation
6. Practical avenues for service

B. Psychological and Social
1. A feeling of security
2. A normal degree of affection, belonging and attention
3. A sense of adequacy, success, and recognition

C. Mental
1. Activity along the line of present interests
2. Challenges to present abilities
3. Opportunities for creative ability
4. Broadening interests and new experiences

D. Physical
1. Healthy vitality
2. Growing independence in health habits
3. Activity for growing muscles

IMPORTANCE OF EMOTIONS

Because whole chapters will be devoted to the other three types of basic needs, only the psychological will be considered here.

In the past too many teachers have been concerned about facts only, about getting the children to sit still so that they can impart to them Bible knowledge. They are content when the boys and girls give back to them this same knowledge. If the pupils recited a Bible verse more or less correctly, it was assumed that the truth was "learned," regardless of the way the pupils *felt* about the words or what they *did* about the words. But familiar facts may be disregarded instead of made essential factors in life if the emphasis is only on outward conformity to outward standards.

In our day the emphasis is turning from the outward and obvious to the inward and more subtle attitudes and motives. How a child feels toward the Bible, the church, and the Lord's people is more important than the facts he can repeat about them. If he likes to be at church, if he is attracted to Christians, and if he is eager to find out more about God's Word, he will be inwardly activated to seek other contacts with them. But if these things of the Lord have become distasteful to him, he will turn away from them as soon as outside pressure is released.

An adult often deceives himself and others by rationalizing to explain his conduct, offering mere excuses, the real reason being that he learned certain emotional habits unconsciously in childhood. In the forgotten episodes of early life lie the reasons for many of our adult preferences and prejudices.

The Emphasis in Scripture. The Bible's central premise is that "out of the heart are the issues of life," that only interior regeneration can work exterior transformation. The first and great commandment is not to *know* or to *do,* but to *love* the Lord with all the heart.

From cover to cover the Word of God provides for the

training and molding of the emotional life by outlets which challenge the whole personality and energy. It continually commends right motives and condemns mere outward conformity. Bible stories abound in incidents of emotional experience to be appreciated vicariously in order that the tragedies and sufferings of the past may help us solve our own emotional conflicts without serious upsets.

The Need for Security. Of all living organism, a child is born the most helpless, and has the longest period of adjustment to fit him to make his contribution in the world. Growing up is just one continual round of gaining security, then losing it to attain new security, maladjustment and readjustment, stepping from dependence to independence. A major emotional need of each individual is a safe feeling that he *belongs* and that he is secure in affection. At each level of development the child should be strengthening his inner confidence to meet life's demands without so much assistance from his elders but with increased dependence on the Lord.

A child feels secure, not when he is being a copy of some one else—perhaps the suppressed desire of one of his parents, perhaps the ideal of one of his teachers—but when his Maker is allowed to develop fully his own unique possibilities. He is not content to gain all his knowledge second-hand through the vague words of others; he must himself reach out to appropriate for himself God's good gifts, to pray through, to renew his strength. Unless these habits are established early, he is already learning to put his confidence in others or in his own efforts, which will always fail.

Our complex civilization creates numerous fine distinctions which bewilder a child as he grapples for security. The Lord's day must be kept differently from other days, and he must learn its special pleasures. What is permissible at home is altogether out of place at church. The meaning of private property, learning what he may and may not touch, is a great source of misunderstanding.

Life is complex indeed for those children whose parents have no interest in spiritual things and yet send them to church for what they themselves have no apparent need. Children have perception, however, to realize that though their parents may provide sufficiently for other needs, spirituality has been neglected. The calm and peace of the Bible school atmosphere contrasted with the discord of many homes will speak louder than words until the child recognizes the authority of the Scriptures.

Faced with a confusion of conflicting standards, it is easy to see how desperately children need stable, consistent training, dependable human relationships, and endless patience.

The Need for Affection. A helpless child's need for love is much greater than that of adults, and he cannot go abroad to initiate his own adventures in friendship. He must depend on a few intimate adults to know him better than he knows himself. He needs a few people who really understand the sensitive inner world of childhood, to whom he feels free to confide both his joys and sorrows, always sure of sympathy and help. He deserves to feel a warm, outgoing interest which acknowledges that he is a personality worth knowing.

It is a peculiar delight for him to have parent or teacher all to himself at times. The teacher should visit the home not only to find out the home background, not only to discover the reason for absence, but also to visit the child for the express purpose of fellowship with him.

What a relief it is for a child to know that the adults whom he loves accept him just as he is, without condemnation! And God, the One who knows him best, is the One who loves him most!

The Need for Adequacy. The third basic reason why people act as they do is the inner urge for adequacy. Stop to analyze how many of a child's overt acts are due to an inner drive to achieve—to achieve status with his own social group and with the superiors he admires. He may even prefer disapproval to no attention at all.

What a person ultimately becomes is largely conditioned by early successes and failures. Unless each individual feels that he is making some progress, failure to achieve may be expressed by introversion, such as shyness and isolation; refusal to try, as in fits of temper or sulking; or by compensations, such as cheating, bluffing, or teasing. Let a human being of any age feel that he is needed, that he has possibilities for success, that increased effort will remove an obstacle, and the goal is as good as won. On the other hand, let a person feel discouraged, unworthy, unlovable, or humiliated in front of his companions, and he lacks sufficient self-esteem to keep on trying.

Almost all children feel inferior in some respect, but the condition is serious only when this feeling is so generalized that they cannot hope to be on a par with their fellows. Discouragement is the devil's best tool, against which God warns, "Provoke not your children to anger, lest they be discouraged" (Col. 3:21), but "bring them up in the nurture and admonition of the Lord" (Eph. 6:4), that they may increase "in wisdom and stature, and in favor with God and man" (Luke 2:52).

Divine provision is ample for each individual, for God has given each of us all the innate endowment we need to fulfill the purpose for which we were created. And the child of God has been given the promise that in all the exigencies of life he shall never be tempted above that he is able to withstand.

But do we not often provoke the children to wrath and thereby discourage them? We bring fragile objects to illustrate new ideas, and if they happen to break or soil the objects reprimand them for exploring and learning about them. We impose on them tasks which make unreasonable demands on their unco-ordinated muscles. We set up for them such high standards and such remote ideals that they can see no present ends that are attainable. Though so-called civilized nations cannot live harmoniously with each other, we seem to expect young children to learn at once to be unselfish.

If a child is to adjust himself happily to our Brobdingnagian requirements, he must have a firm but simple world where order, not chaos, reigns. He must have a few well-known and understood demands consistently enforced, and be able to carry them out without *undue* exertion. This will insure him the balance of success over failure that he needs to go on. Life will always hold frustrations, there will always be struggles and failures. What is joy but surmounting obstacles? Children will profit by failure if they are not harshly blamed, which puts them on the defensive and often leads to rationalization if not to lying.

The degree to which we help a child and the degree to which he looks up to us for approval greatly affect his learning. If we help him too much, he will become boastful and in overconfidence attempt the impossible. We can be on hand to take the bitter edge off failure and to add pleasure to success. The child of God should receive his satisfaction, not from adult approval nor yet from personal achievement, but from the Lord. The fickle plaudits of men will distract attention from the reality of his own achievement, but the praise of God never produces the self-conscious "showing-off" attitude.

TYPES OF INDIVIDUAL DIFFERENCES

After the basic needs of each individual have been envisaged, and case studies have been made of particular pupils, the teacher is then ready to diagnose behavior differences and to begin treatment. Some problems are clearly due to the lack or oversupply of only one of the above basic needs, and remarkable results are quickly effected. Others are more complicated and subtle, with roots buried deep in developmental history and perhaps encased in a guilty or shameful situation which no one involved wishes to disclose.

All too often teachers think of children's misdemeanors as personal, as directed against themselves, and their own emotions are aroused accordingly. A study of root causes takes the problem out of the realm of the personal, and gives the teacher a wholesome objective attitude—calm, and matter-of-fact. When he adopts this scientific attitude, he can then help children to face reality frankly, and develop insight into themselves, without requiring harmful escape mechanisms.

Children are pliable clay in the sense that they may be molded by any influence, but not to the extent that their wills can be disregarded. Teachers must work with nature and not against it, must harness children's wills on the side of the Lord and health. Some clay is too damp and some too dry; some children's wills are too flexible and some too rigid. Yet we should never seek to break a will, for every person needs all the strength of will to fight against evil. The will needs to be guided toward the Lord because His way is seen as reasonable and eternally profitable.

THE TROUBLESOME CHILD

What's his name in your group—the child who seems to delight in attending to anything else but the subject at hand? He has no interest in group activities, but a great deal in being perverse, in disturbing and annoying. He's not really bad yet, though a nuisance to have around; but he is on the road to badness. If a physical examination proves him to be suffering from no organic or glandular abnormalities, and his home conditions prove him to be getting a proper amount of food and sleep, it is likely that he lacks independence, attention, or recognition.

Lack of Independence. "Mamma's baby" who has been overindulged and shielded from all kinds of struggle demands praise and display continually. When the second baby arrives and he is removed from his pedestal, he is likely to develop conflicts and to hate the one who is taking his place. He has been accustomed to finding satisfaction in being the object of pampering and coddling, and outside the home seeks vainly in one way and then another to make up for the lack of petting. His mind is not free to participate wholeheartedly in group activities, but vaguely seeks protection from the give and take of normal social life.

The over-dependent child needs to find satisfaction in growing up and in doing things for himself and for others. The teacher who knows his home will not feel cross with the child; it is the child's foolish or ignorant parents who are to blame. The normal child is ever finding new ways in which to feel bigger and do things that others have previously done for him. Of course, the pampered child can be introduced only gradually to the new idea of independence, but he will soon realize that the Lord and the teacher and his friends in Bible school give him approval for helping rather than in being helped, in giving rather than in receiving. He can be trained to plan special treats for others, and to assume responsibilities.

Lack of Attention. Children are not the only ones who interrupt, make silly remarks, and disobey rules rather than be ignored, for every person normally desires his degree of attention. Most people strive valiantly to achieve it in a socially approved manner, but if that fails, will resort to cruder methods. A child soon learns that the easiest way to get attention is to make trouble, for temptations are always at hand. He much prefers scolding and even punishment to no attention at all. To be called the bad boy of a class gives him at least one type of recognition. Since the older child desires the approval of his own age group more than any other, proof to his friends that he can get ahead of the teacher, even if she punishes, gives him an experience that on the whole is satisfying to him.

Temper tantrums are simply a method of getting their own way that children discover. A child naturally experiments with various types of reaction to see which is most effective in gaining his own ends. An angry scene, especially in public, never fails to bring results. So, of course, that procedure is repeated.

When that happens in Bible school, the mother stands helpless in embarrassment. But the teacher, without a sign of impatience, kindly but firmly, in a tone quite different from the mother's, asks the child, "Would you like to stay here and play happily with the other children, or would you like to go into the next room by yourself where you can scream and cry?" The child is usually surprised to be treated like this, straightens up to consider, and will pay attention to an interesting object which is offered him. It doesn't take him long to learn that in Bible school he gets attention by other means.

Poor Jimmy! He just couldn't do anything right! Constant frowns of disapproval were making a mischievous little boy into a sulky, deliberately bad boy. The superintendent of Daily Vacation Bible School warned his teacher about Jimmy. "You'll have to prove to him that he *can* be good." Praise, whenever possible, and a bright smile were all the encouragement he needed for further effort. When he poked and slapped the other children (his favorite trick), she quietly folded his hands in his lap. He would look up roguishly, to see if she really meant it, and a grave but kind look usually turned the trick. She tried to keep the attitude of taking it for granted that he would "be good," and he did try so hard! At the end of two weeks, Jimmy's mother thanked her for helping him so much, and said he had never been better at home.

Lack of Recognition. The only One to whom a human being can safely surrender his will and self-esteem is the Lord God. To surrender to another human or to conflicting circumstances is to crush and ruin the personality. God has given each child an ego which seeks success and recognition among his peers.

It often happens that an adult's own self-esteem is wounded by a child. He then tries to squelch the child, in the spirit of "I'll put that young one in his place," and tries to force an issue without appealing to the child's sense of justice and reason. The spirit in the child then bounds back up in an effort to protect his own rights and esteem, and the battle is on. The adult may win by reason of superior strength and authority, yet the child remembers the insult, and the next time seeks again to gain the advantage. Only by respecting the personality of a child can an adult expect to train him in the way he should go. In a conflict of wits it is not always the adult who wins.

Everything which tends to encourage a feeling of inferiority is likely to provoke some kind of badness. Inferiority is not to be confused with the commendable virtues of humility and love toward others, nor with acknowledging oneself a sinner before the holy God. The person afflicted with feelings of inferiority exaggerates his weak points and fails to recognize his strong ones. Any perversion of the truth is dishonoring to the Creator, who doeth all things well.

The bluffing bully is an example of this type of behavior.

Many teachers think of the bully as "plain mean" instead of analyzing his difficulties. Sometimes this type is the dull, overage, or overgrown child who cannot succeed mentally, so resorts to using his physical strength to harass others in order "to get even."

Sometimes it is the child who is knocked around at home and made the butt of jokes, until when he escapes from that atmosphere he takes his spite out on those who are younger and weaker than he. He learns to rationalize his acts and blame others for failure. He feels that the world is trying to put something over on him, and he uses what ability he has to resist.

Why cannot his source of strength be used to fight the Lord's battles instead of tormenting others? After prayer and investigation have enabled the teacher to put his finger on the source of trouble, he may talk it over with the child himself. More readily than adults, children will face the issue frankly, and recognize a penetrating analysis of the case.

His teacher may say to him, in effect, "George, I know that there's a lot more in you than most people think. I can see great things in you as a soldier of Christ. Don't waste your strength teasing the children. It shouldn't make you feel important to tease children. There's a lot of sin to fight, and the Lord needs boys like you. Do you remember what Christ did when His enemies accused Him of things He did not do, and treated Him spitefully? He just took it, and prayed for them. We need a boy to keep this room in order and see that we have just enough air coming in the windows. Wouldn't you like to start serving Christ by doing that?" If he is challenged with practical duties in which he can succeed, and is shown the love and approval he deserves, he will no longer feel the need of teasing.

THE TIMID CHILD

Psychologists agree that the children usually considered "model pupils" cause more difficulty later in life than do the troublesome children. Their problems are more serious, more subtle, and more insidious. The normal child is active, aggressive, and sociable. A wise teacher would prefer a child to disturb occasionally if his intentions are good than to sit passively listless and unresponsive, or tense and nervous.

Such is the pressure of competition in modern life that whereas the majority of people possess average ability, all are urged to struggle for the same ideals of perfection. Odious comparisons are made between those of superior ability who easily win the heights and those of average ability who are putting forth their best efforts yet not reaching the same goals. When parents seek to realize their own thwarted ambitions in the lives of their offspring, the poor children are haunted by the ghost of what is expected of them, but which may go against the grain of their interests and abilities.

THE DREAMY CHILD

Though most people do a certain amount of daydreaming, excessive imagination ceases to be constructive, but rather an escape from a world in which there are too few successes to be satisfying. Not trying at all eliminates the possibility of failure.

A child may begin to imagine a great deal when he lies in bed for a long period, when his activities are limited by physical weakness, or when he is led to distrust people who have accused him of guilt when he is innocent. He finds this means a pleasant escape from boredom or inferiority, for in his imagination he can be a hero who asserts himself and does exactly as he pleases. Daydreaming ceases to be normal when it is not connected with some form of activity, when projects started are finished only in imagination.

The dreamy child needs to be guided in visualizing constructive ideas and in carrying them out. He needs to discover that there is more joy in grappling with reality in a give-and-take world. At first he should be given easy tasks, with plenty of approval for what he accomplishes, and then be gradually weaned from unrealities. Life is never all success, and no one should expect it to be, but the Christian "can do all things through Christ who strengtheneth" him.

THE OVERCONSCIENTIOUS CHILD

The child who feels inferior or inadequate in one respect often will overcompensate in another to bolster his morale. He may have a physical deformity, or a speech defect, or be ashamed of his parents, or simply be a social misfit. This type will often work desperately to attain high standards in school subjects. When demands on him are overly strict, to him impossible, he may feel that he is not wanted, and grow exceedingly sensitive to criticism. How hard it is for children when there is conflict at home, with parents incompatible, or divorced, or jealous!

A conflict is sometimes developed between the home and church, the child experiencing the power of the gospel and yet respecting his honorable parents who know not Christ. This is indeed a difficult situation for the child. It is not the authority of teacher or church which is placed in opposition to the views of parents, but the authority of God Himself.

When the home will share no responsibility for the child's Christian training, the teacher will have to give the child more than the minimum of nurture in the faith. He will have to pray often with the child for the parents. The child can very early learn the techniques of tactful witnessing. When such a home situation exists, teacher and child may pray together with great assurance for the salvation of the parents, for surely the Lord will not allow a delicate personality to be pulled asunder in two directions, when all forces should be integrated about Christ in the life.

THE FEARFUL CHILD

Another type of child who is doubtful of his security withdraws from people without making any outward attempt to regain it. Strenuous physical punishment, threats, and loud scoldings may make a child rebellious, or it may make him fearful—fearful of the antagonistic world in which he finds himself, fearful of doing anything to relieve the gnawing agony of apprehension, fearful of anything new and different, and fearful of people, who are all regarded as potential enemies. Insomnia, irritability, nervous habits, stuttering and stammering are all results of emotional tension.

Worry in young or old is the attempt to do something about a dreaded situation when apparently nothing can be done. The remedy for the worrier is to sit down with him, consider frankly whatever is bothering him, and do something positive about it. The Christian can do something about every difficult situation. He can pray to the Lord, he can develop a spiritual philosophy of life which assigns the difficulty to its rightful place of importance, he can leave it in the hands of the Lord and listen to find out what God wants him to be doing instead of worrying, and be at that immediately.

Remove from the environment of the tense, timid child all causes of friction and conflict. Keep the atmosphere cheerful, calm and unhurried. Never make fun of the timid child, or scold him, or plunge him into a fearful situation in order to overcome it. Though it may take time to win his confidence, emphasize what he does well and minimize his difficulty until he regains confidence. Gradually explore the unfamiliar with him in a spirit of play. Introduce him to the Friend who never fails; "when my mother and father forsake me, the Lord will take me up" (Ps. 27:10). Let him feel the Lord's love and power, which always will be with him to help, even in the darkest night and in the hardest situation.

THE SUPERIOR CHILD

He may have been blessed with exceptional special talent, or with general acumen, but along with that capacity should go the same degree of exceptional responsibility. If this added responsibility is kept in mind from the start, this type of child will present less difficulty. The church of Christ needs special talents; Christ has given them to the church for its edification. A group of children readily accept leadership, either adult or juvenile, provided that leadership is worthy and exemplary; but to lead requires great skill and character traits which inspire others to follow.

Problems arise when the exceptional child uses his power to avoid the monotonous, the tame, and the commonplace. If confined to a routine with others far beneath him in intelligence, he manages to get what he wants, but develops a domineering, rebellious and lazy character. Christian life and service present ideals high enough to challenge the most brilliant.

THE HANDICAPPED CHILD

To the unbelieving parent a child who is handicapped in any way is a tragic misfortune. To the Christian it is simply another way in which "all things work together for good." God makes no mistakes; He creates no failures. He gives each soul exactly what will best mold that life for eternity. In fact, sometimes it is the very beautiful child who suffers, for great are her temptations to pride and selfishness. It is the rich child rather than the poor one who is usually handicapped, for his outlook on life and genuine values is usually distorted.

Children who are deformed or defective should feel that their Creator is expecting more rather than less of them, for He is expecting them to overcome the deficiency as well as to contribute their share to the world. Yet most of them expect only to be waited on as they grow sour and useless, hoping only to die and end their misery. They are trained to think only of themselves, never of others. There can be no joy in that kind of life.

These children's attitudes will be exactly the attitudes of the adults who speak of them either with hope or despair. They need the same opportunities as others to develop their abilities, as well as courage and dependence on the Lord. In a group of children they furnish a practical stimulus for developing a wholesome philosophy of life regarding the true basis of glorying.

Every special type of individual should have held up before him true stories of men and women of the faith who overcame the same kind of obstacles he faces, and who won the crown of life: for the child without temporal securities, such a person as William Carey, the missionary; for the timid, young Timothy of Scripture; for the superior, the Apostle Paul; and for the handicapped, blind Fanny Crosby.

1. Which of the basic needs did you have in proper proportion when a child? What difference has this made in your adolescent or adult life?
2. Can you recall a time when you experienced lack of security, lack of affection, lack of recognition, lack of a sense of belonging to a certain group, a sense of fear, a feeling of being differ-

ent, a feeling of shame, a feeling of being superior, a feeling of being handicapped in some way? What was the effect on your personality of each of these emotions?

3. How does each pupil in your group deviate most from the average? How will you deal with that deviation?

4. Design a practical permanent record card to be filed for each pupil in your Bible school. Provide space for home conditions, health, interests, abilities, points of strength, points of weakness, and spiritual victories.

CHAPTER VI

PHYSICAL AND SOCIAL DEVELOPMENT

1. When you are feeling hale and hearty, what is likely to be your general outlook on life? What is it when you are feeling ill and tired?
2. Do you remember when you learned to drive a car, or to use a typewriter, or other motor skill? Did you at first enjoy practicing that skill? What happened if you tried to continue beyond the point of fatigue?
3. Watch a small child and an older child when they are free to play around the house as they wish. Note the type of activity they choose and the length of time spent on each.
4. Have you observed at what age level children seem to be most suggestible, most group conscious, hero worshiping, healthy, spontaneous, easily exhausted, sensitive, interested in gangs, impulsive, imitative, self-centered?

PHYSICAL DEVELOPMENT

"If only Johnny would bring his mind and spirit to Bible class but leave his body at home!" Isn't that the way many teachers feel about their pupils—some of them, at least? No, children's ideas and actions are all of one piece. They learn "all over." Their bodies are as essential a part of them as their spirits. God gave the body as well as the mind for a purpose

Teachers must be optimists who see an opportunity in every difficulty, rather than pessimists who see a difficulty in every opportunity. How teachers would sin against the child if he feigned attention when they failed to meet his needs and interests! It is when forced attention is insisted on that the child wiggles and squirms. When attention is eager and involuntary, his whole being is bent on the subject at hand—he sits on the edge of his chair with face lifted, with eyes and even mouth open. Indeed, he needs to learn to control his body, but that arduous lesson will be learned gradually, not all at once.

When you are bored, do you not react the same as he, only on an adult level? When you sit listening to a sermon or lecture which does not enlist your attention, what do you do? You take some object out of your mental storehouse and play with it. You choose a mental object, for you have learned the wisdom of outward conformity to conventions.

When the child is bored, he likewise finds something to play with; but since his mental life is as yet quite unreal and fragmentary, he takes something out of his pocket, or pokes the child sitting next to him, or simply squirms. It is a great boon to teachers that children show by their very posture what the teaching means to them.

Moreover, if a child acts on the teaching he receives, it becomes a part of his being, and then cannot be taken out of his life. Only as the Word of God is translated into attitudes and action is it truly learned. If the laws with which the Creator has ordained for the child are observed, even his physical nature can be used to further our purposes as teachers.

The Nursery Child. 1. The Nursery child is continually active, for his large fundamental muscles are growing fast. Being constantly on the move is nature's way of insuring physical growth. The urge to activity is the most potent force in the child while he learns to manipulate his own members, to walk, to begin an independent existence. First the large muscles of the leg and then the arm muscles demand exercise by the chubby toddler.

To meet this physical need, the Nursery child must have opportunity and space for activity. Words mean very little to him. He is a "muscle person." Not merely any activity, however, meets his need, but activity requiring a little control —walking about, handling large, heavy objects, carrying chairs, taking care of large materials. He can learn to take off his own coat and hat, and to hang them on low hooks. He needs to be able to change activities when muscles call for a change. Nothing should demand impossible co-ordination of undeveloped muscles.

2. The senses are hungry for new sensations, for they furnish the gateway to impressions from the outside world. They constitute the only real basis for ideas and for words. On their richness and variety depend all future experience and the meaningfulness of symbolic language. On their accuracy of impression and interpretation depend the sharpness of mental perception. If sensory experiences are lacking, words and ideas are mere empty sounds and vague notions.

The Nursery room should provide things to see and hear and touch, sometimes to smell and taste. Children of this age often stand still and just watch what others are doing, or look at a clear outline picture which contains familiar elements. They rub their hands along walls and glass doors, leaving dirty finger marks, but leaving on their minds ideas of smoothness and hardness. They love to feel the soft texture of a fur collar and velvet cloth.

Is a little child naughty because he is always "getting into things"? Do we really wish he would leave things alone? If he did, he would be either sick or defective, for a normal child has been given all his senses to find out about the strange, bewildering world into which he comes with no innate ideas, but with gateways to discover facts for himself. Therefore his Sunday School room should be equipped with materials for him to handle, the commonest of things, which he also finds at home, and which can be connected with God.

3. Reactions are spontaneous, for there are yet few inhibitions. Every Bible school teacher should be required to have a short period of practice teaching in the Nursery, because there *he* would learn, as in no other way, to begin with the interests of the pupil. The young child has not the ability to give polite voluntary attention, but simply gets up and walks off if he is not interested. Attempts at forcing only make him rebellious.

But if we put around the room things he already knows and enjoys, if we follow him to the particular interest center of the moment, and talk with him about that thing in relation to himself and the Lord, his face will light up with a glow which means appreciation and understanding. He may soon leave that center of interest, but if the experience has been satisfying, he will often return to it. Through interests of short duration control gradually will be developed.

4. The Nursery child has a sensitive nervous system. Most of his life, up to this time, has been spent alone and in sleep. How quickly he becomes restless and tense when a large number of people come to his home! In the foreign environment of the church school room with people he is not sure of, there is much to bewilder, even if the emotional climate is kept as calm as possible. Too many children in a room make his contacts too complicated. Noise and confusion and conflict should be kept as far away as possible. The first requisite of the Nursery teacher's personality is confidence and quietness in the strength of the Lord.

All causes of hurry and strain should be avoided. The hour should be planned to proceed at the child's own slow pace, to provide materials sufficient for all without quarreling, and that are sturdy enough for strenuous use without breaking and tearing. Books should be of linen or poster board, which will stand a lot of pulling; wood objects are preferable to paper; pictures should be mounted on poster board and shellacked.

5. Health is frail and endurance slight. The mortality rate decreases every year after infancy. No one can blame a worldly parent for keeping his child home from Nursery class if health conditions are not one of the first considerations, for the child's physical well-being means everything to that parent —spiritual welfare, nothing. Yet how few nurseries are light and sunny and warm, as they ought to be! No teacher should supervise so many pupils that he cannot watch the ventilation of the room, the hygiene of materials, and the careful putting on of wraps. The two- and three-year-old is as yet a delicate plant.

6. Since children grow at different rates of speed, each Nursery group will present great differences in physical maturity. At this age changes are evident each month. The child who last month took little interest in group activities, next month may become a helpful member of the group. The one who tried to do nothing for himself now works hard to dress himself.

The Nursery program must be adjusted to individuals, with a large part of the period given to individual activities when the children are free to go to any part of the room they wish and to stay there only as long as they like.

The Beginner Child. 1. The Kindergarten child is still growing very fast. He lengthens out considerably more than the Nursery tot, and his muscles cry out for him to be doing things which stretch them.

Have we ever said, or at least thought, of this age, "If only you would sit still for five minutes"? Do we really wish the child would sit still for five minutes? When those bright eyes are dull and those eager feet languishing and the active body sick, then we realize how much we prefer him to be his own lively normal self. "Activity must act, explode, or cease to generate." If we wish the child to become a normal adult we must acknowledge that there is no other way of securing physical growth.

It is tyranny to demand attention for a long period. Beginners need four or five changes within an hour, with much variation within each part. They can sit still for a short story if they have been able to stretch their legs and relax previously. One of the easiest ways to discourage a child into feeling that it is hopeless to try to please an adult is for the adult to forget that the child's whole being cries out for movement and change.

The following is the testimony of a teacher who kept a Catholic child going to her Sunday School because an activity program met the physical needs of the young child:

> Alice is an ideal Beginner. After she had been absent for two Sundays, I went to her home. Her mother explained that, of course, Alice would have to attend her own church when she was a little older, but that the child might come to our church now, on that condition. She had taken Alice to St. Rita's Catholic Church several times, but Alice had said she would rather come to Sunday School. She wouldn't sit still, but wanted to get up and do things. When her mother told her she was naughty, she answered, "Well, then you better send me back to Sunday School. I'm good there."
>
> I explained that at our church the children are taught to be reverent at all times and quiet some of the time, but that they are not expected to sit like bumps on a log the whole hour, as that is

a physical impossibility. We teach through activity as well as words.

2. The large muscles are still growing very rapidly. The legs and upper arms mature before the smaller hand muscles.

The Beginner is willing to attempt many things, but possesses little muscular co-ordination. He must have activities not only that can be *performed* by the awkward and clumsy, but even *enjoyed* by the awkward and clumsy, and that do not include fine work. Not that he could do better if he tried harder, or that he needs more practice and instruction; he needs to live longer to acquire more muscular co-ordination.

Much of the handwork suggested for this age has to be done mostly by the teachers. Yet it is not the teachers who need exercise. They do not have time on their hands.

In one large Beginner department several sweet old ladies hang up the children's wraps, pass the offering receptacle, and do most of the other activities, in order to keep the children sitting in their chairs, which are nailed to the floor. The little old ladies are getting all the activity that the children crave!

Teachers should never do anything that boys and girls could profitably do for themselves! They say, "Stand back while I move the rug," instead of, "Let's all move the rug to the other side of the room."

Growth of large muscles demands large, sturdy materials, as large crayons and paper; sufficient room to move about without impeding others, and music with easy rhythm and intervals—music which is not too fast. Only one activity can be expected of the children at a time—they usually stop singing when they do the motions of an action song, or while depositing their offering.

Instead of trying to do handwork which strains their

small finger muscles, Beginners can often play the Bible stories. After they have heard the story of the crossing of the Red Sea, they can play that they are God's people traveling to the new land that He has promised them. They can walk out in the lobby of the church, perhaps, if their own room is too small. The Red Sea can be two chairs pushed together. The wall on one side of the room can be the mountains which hem in God's people. The member of the group chosen to be Moses holds his rod (any kind of stick available) out over the Red Sea. The teacher then pulls the chairs apart. The children talk about the power of the Lord as they walk right through the river bed, and on the other side sing, "Praise Him, praise Him." Thus they project themselves into that experience of long ago and feel the wonder of it.

Or they can follow the teacher as he leads an action rhyme such as the following:

Fishermen four went fishing one night;
Rowed [1] in their boats with all their might;
Threw[2] out their nets in the water—swish!
And drew[3] them up, but found not a fish.
They threw[2] and pulled,[3] threw[2] and pulled [3] some more,
Till their shoulders[4] and backs and arms were sore.
When Jesus said, "Throw," they let down[2] the net,
Hoping at least a few fish to get.
This time the net took four men to pull! [5]
Shining fish piled up till both boats were full! [6]

[1] Row with wide sideward strokes.
[2] Throw out the nets.
[3] Draw up nets, look carefully for a fish.
[4] Rub sore shoulders and arms and back.
[5] Pull the net in with great effort.
[6] All hold up Sunday School papers with colored fishes.

3. The Beginner is learning health habits, and should be responsible for himself to a large degree. A great deal of excess energy can profitably be expended by a child's learning to care for himself and his room. He can put on and off his own wraps, help others with galoshes and buttons, arrange chairs and tables, get out and put away materials, even dust the furniture. If children of this age are discouraged when they want to help—even if at times they are more of a hindrance than a help—we cannot expect them to start later, when they will have more ability.

4. Health is still delicate, and the interest span short. The same precautions are as necessary as for the Nursery age. A slightly better degree of Sunday School attendance may be expected. The program should consist of alternate quiet and active periods, without strain and overstimulation.

The following incident of a teacher's afternoon at a beach demonstrates the importance of changing often the type of activity that is suggested for Beginner age.

> Miss Cole was recuperating by the seaside, wishing she might be serving the Lord, when a five-year old girl came strolling by with her nurse. The child was eager for a diversion, and the nurse was glad to relinquish her charge for an hour.
>
> Since there were several fishing boats near the shore, Miss Cole began by telling the Beginner a story of the Lord Jesus helping His friends catch two boatsful of fish. Apparently the little girl had heard the name of God, but not of Jesus. Therefore the Lord Jesus was often identified as God's Son. After quietly listening to the story, the child needed a more active period. She suggested that *she* would now tell a story, and she told about Peter Rabbit.
>
> Then she was ready for another Bible story, this time the one of Jesus' stilling the storm on the lake. Since the child was idly marking in the sand, Miss Cole suggested that they make

the story in the sand. Soon the child was ready for another story. This time it was the story of the boy who gave his rolls and fishes to Jesus so that He could feed all the hungry people. For a change of activity, they took pebbles and outlined rolls and fishes in the sand.

The final story was the crucifixion of Jesus, emphasizing how much He loved us, even to taking the punishment that we deserve for our sins. So fascinated was the child with this story that at the end she immediately said, "Tell me again how the bad people killed God."

Because the teacher had taken time to consider the child's physical needs, even within an hour, she was able to lead her to a place where she witnessed definite spiritual response.

5. The Beginner still makes large use of his senses in order to understand the world about him. Objects at a distance mean little to him. When a group of children gather about a picture, several who are not immediately in front probably will say, "I can't see," although the picture is only a foot or two from them. And they verily cannot see, not what they call "seeing"—not "seeing" that satisfies them, for truly to enjoy it they must have it in their own hands, with no distractions between.

It is cruel to show small pictures that are frustrating to boys and girls, or to bring into their room fragile objects which they cannot touch, or with which they must "be careful." What if they do want to feel the pretty flower that God made? Why not let them take in their hands one of the soft satin petals, so that they will believe the words we tell them? The only reason we adults are content merely to look at objects that they want to touch is that we already have felt of them and now can "see how they feel" by merely looking at them. First-hand experience must precede verbal concepts.

The Primary Child. 1. Growth is now slower, with gradual development of muscular co-ordination. Girls are usually a little ahead of boys. The toothless grin of the seven- and eight-year-olds is indicative of their uneven and incomplete growth. They have more control of the large muscles than of the small ones. They need practice in using the smaller muscles for skills, yet it is a strain to use them for a long period. They will pursue sedentary mental activities for a short time if they see a need for them, but do not derive much pleasure from them. Although life in general is more purposeful than it was for the Beginner, yet much of their time is spent doing what they love to do for the sake of doing. They crave strenuous play, active but unorganized games, such as tag, and hide-and-seek. It is a joy to chase and be chased.

It is difficult for most adults to get the children's point of view—that they often enjoy doing things for the sake of the process rather than for the results. If they want to do the dishes at home it is not because they want to work, but because they want to splash around in soapy water. Though they start to put the Bible school room in order for the session, they become more interested in putting the chairs in place by making a train of them.

What do Primaries like best to do? To work and to play, but they work very hard at their play, and their work is such fun! When asked what they like best to do, many Primaries answer, "To clean house," "Sweep the floor," "Do things for Grandpa," "Take care of other children," "Work in the garden," and "Wash dishes." When the activity itself is satisfying, when they receive approval for it, and by engaging in it enter the realm of grown-up life, why should not work hold great appeal for them? They learn to distinguish the terms "work" and "play" according to adult usage; yet, left to themselves, they would make no distinctions, for almost anything active is interesting.

Although the Bible school program for this age cannot be one of run and chase, neither will it be all passive listening. And teachers will be sympathetic when they run instead of walk to their chairs. Handwork may now be employed purposefully—not intricate complications, but something simple which they can do about the lesson, or something they want to keep for themselves or to give others. At Primary age a great deal more is possible in the practice of accuracy and observance of detail.

2. Energy and vitality fluctuate, with a tendency to overdo. Because the Primary is so much stronger than the Beginner, and often feels an urge for strenuous activity, it is very easy for him to run too long and attempt too much. Especially is this true of the eighth year, when the lungs and heart are small in proportion to the rest of the body, and must supply more oxygen and blood than usual, since growth is uneven. One minute the Primary will be wholly absorbed in some activity; the next, he will drop onto the floor exhausted, or sigh with weariness.

In our work with him we should always stop before he is weary of an activity; then he will always want more, and never remember it as overdone. When he attempts to do more and harder things than he is capable of finishing, we should be ready to suggest simpler, less strenuous activities which will be as satisfying to him.

3. Sustained attention is no longer a physical impossibility if based on needs and interests. Yet Primaries need three major changes of activity within the period of an hour with variation in each part. They need a Bible story and discussion, worship activity, and something to do about the desires which have been stimulated.

While the attention span of Primaries is longer than for the Beginner, and the public school is training them to do sedentary work, yet too much must not be expected of them. Their nerve cells are not fully grown, nor their nerve centers perfectly co-ordinated. Any good thing soon becomes too much of a good thing. Teachers of the old school would deprive a child of recess for punishment, when all the overactive child needed was recess a bit more often.

4. Disease resistance is almost twice as great as for Beginners. Yet Primaries need protection from the danger of contracting a contagious disease by more contacts with others. The Primary teacher should ever be on the lookout for symptoms of colds and disease—running nose, red eyes, unnatural coloring, coughing, and sneezing. These cases can be tactfully isolated from the group and have special tasks given them.

5. The senses report a wider range of impressions, which the mind is kept busy sorting. Now many items are noted which the Beginner did not even notice, because he had no experience to interpret them. If Primary occasionally sits with a thoughtful look, he is no doubt pondering in very literal terms and trying to integrate some of the inconsistencies of his widening world. After learning the likes and dislikes of his mother, he expects his teachers to act the same way, but they do not. Perhaps mother lays down no principle, but proceeds according to whim and present feeling. We trust that the Bible school teacher is always consistent. A child's early years are spent largely in discovering by direct experience how he can express his own inner urges without incurring the displeasure of others in such a strange, bewildering world. Understanding still comes largely from first-hand contact.

The Junior Child. 1. Growth has now reached a slower, relatively stable stage. The physical gain made by Juniors is more in weight than in height. This slight pause for physical relaxation before the adolescent spurt gives the body a breathing spell, and allows it to muster its forces to acquire strength. Juniors almost worship power and strength in any form. A girl may be as strong and brave as a boy. The problem of the Junior who is physically weak is sometimes a serious one, but he can learn to find success and approval along other lines.

Boys are a little ahead of girls during the first half of this period, but then the girls spurt ahead until the largest in a good-sized department are girls and the smallest are likely to be boys. This fact of physical anomalies in itself tends to produce sex antagonism, for at the very stage when the boys are most interested in masculinity the girls their age are larger than they.

2. There is slower adjustment of the smaller, finer muscles. Not until the finer muscles co-ordinate are control, speed, and endurance possible. Now the Junior feels the need of practicing skill and control. Do you remember the games of competition which you yourself devised at the Junior age? Even girls practice until they perfect bouncing and catching balls, jumping rope, shooting at a target—almost anything which requires skill, strength, and speed.

Nothing is too hard for the Junior, if only it is put in the form of a challenge to his growing powers.

These very characteristics make the Junior a fascinating pupil if only the teacher lets his interests lead the way. If life in Christ is presented as a battle against sin, in which there is no place for "softies," he is ready to give himself wholly to it.

Capitalize on the Juniors' love of skill in teaching them to use their Bibles. Instead of letting them slump in their chairs wishing they were out on some adventure, keep them alert to find God's answers to their own problems. Instead of repeating directions twice, expect them to listen to the book, chapter, and verse, and to settle their own disputes by referring to the source of authority.

3. The Junior has exuberant energy to harness for the Lord. He will not walk when he can run, nor run when he can jump over a hydrant, nor jump when he can be sliding down hill. "Imagine yourself getting up some crisp morning after a good night's sleep, with ten times as much strength and energy, ten times as hungry, ten times as good-natured, ten times as full of mischief, ten times as ready to shout and sing, ten times as ready for the next act!" Is it any wonder that adults cannot keep up with Juniors?

The motto for the Junior department is rightly, "Be ye doers of the word, and not hearers only" (James 1:22). It is just the opposite of "Come unto me, all ye that labor and are heavy laden, and I will give you rest" (Matt. 11:28).

The problem with Juniors is to direct their great energy into learning of and adventuring with the Lord. Their energy, their abilities, and their growing independence, all warrant their taking over a great deal of their own Bible school session. They need to assume responsibility, and need a teacher whose supervision is forceful but unobtrusive.

There is practically nothing that Juniors are not able to do if they set their minds on it. How laboriously they slave to build a hut for their gang or a snow fort to engage the enemy; yet how bored they are to use the same energy in performing the routine chores of mowing the lawn or setting the table! Bible school may be either the enticing project or the routine chore, according to the leadership. A Junior session should be alive with activity, not dead with suppression. Juniors should be searching the Scriptures, memorizing Scripture, discussing problems, righting wrongs, helping the unfortunate, making picture maps, making flannelgraph stories, Bible bookcases, preparing the room for worship, illustrating Scripture and songs, and making tracts. Like their younger brothers and sisters, they too need many opportunities to grapple with the realities of life on their own level of interest.

4. This is an age of sturdy health. The husky youngsters love noise and roughhouse; they are inclined to shout instead of talk, or, in their quieter moments, the girls giggle and whisper. They are particularly fond of primitive outdoor activities—exploring, hunting, camping, and scouting. They are always hurrying somewhere, too busy to care about appearance. Because they love to go to places and are no longer dependent on parents, they will attend Bible school regularly and give concentrated attention if it is challenging to them. The Junior should be the largest department of the Bible school and the one with the best attendance record.

If Juniors have any lack in health, it may be that they need sleep, for they are always too interested in something to want to go to bed, and try to resist attempts to curb their liveliness. Because of their adventurous natures, most deaths at this age are caused by accidents. Nothing is so enticing as jumping from one roof to another, or discovering how an engine works.

5. Though Juniors now have finer perception, they are impulsive and impatient because of their great energy and growing independence. The senses have become more accurate, yet give vigorous response. Often juniors are accused of disregarding the rights of others, and need a great deal of training in this form of practical Christianity. When Jim hears a war whoop outdoors, he jumps up from the dining table with a mouthful of food, upsets a teacup, and grazes Mother's head with the jacket that he flings around him as he goes. The few social graces acquired in early childhood now seem to disappear.

Yet Juniors are sufficiently conscious of details to be

critical of their own efforts as well as those of others. They often destroy their work and begin again, for they lack the persistence and skill to attain their own standards. They sound very impertinent when they flatly contradict their elders. It is a satisfaction to them to be sure of what they say or do, whether it be a vital or a trivial matter, or whether or not they are talking about the same thing that Father is talking about. In Junior fashion they assert the truth without considering the courtesy of the situation or the value of the fact they are defending.

SOCIAL DEVELOPMENT

The Nursery Child. Because the former life of a Nursery child has been primarily one of eating and sleeping, with a few social contacts, he may be timid, self-centered, individualistic, and dependent. In infancy he had to be the center of his universe, but already at home he has learned that the other members of his family must also be considered. Yet at home the older children and parents seldom want the same things that he wants, though they do not always gratify his desires. Church may be the first place where he comes in contact with children his own age and discovers that they too have rights and feelings of their own.

He may still prefer to play alone, although he enjoys doing the same thing side by side with others. There is little co-operation, however. It is usually when children conflict over wanting the same objects that they are drawn into close, personal relationship.

Though imitative, affectionate, and eager to please, the three-year-old often gets a negativist streak when he discovers himself to be an independent personality. It is quite revolutionary to him to discover that he can say "No" as well as be meekly led by adults. It is physically easier to shake the head sideways than up and down—easier to say "No" than "Yes." He begins to experiment with "No," and that one word does wonders in getting him what he wants. The wise teacher gives him little opportunity to refuse.

She doesn't ask him whether or not he wants to do this or that. She merely surrounds him with things he likes to do, and doesn't force his choice.

Only during part of the hour is he expected to conform to the rest of the group. At that time group activities are made so fascinating that he can't bear to miss them.

Therefore he soon discovers that he gets farther by regarding what others want than by considering only what he wants. By experience he learns that when he gives up his own way, he receives greater satisfaction from the approval of mother and teacher and God. If approval from these sources is consistent and can be depended on, the child is on his way toward becoming a social creature.

The Beginner Child. Unlike the Nursery child, Beginners like to help others and to work together on the same materials. Their growing awareness of the social group affords many opportunities for practicing habits of working and playing together. An occasional child may not realize that he is included in a group suggestion, but when we say, "Tommy, you come, too," he readily complies.

This age marks the height of suggestibility and imitation. "Let's play that we are the boy Samuel," or "Wouldn't you like to make sick Johnny happy?" is accorded hearty and immediate approval. What a responsibility it is for the teacher to furnish the right examples of conduct, the right tone of voice, the right attitude toward problems that arise, when such absorbing natures are ready to pick up every impression and make it a part of themselves. Many a teacher has prayed, "Oh, Lord, let nothing come into the room this morning that should not be built into behavior patterns. Guard the spiritual atmosphere, the factual material, the vocabulary that I use. Let no impression registered on these children's sensitive natures be untrue or unworthy."

The Primary Child. "I am no longer a *little* child, I'll have you know!" is the attitude of Primaries. Especially do the seven- and eight-year-olds lose respect for the teacher and the Bible school which still think of them as the "dear little ones," and insist on their singing such songs, as "Praise Him, praise Him, all ye little children." The word "happy" may be substituted for the word "little" in recognition of the fact that they are growing up.

Primaries begin imitating grown-ups, and for a year or two take great delight in proving to themselves that they can act as grown people, at least in their own eyes. Their ways are quite different from the babyish ways of the Beginner. They feel like different beings when they begin to read and write and take care of themselves. They begin to assert themselves, to be more individualistic, and to desire individual recognition in the group, at the same time preferring group activities to solitary ways.

The great opportunity at this age is to respect the individual personality and yet help the boys and girls develop responsibility and co-operation. Now that they see a need for subordinating themselves to the well-being of the group, they will practice self-control and inhibition. Each one needs to feel that he belongs to the group and that he is responsible for its success.

Moreover, Primaries' sympathies are easily aroused for groups outside their own. They should have contacts with people different from themselves, and learn to understand and to help them without a spirit of superiority. They can begin to play games with rules, in which they learn the importance of each player and yet his subordination to the team as a whole. Yet in their games they are more interested in activity for its own sake than in rivalry with others.

The Junior Child. After the Primary has proved to his own satisfaction that he is no longer a baby, as a Junior his interest in adults wanes in favor of his own noisy, carefree, and sometimes silly pals. This is often termed the "unknown age," because there is less sympathetic understanding between Juniors and adults than at any other stage. Being in a healthy period of slower growth, they are no longer as dependent on adults as formerly. Neither do they feel the interests and problems of adults as they will feel them during the period of youth. They desire to live their own lives, to think for themselves, and to be free from former restrictions. This is as it should be, for they need to learn independence and control.

Juniors seek friends among their own age and sex, and often form temporary and unorganized gangs, as occasion arises, to enjoy each other's company. Small groups spontaneously get together for fun and adventure, and break up when another interest involving other children looms up as more exciting. They are very fond of secret names and passwords, fancy regalia, and badges of honor.

The boys and girls naturally separate themselves at this stage, for though they are both active, the boys think of themselves as stronger and braver. Because they make a contest out of almost everything they do, the other sex constitutes a natural rival. It is thrilling to have an enemy and try to outwit him. Friendly rivalry in the Bible school may be encouraged if the boys and girls are well matched.

The team work is attempted and should be promoted, yet not too much should be expected in the way of subordinating individual preferences for the good of the team, and in graciously acknowledging that one is on a losing side. Even temporary defeat is an experience the robust Junior has not conceded for himself.

Though Juniors tend to ignore most adults, the adults who do the things they long to achieve are now their heroes. It is characteristic of them to do everything so wholeheartedly that they both love and hate with vehemence. And the persons they love, they worship.

Along with hero worship goes a healthy respect for authority when it personifies the justice and loyalty which the Junior has come to prize. With ambition of his own for leadership, he can project himself into the rôle of the leader, and genuinely admires the teacher who can command control because he inspires obedience. Of course, he will often resist this authority, yet deeper than his love of vigorous independence is a realization that fair play and equal rights must be safeguarded. He has met enough of the world to have a degree of caution and skepticism.

Although the qualifications for a teacher of Juniors are very exacting, no age pays greater dividends in spiritual results and personal satisfaction. The teacher should be one who is their hero because he is succeeding in his life work, one who cares enough about them to enter their ball games and exploits, one who becomes a real pal and one of their gang, and who shows them that honor and justice are practical.

Enlist the gang under church supervision. Let them take responsibility in their own class organization. Let them find out that in this game of life the greatest adventures are to be experienced alongside the greatest of heroes—the Son of God Himself. Present Christ as the King of their lives, who, single-handed, drove the moneychangers from the temple, and suffered the most intense agonies for His friends. He said, "Ye are my friends, if ye do whatsoever I command you" (John

15:14). Human heroes fall from their pinnacle, but Jesus never fails. In their language, "He never lets a fellow down."

1. Select four children whom you know well—if possible, one at each age level—and analyze in what respects they are average physically and socially, and in what respects they deviate from the average.
2. How would the personality of the ideal teacher of Nursery children differ from the personality of the ideal teacher of Juniors?
3. In what ways could your department, or one you observe, better meet the children's physical and social needs?
4. In question four at the beginning of this chapter, were all four departments represented in the characteristics? Why, or why not?

CHAPTER VII

MENTAL DEVELOPMENT

1. Give the following questionnaire to as many children as you can, tabulate the answers, and summarize results. What difference should this information make in your teaching?

   (1) What do you see in this picture? (A Bible picture with both central action and minor detail).
   (2) What do you like best to do?
   (3) What is the most wonderful thing you can think of?
   (4) What is the funniest thing you can think of?
   (5) What kind of teacher do you like best?
   (6) What does it mean to pray?
   (7) What does it mean to praise?
   (8) What is sin?
   (9) What is faith?
   (10) What is your heart?

2. Why is it that object lessons given for the children in a church service often mean more to the adults? What part of an object lesson are the children most interested in? What part the adults?

3. Try to analyze your thinking on various subjects, whether you think in terms of words, or pictures and happenings?

4. Can you recall a time when you arrived at wrong conclusions in your reasoning? Explain why.

Just as the normal child craves physical activity, so he also craves mental activity. God has put within him the urge to develop mentally as well as physically. If he is lazy physically, he is sick; if he is lazy mentally, we have made him so. He is normally a budding scientist, eager and alert and curious to explore and investigate and experiment continually. Along with the handling of material things goes the need for insight and understanding and interpretation of the world.

Mental activity is the manipulation, not of the objects themselves, but of the symbols representing them. Of course rich mental activity requires rich sensory and motor experiences with which to work. It is these material objects which provide the problems and the stimuli for thinking.

REASONING

When does a child begin to think purposefully in a broad practical sense? Is the reasoning process of children different in quality from that of the adult, or is it the same essentially, though on an immature plane? What is the earliest case of reasoning that you can recall?

The infant learns to cry if he gets attention thereby, but to play happily by himself if his crying avails him naught. When the toddler gets bumped in his play, he looks first to his mother to see whether or not she seems to be in a mood to give him attention and sympathy if he makes a fuss about his hurt, and acts accordingly. About the age of seven or eight, children begin to reason verbally, but they have been reasoning concretely long before that.

Why is it that children so often are inconsistent and contradictory in their thinking? If a perverted process is not responsible, upon what can the blame be laid? Upon the same lack which conditions so many of their other immaturities—the lack of experience. When one or more pertinent facts are totally absent from a proposition, of course the conclusion will be faulty. When children's reactions seem irrational and bizarre, they lack essential data for adequate judgment.

When a child reasons with the same data as an adult, he reaches the same conclusion, because he uses the same process. Teachers, therefore, should help children to muster sufficient data concerning the most vital of all problems, their relationship to the Lord. Great damage is done when children are considered too young to think and reason. They will not reason with abstractions which mean nothing to them, but they will turn the community upside down to solve a problem that is real to them. For instance, they are ready to do one thing after another that will help bring Jim's father to the Saviour so that he will no longer use his money for drink and mistreat the boy and his mother. They have a personal interest in their friend Jim; they reason that the Lord is the only One who can save and straighten out the father, and that Christians will have to show him that they care and that they are kind. They meet for prayer on his behalf, they help Jim do all sorts of chores around the house, and they write Jim's father letters showing him what God says.

The work of the teacher is to see that each age is confronted with problems which are not too easy and not too hard, that lead boys and girls into broader and deeper fields without expecting too much of present abilities. Especially do Juniors need the challenge of practical problems which require digging into every resource they possess. If trained, they can put forth strenuous mental exertion as well as physical. Above all things, they loathe having a teacher "talk at them" while they merely listen. That kind of teacher is an "abomination" to many Juniors; the passive type of goodness is only for "sissies," and that kind of Bible school is "not for them."

If we wish each child in a class to think about the answer to a question, we shall ask the question first, then name the child. If we name the child first, only he will do the thinking.

WIDENING WORLD HORIZONS

The young child's attitude toward the unfamiliar is one of fear, since everything in his environment is strange and new. It is almost impossible for adults to conceive of such a situation, for even if they were set down in the midst of a cannibal civilization that would be much more familiar to them than ordinary life to a young child. He needs to feel the security of a great deal of repetition, until, at least with a few things, he can relax in the assurance of knowing what comes next.

The Beginner's world is also very narrow. What makes teaching difficult is that each child brings to church with him a narrow world that is different from the others, and we can expect him to be interested in and understand only what is real there. What a difference in background there is between the pupil who has never been outside his own farm and the one who has lived in a foreign land with his missionary parents and traveled halfway round the world with them; between the one from a wealthy home and one from a very meager home. The latter may be richer in personal relationship, but not in broadening experience. The child who grows up with many brothers cannot be treated the same as the one who lives quietly with his grandmother. Yet a few common elements are familiar to almost all Beginners—home, children, pets, and daily activities. These are the bases for Bible teaching.

Though Primaries are now adventuring toward new experiences, ideas still need to have a personal reference. Through school contacts the world widens immensely, and multitudes of things arouse curiosity and questions. Something new every day must be investigated and fitted into its place in the previous scheme of things. Yet all is quite personal—the relation to "me and my life and what I shall do about it."

The Junior for the first time takes a world view. He can conceive of all the nations of the earth on a globe and their relationship to each other. Avid for facts, he often wants to know just because he wants to know, and that was not true earlier in his life. Like the Greeks of old, he spends his time either in telling or hearing some new thing. When someone mentions a new person or place, he interrupts to ask about it. Then he has gone in search of something else he has not yet heard or done. For him the teacher needs a wide range of illustrations from all over the world, from all kinds of occupations and customs, from all points of view. If he cannot be a world traveler and explorer as he would like to be, then he will travel through the world vicariously.

FINER DISCRIMINATION

At first, "mother" to the infant means eating, and that's all. At first, "people" are represented by mother, and that's all. To the Nursery tot God is the only answer to many of his questions—the true answer and the satisfying answer. To the Beginner child birds are birds; but to the Primary child birds are robins and sparrows and starlings.

Gradually, the basic distinctions between right and wrong, mine and thine, lovely and ugly, are developed. At first, Jesus is not distinguished from God. Often the Christmas "Baby Jesus" is not connected with the Man who loved little children unless teachers definitely show that the Baby grew and grew.

One of the fundamental distinctions which must be made clear is that Jesus loves me; He hates sin, He hates my sin, but He loves me even when I sin. Another is that though Jesus wants us to ask Him for help and will do what we cannot do, we must do what we can, too.

The Junior is keen and critical, with senses and intellect sharp enough to love puzzles and problems and riddles and games. He is quick to detect absurdities, but also quick to jump at conclusions before he has thoroughly considered a case. If the teacher abruptly asks a group, "What do you think of Sunday games?" the Juniors will each have a snap answer, and they will insist on that answer, for self-esteem will force them to abide by their opinion, no matter what strong reasons are advanced for the opposing side.

Their great need is to form the habit of suspending judgment until both or all sides of the question have been weighed. When the problem is broached, they should give all the points they can think of on both sides, so that they may objectively see the balance. They will then be trained to do their own independent thinking, will not feel the repugnant restraint of outside influence, will be developing their own inner controls, and will be constrained to abide by their own decisions. The habit of clear, independent thinking is as valuable as the specific judgments formed.

What children see and draw in pictures is a significant index to their discrimination. When shown the subject of Moses at the burning bush, the Nursery child may actually see nothing at all, for there may be nothing in the picture familiar enough for him to identify and name. If shown a picture portraying his daily life, he will name separate objects, a mother and a baby, no matter what the mother and baby may be doing. Most relationships elude him.

At Beginner age, he will probably note that the mother is bathing the baby. When Beginners are shown the picture of Moses at the burning bush, many of them remark first about the sheep rather than the central action. Why is that? A bush aflame is quite foreign to their lives, male Bible characters dressed in the flowing oriental garb look to them like women. All but the sheep are strange. Not only what they see first, but their vocabulary and associations are most revealing.

Primaries enjoy enumerating all the details they can find, with a higher degree of interpretation than Beginners.

Only at Junior age are the children likely to note relationships, and why thus and so is happening. Of course, their interpretation always depends on the richness of background which they bring to the picture. Maturity and experience are necessary to select significant elements from a mass of details, and to relate each of the minor details to the main message.

That young children are not deficent in visual acuity is shown by the fact that in pictures they pick out small details which are prominent in their own narrow lives. They will notice a tiny train in the midst of other toys, and wonder why a boy in a Bible picture is not wearing shoes.

SCHOOL ABILITIES

If the Bible school is to be a school worthy of the name and not a travesty on the word, it must be cognizant of the secular experiences which its pupils are having, and be building upon the same habits and skills. Bible school teachers should often visit the secular school to keep up with its activities and interests. They should often refer to what is being done in public school, and be alert to interpret those activities spiritually, since the hand of God is not usually recognized there.

Language. Words are a relatively unfamiliar tool to the young child. Some of the most active and dramatic of children do not early put forth the effort to learn to speak because they can learn to get what they want without it. Many Nursery children can be helpful members of a group without uttering a word the whole hour. Neither should the teacher rely much on words, but rather on doing and feeling.

Young children like similarities of sound, and words with sound effects. Two-year-olds often repeat exactly what is said to them. If their everyday life can be interpreted spiritually with the rhythm and rhyme and repetition of Mother Goose, great truths will seep into little minds. They can themselves pretend to be the things which God created, as they sing:

God our Father made the trees to grow and grow and grow;
God our Father made the wind to blow and blow and blow.

God our Father made the birds to fly and fly and fly;
Down they fly upon the ground, and up into the sky.

God our Father made the flowers, yellow, red and blue,
Nodding, smiling, bending down, as God meant them to do.

Since language has meaning for children only when built on personal experience, Bible vocabulary should be carefully graded and limited to a few new terms which are built into the vocabulary and inner experience of each department. A questionnaire dealing with biblical language revealed deplorable vagueness and inaccuracy regarding the most fundamental concepts. Only 10 per cent of Beginners, 8 per cent of Primaries, and 34 per cent of Juniors gave satisfactory answers when asked what it means to praise. Adequate answers range all the way from mature concepts such as "adore," "admire," "bless God," and "give glory," to such childlike expressions as "like the guy," "tell God He is nice," "think someone is wonderful," and "someone did something good to someone and he pats him on the shoulder."

Of course, people at all ages have a feeling for more than

they can adequately express in words, yet the basic concepts of the Christian faith should be so clearly understood that children can express them in their own words from actual experience.

Build up new Bible vocabulary in each department:

Nursery—God, Jesus, God's Book, love, give, help, thank.
Beginner—God's Son, the Bible, sin, heaven, obey, pray, share.
Primary—heart, holy, trust, believe, worship, lost, saved, died on the cross, everlasting life.
Junior—faith, grace, righteousness, mercy, glory, Spirit, temptation, redeem, crucify.

Not that the abstract terms are not used occasionally in context in younger departments, but one department should assume responsibility for weaving them into the warp and woof of the child's existence. If a Primary asks concerning the Trinity, of course we will explain to him that just as there are three members of some families, Mother, Father, and Son, yet all one family, so there are the Father, Son, and Holy Spirit, yet one God.

But there is usually little interest in the Trinity before the Junior department. The Junior enjoys finding illustrations of other things that are three in one, as water and steam and ice are one substance in three forms, as a girls' braid of hair consists of three distinct strands yet one braid, as a man may be at the same time father, son, and husband. The Junior appreciates the answer of the Christian who, when chided that he was trying to say that one plus one plus one equals one, replied that instead he was saying that one times one times one equals one.

Not until Junior age do we speak of Palestine; that country is the Holy Land to Primaries; to Beginners, the land where Jesus lived.

An excellent activity for Primaries is to make a Bible dictionary of the new words they use often, and to illustrate the new words by pictures which they cut out or draw.

Reading. In a college community where books are one of the prime factors in life, where books are everywhere carried and read and pondered and talked about, it is no wonder that Nursery pupils are as fond of their picture books as their toys. Although this is not true where books are lacking in the home, yet in Bible school the young child may learn a great deal from "reading" one bold outline picture on a page which does not tear, in a book whose pages turn easily.

From the Nursery class on, each department should contain a browsing table with the kind of books that a child of that age enjoys. Publishers are increasingly giving attention to lovely new books with a spiritual tone.

The Junior department, and perhaps the Primary, should have its own library, organized and conducted by the pupils themselves. Very few books will be lost, and the reading will be valued more if they themselves work out a simple checking system, and feel responsible for keeping their library intact and for telling their friends of the good things they have discovered in the books.

Picture books with good print and bindings are not among the cheapest books, but when the children's tastes are being formed, the finest editions are none too good for them. It should be the heritage of each child to own and take pride in beautiful and well illustrated copies of the masterpieces of literature on their level. It may be that a church group will decide to keep the most valuable books at the church, to be used only there, lest misfortune befall them through accident.

The Primary department of the Bible school exhibits a wide range of reading ability, from the very beginning to a fair vocabulary of common words. Books with spiritual emphasis on the Primary level are scarce, but teachers and pupils can co-operate in making their own. The children can look at home for pictures that interest them, and they can compose short stories which the teacher will print in large letters. They also can draw pictures. The content they prefer seems to include essential action without much detail, a surprise element, animals, conversation, their type of humor, outdoor activities, and simple problems.

Though the Junior may be a "good reader," he should not be called upon to read Scripture without sufficient practice to convey the message forcefully. Nothing kills interest in Scripture quicker than having a person stumble over words and mispronounce them. Words written on the blackboard for boys and girls to read should be printed in large letters and not crowded.

Juniors will read many books even when they should be helping around the house, and the quality of their reading may change the course of their lives. The right book put into the hand of the Junior at a critical time may give him a new vision, which will arouse motives, which, in turn, will set the direction of his powers.

The following are testimonies of young people as to childhood books which made lasting impressions on their lives:

> *Story of the Bible*. I well remember when Mother bought Hurlbut's *Story of the Bible* and how well I liked the pictures. Mother never let us children play with it as we did our other story books, because she knew we would tear or misuse it. On Sundays or evenings, she would sit down and read a story to us, or just page through it explaining the pictures, which were the main thing for me. I always felt so sorry for the two people who were bad and had to leave the lovely garden. When Abraham was about to offer Isaac, this seemed strange to me—I just couldn't

understand it all. It was wonderful how God helped Noah build the boat which saved all his family.

I think I would have accepted Christ as my personal Saviour as a young child if I had been approached about the matter. Above all things, my brother and I loved to play church with our dolls as the congregation. We would sing our Sunday School songs, read Scripture, pray in our childlike way, and then Brother would give the story or sermon. We were very disappointed if Mother or someone else came and disturbed our service. When I remember just what I liked as a child, I try to see that the children I contact get the same.

The Wrong Book. As a child of twelve years, my parents being dead, I was living in a home where many essential things that should come into the life of a child were overlooked. During my leisure time I was always to be found deep in the pages of some book, usually fiction. One day when a number of books were brought into the house, eagerly scanning through them I found one called *The Hidden Hand.* Soon I was buried in it, and found it to be a very frightening story. In one part eyes from under a bed were seen in a mirror. From that day on through college, yes, even further, I never went to bed alone in a room without first looking under the bed in fear and trembling. I didn't tell anyone until the last few years, for I was ashamed of it, and was afraid of being laughed at. There wasn't a bit of humor in the situation for me, and I don't believe I shall ever entirely forget it. However, I don't look under the bed now, for my complete trust is in the Lord. May other sensitive children be saved similar experiences through the wrong book!

Writing. Can you remember writing something which was very difficult for you—a dreaded letter, or report, or composition? Even after muscular co-ordination is acquired, a writer must consider sentence structure, capitalization, punctuation, spelling, grammar, unity, coherence, emphasis, and the reader. When a child writes, he has, of course, never heard of such requirements, though he has a feeling for some of them, and, in addition to that, does not even make the letters with ease, and finds that his hands don't always obey his mind. It is no wonder that Juniors do little writing in which they really take pleasure. Higher processes are involved as well as physical refinement.

It makes the Primary feel big to copy a few words if only a few will accomplish some purpose.

Difficult it is indeed to suggest handwork for Beginners that is valuable and not just "busy work." Beginners cannot read or write, but they can cut, color, draw; paste, with supervision, and mold clay.

Time, Space and Number. Why is there no better beginning for young children's secular stories than "Once upon a time"? A narrative naturally starts with the setting in time and place for orientation. What does the young child know or care about time and place? To him things happen before or after others. The only time he knows is "time to go," dinnertime," and "bedtime."

The following conversation between a four-year-old and his mother after his first experience in Sunday School shows how much numbers, as well as other concepts, mean to him:

Richard: Oh, Mother! I went to Sunday School, and I was a good boy!

Mother: What did you do there?

Richard: We didn't sit still in our chairs. We stood up, too, and walked around, and the teacher told us a story.

Mother: What did she tell you?

Richard: It was about Jesus. They were making something for him, a big church. There was a big tree as big as this (arms outstretched). And all the people tore it up and knocked it down to fix it for Jesus. And they had big white stones. When they got through, *all the people went in there—five.* And my teacher had a red hat, and glasses.

To Richard, five was so many more than one or two, probably conceived of as one or two cookies, that it seemed like the number of all the people. Because a child can count to a certain number does not mean that he comprehends those numbers. The rhythm is fun by rote memory. At first, the number five means nothing at all, unless one refers to five apples or five balls or five children.

> A first grader once came home from school proudly informing his mother that two apples and two apples together made four apples, for the teacher had received four apples that morning. "Well, then," asked the mother, "how many are two mittens and two mittens?" "Oh, I don't know that," answered her son. "We haven't done mittens yet."

Since all the Bible people lived long ago, but at the same time to children under Junior age, Bible subjects for them should be organized around needs in their daily lives, as Jesus our Saviour, or learning to obey; or around characters, as David doing God's will, or God's people going into their new land.

Juniors for the first time are studying history and geography in school, and should be helped to place Bible times and places in relation to what they already know. Then, for the first time, lessons are arranged chronologically, with surveys to see in their true perspective what previously have been isolated details.

GENERALIZATION

Would you want your department superintendent or supervisor to visit your Bible class and make a generalization as to the quality and effectiveness of your teaching after one visit? Why not? Adults tend to generalize, often too quickly, but not the children. They would say, "We had a good time today," or "I'm tired of school."

Objective Happenings. Being realistic and literal-minded, children think in terms of concrete pictures and happenings rather than in general ideas. Does any statement sound plainer than "God is everywhere"? Yet that generalization may be simply words to a Beginner. Have you ever watched a child himself put meaning behind such a statement? One boy began, "Do you mean God is right here with us?" The teacher assured him that He was. "Is He at home with Mother?" "Is He at work with Father?" The teacher kept answering in the affirmative. "Is He upstairs in Brother's class?" "Is He outdoors with the birds?" "Is He even there in that box?" Then for the first time the boy comprehended those simple words, "God is everywhere."

But not all children take the interest or initiative to follow through that process. They simply continue to think concretely, unless their teachers take time to go through it with them.

Mother Whittemore tells of the use of a Bible verse worded concretely which a child did not generalize:

> A small kindergarten was opened on the west side of the city. It brought many a ray of comfort to the hearts of the poor little waifs who were living in destitution, and who suffered much at the hands of negligent and often cruel parents. But for our kindergarten, many of them would have had no schooling whatever. Each day we gave them a warm dinner, and the simple meal was followed by a brief talk.
>
> One day the subject was, "How to Pray," and they were told of its necessity. The passage read told of entering the closet and meeting God there and then He would reward them later (Matt. 6:6). The following morning when Willie, one of the poorest boys, entered the hall, the leader asked him whether he had remembered what was said about the closet and prayer the day before, and if he had prayed that morning. He shook his head somewhat sadly and replied, "I couldn't; I just couldn't."

> "Why, my dear boy," Miss Horace said, "we can all pray; we must pray. I hope you will not forget it after today." With this, the little fellow began to cry and at last, through his sobs, managed to give her the reason for his neglect. "I couldn't, teacher, because the only closet we have in our house is full of old boots and mother's scrub things what she works with."
>
> She lovingly endeavored to explain more simply what it meant to shut oneself up with God. She thought he understood. The next morning he hurried up the aisle with a smiling face, and waving his hand triumphantly said, "I did it, I did it." When asked what he had done, his answer was joyously given, "I prayed, I prayed, teacher. I did what you said." She placed her arm around him and asked how he did it. "Why," he said, "I just climbed in on top of the boots an' scrub things an' all, and prayed all alone in the dark closet."[5]

Here is another example which should put teachers on their guard:

> A teacher was giving an object lesson on temperance. He used a glass of pure water and a glass of alcohol. Into each was placed a healthy, squirming worm. The one in the water kept swimming in a lively fashion, but the one in the alcohol slowed his pace, and finally grew inert. Thinking that the point of the lesson was clear enough, the teacher allowed the boys and girls to state it themselves. "What does this teach us?" he asked.
>
> A bright little fellow immediately answered, "If you have worms, take alcohol."

When children are asked, "What does faith mean?" It should seem easy for them to say "trusting," or "believing." Instead, many give some specific instance of the use of faith:

> When Mamma thinks I'll be good.
>
> If your mother would promise to give you five cents.

Daddy said he was going to bring candy home, and we believed it.

Believing that a footstool will hold you.

If you have faith in someone, you know he'll do it.

When you are down in the dumps and don't have food and clothing, and you know God will pull you through.

Although generalizations are a part of developing maturity, yet children's very concreteness makes it easier for them to acknowledge themselves sinners in the sight of the Lord. If they glibly recited the fact that sin is being bad or doing wrong, one might wonder whether or not they made any personal association, and connected the term with their own behavior. But when they say that sin is specific wrongdoing, such as "being bad, like talking back to Mother," then they are referring to their own sin. Lying is the sin most often mentioned by children. Then, disobeying, saying bad words, stealing, drinking, and such individual matters as copying examination papers, breaking a window, being mean, etc.

Questionnaires indicate that some children have gleaned very unfortunate ideas of Bible terms, chiefly no doubt from the use of ill-chosen object lessons. Some answered that sin was "black dirt," "inside of us like a bone," "like a dark den," "Jesus will put a big black mark on your soul," "You're going to get bad luck and you'll die when you're about twenty or twenty-five years old."

Though children's ideas necessarily will be partial and concrete, they need not be distorted and perverted. We must be sure our illustrations truly illustrate the truth instead of clouding it. Boys and girls need to multiply accurate concrete views until all of them together afford a rounded general impression because they have distinguished the significant elements in each. Only through experience in a wide variety of situations can they discern the generalization of them all.

Concrete to General to Concrete. Because children think concretely, teachers must begin with the concrete in their approach to the Bible—begin with a life problem which arises, which they have observed, which they have been told, or which they know to be typical of the age. The solution to this problem lies in some relation to the Lord or His will for His children, to be found somewhere in His Word. For children younger than Juniors, this part of the lesson will be a specific Bible

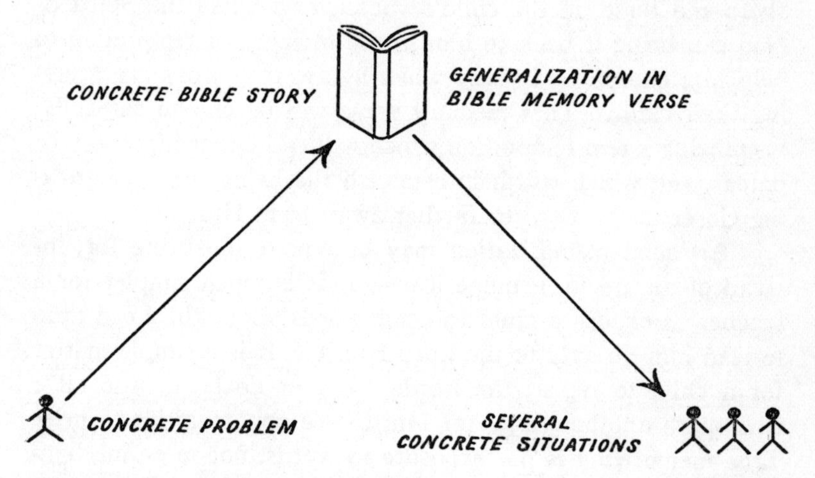

story—still concrete. For Juniors it will be discussion and searching their Bibles.

If this particular problem were all the teacher was concerned about, the lesson would now be finished, for the Bible has solved the difficulty. But being concrete, this one problem alone would be met. Other similar problems would remain untouched, for the child does not automatically transfer this experience over into another situation. He does not perceive the points in common between this situation and the next in which he needs the same principle. He may have learned one set of habits at home, and an entirely different set at church. His conduct is based mainly on specific habits which have received approval.

The general principle, which gives help in this problem and also in others of a similar nature, is expressed by Bible words called a memory verse. If the child is actually to use the verse the next time, it will not be a long, involved, obscurely stated sentence. Such he avoids whenever possible. It will be short and terse, in the child's vocabulary. Then the Spirit of God can bring it back to him in the moment of temptation to help him choose God's way when less worthy ways are pressing their claims. That memory verse will be chosen carefully, visualizing a real temptation which will end either in victory or defeat, and which will help establish the habit either of growing closer to the Lord or farther away from Him.

Artificial memorization may become a substitute for, instead of an aid to, genuine learning. It is much simpler for a teacher to expose a child to some words about the Lord than to lead him directly to the Lord Himself. It is a simple matter for a child to repeat the words, "Let us do good unto all"; it is quite another thing for him to see opportunities to help. True memorizing is not exposure to words, nor mere mechanical recall. It is the active translation of Scripture into one's own experience.

Because children fail to apply generalizations, the teacher must take time to make definite transfer to new situations, the more the better, until the boys and girls sense the outworking of the principle. Of course, the best conclusion of a lesson is to lead the pupils to practice the generalization right then and there. They can discuss what they will do during the week when they find this and that happening which require the principle. They can draw what they would do. They can learn a new song which will bring it to mind. They can dramatize what often takes place. In as many ways as possible they should visualize the difference it will make in their lives at home and school and play, with Mother and with Grandmother and with Susie, when they get up in the morning and eat lunch at noon and go to bed at night.

Symbolism. The word "symbol" is derived from two Greek words meaning to throw together. It implies the putting together of the concrete and the abstract, illustrating the invisible by the visible. The symbol or sign serves to represent the abstract not by exact resemblance, but by suggestion. Of course, no illustration borrowed from earthly things can bring out the fullness of the things of God, but some of them forcefully illustrate certain aspects of divine truth.

> A little mountain girl discovered one evening that she had left her hoe at the foot of the hill where she had been digging in the garden. The missionary with whom she lived told her that she must bring it to the house. The deepening shadows caused the child to hesitate, for after dark, familiar and friendly things seemed strange and fearsome to her. When she continued to make excuses and tried to persuade the missionary to go with her, the woman gave her this verse from God's Word, "Thy word is a lamp unto my feet, and a light unto my path."
>
> "Yes, that's what I need, a lamp for my feet!" exclaimed the child. "If I take my Bible outside, will it shine in the dark?" she asked, ready to accept every marvel from the God of miracles.

Many similar incidents could be cited to illustrate the working of the child mind. It is concrete, literal, realistic, and matter-of-fact. Those pupils who are saved often show deep spiritual discernment which transcends what can be expected on the natural plane. But the very ones we are most eager to reach with the gospel are the ones who will probably miss the point of abstract teaching. When we have only one hour a week to teach the Word, should not our teaching be so clear that the children cannot miss the way?

In our earnest attempt to illuminate the truth and make it concrete, we use object lessons, and a very fruitful ministry they often have. But instead of illuminating the truth, the object lesson sometimes obscures it when the teaching is far-fetched and not closely tied up with the object.

Because a group of children are always attentive to the interesting and mysterious manipulations of objects, we take it for granted that the objects have fulfilled the purpose for which they were intended. But when individuals are questioned concerning the spiritual application, very often their responses are not satisfactory. When a child is asked in our hearing to tell his mother about the lesson, his interest may be wholly in the objects, rather than in the truth we tried to demonstrate. Of course, the children will be with us on the material plane, but our time in Bible school is too precious merely to entertain, if the truth fails to reach the heart.

> Attractive folders were one day passed out to children as they came from school, inviting them to a children's meeting. The outside of the folder bore the words, "Are you hungry? Come, feast on the bread of life." Later, one of the boys came to the church inquiring, "Is this the place where you're giving away sandwiches?"

It is not easy for us as adults to select the milk of the Word for our children when we ourselves so thoroughly enjoy and profit by the meat which is woven into the warp and woof of Scripture. We have spent hours and hours meditating in our private devotions and listening to sermons on the symbols of the Bible, such as those which the Lord Jesus used to describe Himself and the Holy Spirit—the light, the bread, the water, the vine. It is most likely that these deeper meanings were taught concretely by the Lord: the light after He had restored sight to the blind, or at a feast as He stood near a colossal golden lampstand with its multitude of lamps; the bread after the feeding of the thousands; and the water after conversing with the Samaritan woman at the well, or at the ceremony of the filling of the golden pitcher from the pool of Siloam.

Christ knew that all His words could not then be comprehended by His disciples, but that later the Spirit would bring all things to their remembrance. He used symbols and illustrations to conceal as well as to illuminate the truth, as early as John 2:18-21 (see also John 16:25). Nicodemus, a ruler of the Jews, had only a literal conception of being born again (John 3:4). John, being the profoundest Gospel, is full of symbolism. What was the response of the disciples at the end of that great discourse on the bread of life in John 6?

> Jesus said, Verily, verily, I say unto you, Except ye eat the flesh of the Son of man, and drink his blood, ye have no life in you. . . . For my flesh is meat indeed, and my blood is drink indeed. . . . Many therefore of his disciples, when they heard this, said, This is an hard saying; who can hear it?

Figuratively, the thought was not intelligible to them; literally, it was not practicable.

Our children today feel that same way about figurative teaching, "This is a hard saying; who can hear it?" The Oriental mind, moreover, has always been more symbolic and metaphorical than the Western.

Perhaps the reader is wondering what is the difference between symbolism and imagination, and why a child cannot use his vivid imagination to change the concrete into the abstract, for imagination is natural to the child mind. Is not this the distinction: imagination is transforming one concrete thing into another concrete thing, while symbolism is transforming a concrete thing into an abstract idea? [6] The difference is vast indeed. Children at their play take a block of wood and call it a train or a car or an airplane or anything else concrete that suits their fancy. But it remains something concrete, free from abstract and mystical implications.

Let us therefore be alert to distinguish and choose for the children the concrete and literal rather than the abstract. Let us continually ask ourselves, "How will the children conceive of this literally?" "Is the thought left with the child literal or abstract?"

Let us choose Bible verses which can be comprehended literally with their intended meaning. "Light" to children is physical light, as the sun; Christ Jesus will be that kind of light in heaven, but as the light of this world, the meaning is figurative. If we decide to use a metaphor, let's first turn it into a simile with "as" or "like," and then proceed to point out the points of likeness—otherwise what was intended to illustrate may bewilder instead.

And after we have gone to all that trouble, we often conclude that our choice should have been a literal verse in the beginning. When eternal issues are at stake we cannot run the risk of not being understood. The literal verse expresses the truth in a way children cannot miss. Instead of telling the mountain child (p. 153), "Thy word is a lamp unto my feet," why did not the missionary tell her simply in her own language, "God says, 'I am with thee and will keep thee in all places' "?

If symbolism is used, we must take time to make definite association with daily life, lest the teaching be left up in the air in the realm of the hazy and abstract. A few basic Bible concepts must be built up early, thoroughly taught, and illustrated from many angles; other concepts can better be left until adolescence, when the mind is more meditative and theoretical.

If only teachers knew what children were thinking when they ask them to invite the Lord Jesus to come into their hearts! A few, but only a few, think of it as their real self, or "a loving thing inside of you," or a "place where you keep things that are very precious." They naturally think of the physical heart which beats. A Beginner asked, "Did you ever hear anything ticking inside?" Several said it was their stomach, or something inside you that digests your food.

Teachers should make perfectly clear the Scriptural connotation of the word "heart." This outside body of ours is only the house in which our real self lives. It is our real self which feels and sees and hears the outside world. Have you ever seen the dead body of a bird or animal? What makes that dead body different from the live one? The outside body is just the same, but the inside part that told the body what to do is gone.

Our real self, which the Bible calls our "heart," tells our hands and feet and eyes what to do. It thinks and loves and knows. It cannot be seen, and it knows and loves God, who cannot be seen. When you love someone, what part of you loves that person?

Now that Jesus has gone back to Heaven, He is a spirit who can be everywhere. He wants to take charge of your real self. He wants a place in your real self. He wants you to give yourself and your love to Him.

Even with explanation, however, this approach to salvation is harder than that of Christ's taking the punishment that we deserve for the things we have done wrong.

IMAGINATION

Do you like to work with people who are void of imagination? Probably not. Although the Beginner level represents imagination at its height, adults need it too, particularly those who work with young children. How barren and drab is life without it! How easily it makes a game out of tedious routine and unpleasant tasks! What an enormous problem it would be to teach children with their lack of mechanical skill, their narrow world, their lack of conventional habits, if teachers could not count on that ally, the imagination. How often teachers say, "This is a poor specimen of what I am trying to show the children, but they will use their imagination!"

Distinguishing between Fact and Fancy. When Bobby comes running to you for protection because "a lion is chasing him," is he trying to lie to you? As a large, shaggy dog starts toward him, setting every nerve of his body aquiver, the total effect is certainly that of the lion which he has heard about in connection with Daniel. Up to that time, a dog to him has been the smaller type which is more gentle than the leaping beast who looks as if he is going to eat him up. Though assured that it is just a dog, still to Bobby "lion" best describes the beast as he saw it coming toward him.

Young children have had so few experiences, and those few have carried such specific meaning, that they are lacking the checks on the imagination which are exercised by adults. In their imagination they can picture a blue lion because they have seen so few tawney lions. They can think of a little man, because men at a distance look so little. They seldom willfully lie. They are easily confused because the real world is so full of wonder and amazing new experiences, and because their observation is inaccurate concerning details in which they are not personally interested.

What they need is more opportunity for contact with real things, opportunity to explore the unknown in dark corners and shadows, and to investigate personally things under guidance, which gives healthy interpretation. They can stand at a window, and compare large dogs with small ones, and contrast various colors.

If we quench their ardor when they come in all agog with tall tales they may hesitate in the future to bring us their confidences. We can enjoy their point of view with them, and then take the attitude, "That was a wonderful story. Wasn't that funny! But of course it did not really happen. Now I'll tell you one that really happened. Can you tell me something that really happened?"

Unseen Realities. After living in the prosaic, materialistic world of adult life, it is very refreshing to work with children to whom all is new and possible. If we happen to want something which is not at hand, we simply use something else or nothing at all, and just pretend we have what we want.

The varnished floor around the outside of a rug makes excellent water in which to place the baby Moses in his basket which we have made. First, we are all the mother of Moses, who puts the basket in the water; the next minute there is nothing at all incongruous about changing to the princess, who comes down to the water and discovers the baby.

In imagination children can project themselves into the experiences and feelings of others, thus gaining much insight into events they could never directly experience. In imagination they can gain more mature relationships and more spiritual values.

Many young children have imaginary playmates to whom they give personality, character, and appearance. How much more wonderful to experience from early years the companionship of the dearest Friend of all children, the Lord Jesus Himself! That is the time for Him to become real and personal to them. He is with them in the dark room, and when parents need to leave. He can control forces when parents are impotent. He knows about things that are too intimate even to tell parents. He ever understands and is ready to help. They love to sing, "Jesus, Friend of all the children, . . ."

It is a mistake, intentional or unintentional, to give children the impression that God sees them only for the purpose of spying on them and noting their sins. In that case they do not want Him around, but try to put Him out of their thoughts. He is surely present to see all they do, but they should feel that He is even more ready to forgive and help them do right than to punish them for doing wrong.

In 1829 the great Scotch preacher Dr. Alexander Whyte wrote the following letter to one of his children who was ill. It is a dialogue between the lonely father and the children's canary:

> Dear Janet: I was out beyond Carstorphine visiting this afternoon and had to telegraph this: "Douglas, 7 Charlotte Square. Home at 8. Dr. Whyte."
>
> On my way home I got some nice chickweed for Dick, and when I took it to him, he was just saying his prayers before going to bed. "How are Janet and Aird?" he asked, as he nibbled a little fibre of grass. "Better, I hope, Richard," I said. "Tell them," he said, "that I whistle to Jesus every morning to ask Him to make them better." "My dear bird," I said, "I did not know that you could speak to Jesus." "Oh, Dr. Whyte," he said, "are you a minister and have you forgotten the 148th Psalm?" "I shall read it when I go upstairs," I said. "Very well," he said, "good night. Thank you for this nice chickweed, and remember my love to Janet and the Moderator." As I shut his door, he said: "The Lord is my Shepherd," and popped his head under his wing.

I came up and read the 148th Psalm. And, sure enough, David must have had a canary like us. With Dick's love and Father's.[7]

True Hero Stories. Does the realistic Junior also enjoy using his imagination? Yes, though in a different way from the younger child. He wants true hero stories, but he puts himself into these true stories as the hero. Living in a realm of vigorous realism, he likes to see things happen, and the livelier and speedier, the better. Tales the Junior prefers seem quite impossible to the adult for the reason that in everyday life things do not happen so fast and so often except in times of extreme exigency. Yet that is the way the Junior pictures ideal existence, and adventures cannot be too thrilling to suit him.

The Junior teacher should be collecting for his file many true incidents of spiritual victories, especially concerning the people Juniors consider heroes, such as the figures in their history books and in the world of sports. When we want to illustrate a principle, we can find an incident from the life of Washington or Lincoln, Gill Dodds or Eddie Rickenbacker.

For the Primary, teachers have a wider latitude of choice, for the Primary enjoys both the real and make-believe, yet clearly distinguishes one from the other. Stories can be concocted to fit his special needs. At eight years the fairy tale is in full glory, but interest in stories of real life is also apparent. The "really-truly" character of the Bible stories should continually be stressed.

The Junior is finished with made-up stories which never happened. He wants to identify with real people the illustrations he takes to heart. He wants to have incidents truthfully related, even to the exact words which people spoke. He is quick to detect stories which are merely doctored up for the purpose.

Juniors need the following type of illustration:

In July, 1863, Abraham Lincoln rode horseback from his summer home to call on General Sickles, who had a leg amputated just after the great victory at Gettysburg. Mr. Lincoln wore a long linen duster, with a stovepipe hat, his trousers stuffed in the tops of his tall riding boots, and his spurs on.

He sat down and talked with General Sickles as man to man, not as the great President. They talked about the war and the battle of Gettysburg. In reply to a question from General Sickles whether or not the President was anxious about the battle at Gettysburg, Lincoln gravely said, "No, I was not. Some of my cabinet and many others in Washington were, but I had no fears."

General Sickles inquired how this was, and seemed curious about it. Mr. Lincoln hesitated, but finally replied:

"Well, I will tell you how it was, but I would rather you wouldn't say anything about it just now, for the people might not understand. In the pinch of your campaign up there, when everybody seemed panic-stricken, and nobody could tell what was going to happen, oppressed by the gravity of our affairs, I went to my room one day, locked the door, got down on my knees before Almighty God, and prayed to Him mightily for victory at Gettysburg. I told Him that this was His war, and our cause His cause, but we couldn't stand another Fredericksburg or Chancellorsville. I then and there made a solemn vow to Almighty God, that if He would stand by our boys at Gettysburg, I would stand by Him. He *did* stand by our boys, and I *will* stand by Him. After that (I don't know how it was, and I can't explain it), a sweet comfort crept into my soul that God Almighty had taken the whole business into His own hands and that things would go all right at Gettysburg. That is why I had no fears about you."[8]

1. From your experience, reading or conversation with others, how many actual experiences and illustrations from childhood can you find of the principles discussed in this chapter?

2. For the age group which you teach or are particularly interested in, list some mental distinctions they make but which are not made by the department below them, and also some which the department above them makes but they do not make.

3. Show by a specific Bible lesson how one proceeds from the concrete to the general and then back to the concrete. Start with a child's definite problem, select a Bible story which suggests the solution to that problem, a short Bible verse which generalizes the solution, and several ways of carrying the same principle over into other daily situations.

4. In our teaching, how important are the past experiences of each child? List ten ways in which they will make a difference in our methods.

5. Make up an illustration which exactly meets a spiritual need of a Beginner or Primary, and find a true incident which meets a spiritual need of a Junior.

CHAPTER VIII

SPIRITUAL DEVELOPMENT

1. What reasons can you give for there being so many church members today who show little evidence of spiritual life?
2. What do Matthew 18:6 and 10 suggest as to the church's general attitude toward children through the ages? Is it possible to go to the opposite extreme at the period when that fault is being recognized and corrected?
3. Does the Bible specify the age of accountability? Why do you think it does, or doesn't?
4. Amy Carmichael, director of the Dohnavur Children's Home in South India, fervent lover of Christ and children, makes this statement, "There is nothing more fatal than to hustle souls." [9] What do you think is her implication?

No doubt the most significant statement ever made about child training is recorded in the greatest book on the subject, the book of Proverbs. "Train up a child in the way he should go: and when he is old, he will not depart from it," we are admonished in Proverbs 22:6. The word translated "train" is, in the original, a military term; train a child as a soldier, to keep file, obey the word of command, and carry his weapons. "In the way he should go," implies vastly more than teaching or telling of the One who is the way, the truth, and the life. It means continual decision in favor of Him who is the way to God, personally seeking the truth of God, and daily living in the will and power of the Son of God.

Parents and teachers are to train up a child in the way he *should* go, not the way he *would* go, for the bias of inbred sin, strengthened by actual sin, tends to direct his actions in the downward way. Although some of us may be called *eccentric* —and we surely are out of center in the opinion of many educators—yet we are more interested than they in integrating the personality; but, whereas they put "self" on the throne and magnify "self," we seek to build a life with Christ Jesus magnified and enthroned in the heart of each child.

The church of Christ is finally waking to the fact that it should first conquer from within rather than let its own children fall away, to be rescued after irreparable damage has been done. Formerly the church had the audacity to let sin ripen before doing anything about it. Yet a few wise leaders in every age have sensed the absurdity of such procedure, and have led the children to Christ and onward into service as soon as their hearts were ready.

It is the Lord's intention that parents should early train their own children diligently, "when they sit in their house, when they walk by the way, when they lie down, and when they rise up" (Deut. 6:7). It is not His way that sporadic efforts should be made intermittently when outside evangelists are brought into a community. It is His way that every day should give the spiritual training needed for that day, that spiritual development should be an ongoing process as is physical and mental development.

Just as there are spurts in physical and mental life, so the spiritual will have its moments of mountain-peak crises. Regeneration is one mountain peak in life's journey, but the hillsides must be scaled before that height is reached; and after life in Christ is accepted, other more majestic peaks loom ahead in the distant clouds for those who are not content to stop growing.

Spiritual training cannot begin too early nor stop too late. Since children are compared in Scripture with plants (Ps. 128:3; 144:12; 92:13,14), spiritual development may well be described by the figure of plant life. First, the ground is plowed; then the seed is sown. Sunshine and rain are necessary for the new life or spiritual crisis. Healthy growth is followed by fruit bearing.

When spiritual training is neglected during the early years an older child may be ready for an accelerated program. Yet we must beware of mushroom growth without roots.

PLOWING THE GROUND

Even in the most favorable of soils furrows must be made as repositories for the life-giving seed.

Natural Birth and Spiritual Birth. After hearing a statement of a child's two birthdays, one boy remarked, "First I was born from heaven to earth, then from earth to heaven!" "Between the natural birth and the spiritual birth there is not a moment to be lost." Spiritual birth *should* correspond to physical birth, although this is not usually the case. The young child *should* be protected by parents and teachers as he forms habits and attitudes which will be ready to function when he slips over into eternal life. Prenatal care of the young *should* be as diligently guarded in the spiritual life as in the physical life. The young child needs shielding more than testing as he forms habits of dependence and reverence and gratitude and prayer.

He needs not only to establish confidence in his parents and teachers, who do so much for him, but also to kneel with them and together seek help from One who is infinitely higher than any mortal. How fortunate that boy or girl who cannot remember the time when he did not love the Lord Jesus and try to obey Him! How fortunate that child whose affections have been set on things above from the earliest years, who, from a child, like young Timothy of old, has known the holy Scriptures (II Tim. 3:15)! In later life, instead of being continually annoyed and discouraged by selfish and evil habits which have clung to him from childhood, he can forge ahead in manlike stride to a life of glorious service!

Self-Centered Love. Although childhood is the period of development which can boast of natural faith and dependency, still a young child's love is immature. It is naturally centered in himself, and is given in response to love and attention. Childhood's creed is best expressed in the verse, "We love him, because he first loved us" (I John 4:19). The child should feel that the love of God has always been calling and beckoning him.

It is hard for us in this day of child nurture to imagine the amazement of the disciples when Jesus turned from the Pharisees to bless a throng of children—children who were merely infants, children who were not even sick. Jesus took time to fill their hearts with the love of God, for this would be their best defense against temptation. In the presence of the Saviour a child never feels that he is a stranger, or fails to be attracted to His person.

The love of God must overshadow every other teaching. H. G. Wells was early alienated from God because He was portrayed as a stern judge and an everlasting spy. God and His hell were the nightmares of Wells' childhood, He hated God, while he still believed.

Although holiness is God's basic attribute, it is by way of His love that His holiness should be approached when teaching children. The first and great commandment is to love the

Lord with all the heart. All other doctrines of Scripture must be built on the foundation of God's love, which is from everlasting to everlasting.

Attitude toward Sin. Just as disease germs are always present in the body, and develop when resistance is low, so sin is ever present in the human race. Even small children can understand that all of us get dirty as we work and play, but the disgrace is failure to wash and make ourselves clean. Just so, all have sinned—the very best of people, the ones we love best—and they do not hesitate to confess it. Neither are they overly strict when the children sin, but simply face the fact frankly, call departure from any known law by its rightful name, and inculcate the habit of doing something about it. The very act of calling wrongdoing "sin" is in itself a prophylactic for the rampant false cults of the religious world.

If children get the idea that adults consider themselves perfect and are ready to condemn the younger generation because they are not, they probably will try to conceal their wrongdoing. But if adults also confess their shortcomings and mistakes, and are more ready to forgive a penitent than to punish, practically all children will readily admit their personal sins.

The following seems to be the typical attitude of childhood toward sin:

> As a child, I was never permitted to attend movies, though I often begged to go before I was saved. When I was nine years old I was invited to a birthday party. I didn't know until we were on the way that it was to be a theater party. I was panic-stricken, but afraid to say anything. My girl friend, who knew I didn't go to the movies, tried to coax me into going to this one, explaining that it was very funny and I'd enjoy it.
>
> At the theater, three of us were left to wait outside while the others were being brought. I looked at the publicity pictures,

but I felt sick, because I knew I couldn't go. At last I whispered to my girl friend, "I'm going home."

I ran all the way, a mile and a half, crying and praying. I felt so relieved when I got home, but I was also disappointed. My mother was proud of me, but said, "I think you could have gone this once."

I've wished so often that she had not said that, because I was firmly convinced that there could be no exceptions. I regret also that my father gave me a silver dollar as a reward. I didn't want any reward, and I felt as though I had accepted something I did not deserve.

SOWING THE SEED

Revelation 21:21 speaks of the city of God with its twelve gates, every gate a pearl. By only one gate does a person enter the city, to tread the streets of gold. Yet if that person has also viewed the other gates, he will be all the more appreciative of the holy city. Not until, face to face, we behold Him who is the truth, shall we see all angles of the truth simultaneously. But children need to approach the meaning of salvation by grace through faith from many angles. Because of their limited experience, some gates to the city may mean a great deal more to them than others.

1. The Lord has done more for us than even our parents; therefore, we love Him most of all.
2. God adopts into His family those who receive His Son.
3. Each year firemen save *some* people from burning, policemen save *some* people from accident, lifeguards save *some* people from drowning, but God needs to save from sin *every* person born into this world.
4. Only that which is clean and holy can enter God's presence, for heaven wouldn't be heaven if sin were allowed there.
5. Christ became our substitute, as when a mother takes punishment which a child deserves.

6. "All we like sheep have gone astray"; Christ seeks the lost at the cost of His life.
7. We first believe; only then with the help of Christ can we be good.
8. After we believe, we become new creatures in Christ.
9. How can God love us very dearly and yet punish us for our sin?
10. Miracles are very easy for God's Son, but taking all our awful sins on Himself was very hard.
11. Salvation is free to us, although it cost Christ so much.
12. Salvation is free, but Christians can work for Jesus.

SUNSHINE AND RAIN

It is the benign influence of God's sunshine and rain which works on the forces within the hard shell of a seed and causes it to crack open and germinate.

Moral Training. Is moral training ever to be discouraged for the saved or the unsaved? Did you ever know a child who was not taught to pray until after he was saved?

In preparation for rebirth, Bible verses and stories portraying conduct serve as did the law of old to give knowledge of sin. Children should realize that God speaks definitely to them in His Word: "Children, obey your parents in the Lord," "Be ye kind one to another," and "Do all things without murmurings." God expects children to keep His commands.

But even when they try hard, they sense that they are not able to keep the clear statements from the Book. When children see how high are God's standards and how far short they have fallen from keeping them, they acknowledge themselves genuine sinners. All conduct teaching can demonstrate the need of One stronger than they are to help them.

We should never disparage early moral training. It has been likened to a well-laid fire. Though the careful laying of sticks can in no way produce a flame, yet this kind of preparation causes the fire to burn up more brightly when the spark is kindled from outside. The ultimate aim, however, is expression of a new nature as well as redirection or suppression of the old.

Opportunities for Decision. If we provide small children frequent opportunities to say "Yes" to Christ in accordance with their limited comprehension of Him, we shall never err by hindering them from coming to the Saviour, nor by being responsible for their making a mere profession before the Spirit has prepared the heart. We shall never be guilty of going to either extreme if we give our groups of children numerous occasions to confess their love of Christ, and then deal individually with those who seek salvation, a miracle which happens once for all time and eternity.

The whole group may be invited to express their love—love even surpassing love for mother and father, and their desire to do anything the Lord wants them to do, no matter how hard. If the spiritual needs of boys and girls are met from week to week, even before rebirth we shall see evidence that the truth is being assimilated. "In God's economy every feeling has its work to do in every stage of development."

When a child has been trained from his early years, it is sometimes difficult or impossible to know the date of regeneration. "The wind bloweth where it listeth, and thou hearest the sound thereof, but canst not tell whence it cometh, and whither it goeth: so is every one that is born of the Spirit" (John 3:8).

Though the new birth is an instantaneous experience, the turning about of conversion may be a gradual process. Choosing the things of God in preference to one's own natural way, the child brought up in a Christian home may day by day be redirecting his tendencies upward toward the Lord. Supernatural forces are continually working on him as he witnesses godly examples, hears the words of Scripture quoted frequently in familiar discourse, forms habits of daily devotion, and depends on God for the daily supply of his needs.

When in 1938, a study was made of the regeneration experiences of 732 Christian students of Wheaton College, a Christian institution in Wheaton, Illinois, approximately half of the young people knew little or nothing concerning their second birth. Most of those who were saved before the age of twelve were unable to give any exact information concerning their experience. Thirty-seven per cent could not state the time of the regeneration, since it occurred early in their childhood. Approximately 73 per cent of the students had come from strong Christian backgrounds, 23 per cent from nominal Christian homes, and 4 per cent from non-Christian homes.[10]

One of the students explains the situation in his case:

> I am a Christian and cannot recall any time when I was not a Christian. Having been reared in a Christian home, I have continually loved the Lord as He has led me step by step.
>
> As a child, I listened with eagerness to His message, yielded Him my allegiance, and responded to His call to service by participating in numerous phases of His work. I was greatly interested in Junior League work at the age of nine, and started teaching in the Junor department of the Sunday School at the age of thirteen.
>
> The calling of an older brother to the mission field had a marked influence upon my life. As a senior in high school, I consecrated my life to the Lord. From that point, He has led me into full-time service for Him.
>
> My answer to the question, "When were you saved?" thus is: "I do not know, for Jesus Christ has always been in my life."

Even when a child has responded to the Lord since infancy, it is salutary and satisfying, nevertheless, for salvation to be made definite. If a child assumes that he belongs to the Lord and the question arises, ask him, "Have you ever told the Lord Jesus that you give your whole self to Him once for all? Are you ready to do that now? What has Christ done to save you? What is your part?"

> Frank and James (Primaries) grew up in a home where daily life in Christ was practical and joyous. The happiest times of their lives were connected with the things of God. He was as real to them as members of the family "with skin on."
>
> One morning at the breakfast table the two boys were wondering whether or not certain people belonged to the family of God. As they discussed with their mother the evidences which one boy showed for and against salvation, James suddenly remarked, "Well, I'm not perfect either, but don't say I don't belong to God." The mother then asked them if a person had to be perfect in order to be a Christian. They answered that of course everyone had to believe on the Lord Jesus Christ to be a Christian.
>
> "Just what is believing?" asked James.
>
> Mother explained, "It's giving your whole self over to Christ, asking Him to take away your sin, and entrusting Him to make of you what He would like to."
>
> James answered, "I often tell Jesus I love Him, and ask Him to keep me from sin, but I guess I've never given the whole thing over to Him. I'll do that now." Dropping on his knees, he made the transaction definite then and there.

After an older child has voiced his own prayer for salvation, assurance should be given him from his own Bible; then he may write in it, for instance, "On March 19, 19___, I accepted Christ as my own Saviour." He should mark and be able to turn immediately to a few verses which have become personal to him. With these he will be able to answer the objections of any who doubt, or any mixed feelings of his own.

He has assurance on the authority of God's Word. For instance, "God says, 'To as many as received him [Christ], to them gave he power to become the sons of God.' I believe in Him. I have received Him, and so God says I am saved."

One morning a Junior girl had a deep experience with the Lord. She confided to her aunt with whom she lived, "You know, I think it was this morning that I was really saved! But don't tell anyone at church, for they all think I am saved already."

On the next to the last day of vacation school, when the older departments were having decision services, a Primary superintendent wanted to give her boys and girls an opportunity to take a step toward Christ. This was her first vacation school, she knew not how to proceed; she knew not how to pray definitely, but sought the Lord importunately that He would give these children a definite experience with Himself. One thing she had—a story. The rest she left in the hands of the Lord, to be directed when the time came.

The story pictured a boy from a poor home having a precious quarter of his own, and debating what he should do with it. He thought of all the fascinating things he might buy for himself—an airplane, a ride on a pony, a new cap. He looked in the store windows at the pretty handkerchiefs and stationery which he might buy his dear mother. But after a struggle he decided to give it to the person who had done most for him, who had given His very life for him. So he often fingered the coin in his pocket, but never let it stray until he put it in the offering basket at church on Sunday morning.

When the story was finished, the teacher breathed a prayer, "Now, Lord, what next?" She asked those who had already accepted Christ as their own Saviour from sin to stand at the front with her. Then as she continued to tell how much Christ had done for them, and as the ones in front told how much they loved Him, to her surprise she saw, first, Marvin and, then, Adele and, next, Helen coming up to stand with those who had taken their stand on the Lord's side. One after another they kept coming, until the last boy had left his seat! There was that whole group assembled in front! There they were without an invitation! The teacher was a bit overwhelmed! Could they mean business with the Lord? All of them? She searched their faces. Every one was dead in earnest, without natural thought for the child who was standing next him. Not at all the way Primaries usually gather informally in a group.

Recognizing that the needs of the group were different, the teacher then suggested silent prayer, to tell the Lord why they had come. She closed with a few words of audible prayer. Sensitive to the fact that they now needed expression for this new step, she suggested singing a song which afforded an enthusiastic outlet. Before they took their seats, they each thought of one thing they wanted to do for the Lord that week. The deeds mentioned were childlike and practical.

Though the way of salvation had been previously made very clear and plain, as the teacher watched those same children for six years afterward, she felt that they were not all saved at that hour. It was truly a definite step forward for all of them, but the individual moment of salvation came later in most cases.

It is often said that children are responsible to God after the age of accountability. What is that age? The church has sometimes assumed it to be the age of twelve, when the Jewish boy became a "son of the law." Until twelve, therefore, it formerly neglected the child and allowed him to stagnate spiritually. May not the age of accountability vary with individuals and with environmental conditions? May not the age of accountability be considerably lower in our day in cities than it was previously on isolated farms?

II Chronicles 36:9 records that "Jehoiachin was eight years old when he began to reign, and he reigned three months and ten days in Jerusalem: and he did that which was evil in the sight of the Lord."

SPIRITUAL CRISIS

The Requisite for Salvation. The church is already too full of mere *professing* Christians who are not *possessing* Christians, without adding more *professors* to the ranks. If a child professes to accept Christ as his Saviour from sin without true rebirth, then realizes later that there was nothing to it, he will be much harder to reach a second time. It is indeed a delicate matter to deal with young souls in the greatest issue of life, and yet it is not too delicate for those who are filled with the Spirit. May we watch and pray lest we be tempted to deal with children in the flesh rather than in the Spirit!

It is dangerous to err on either side of the straight and narrow path—to offend the little ones by hindering them in any way from coming to Christ, and, on the other hand, to lead them through the outward motions without their becoming new creatures in Christ. The church of today has awakened to the fact that it has been hindering the children from coming by considering them too young until they reach the age of eleven or twelve, or at least the age of nine. In our zeal to gather in the children let us not go to the other extreme and hinder real regeneration by being content with mere outward form.

Though children are naturally more ready for salvation than adults, because of faith and dependence, rebirth is always supernatural. Preparation of heart, not a certain age, is the condition for salvation.

Force of Adult Personality. Force of adult personality alone will gain a decision from a child ninety-nine times out of one hundred. He is taught to please his teacher, and he greatly desires his approval. However, his personality must be but a mirror for the personality of Christ.

Plants bear the best blossoms when they are carefully and regularly tended, watered, cultivated, and pruned. As plants, children's natures are such that they can be easily transplanted into God's garden. The transplanting of children from the earthly to the heavenly garden is the work of the Spirit. To attempt to force a feeling before it is prepared by the Spirit is like prying open the petals of a bud to hasten God's process.[11] We sometimes try to hasten the unfolding of a rosebud so that it will be in full bloom for some special occasion. What is the result of being impatient with God's time? Every touch made by our human fingers on the delicate satin petals leaves an ugly, dark blemish.

In the fullness of God's own time the Lord Jesus was born into this world, though His coming was long awaited by pure hearts. In the fullness of God's own time, likewise, do we want Him to be born into the heart of each child. A child born prematurely has a harder struggle for existence than the others. Forced development at one stage means arrested development at a later stage.

Balance between the Head and the Heart. Both the head and the heart must respond in salvation. The head must know the facts of Scripture, and the heart must appropriate them with affection. Although neither is sufficient in itself, Christ summed up His commands with "love" rather than "know." When we give children an appeal for salvation, let us be careful to reserve the proper balance between the head and the heart, for children's emotions are both intense and transitory. Their feelings can be very easily stirred, so fleeting and superficial are they. In the early years laughter and tears are very near the surface, and may follow each other in rapid succession. If we overstimulate children's feelings beyond what can be expended in action, the result is likely to be a weakening and reactionary effect.

Spurgeon gave an apt illustration of this overstimulation. He related that as he rode down the street in his carriage, he sometimes stirred up much dust and sometimes very little dust, depending entirely on the kind of street. He was not concerned about the amount of dust he stirred up—his concern was to ride down the street to his destination. Our concern in dealing with children is to lead them to the Lord Jesus; little or much emotion may be aroused—depending on the nature of the child—which is not our concern. But, says Spurgeon, some people go out into the road with a broom, and deliberately sweep up the dust; some speakers unduly play on children's emotions. Results cannot be judged by the amount of emotion aroused. Not being great sinners, children often need no great upheaval; just a quiet committing of themselves to the Saviour.

Active Acceptance. At the other extreme children are led through the outward motions of salvation without an inner experience. They sometimes imitate the outward manifestations of a feeling. They are so ready to change their bodily positions and do something different that they welcome any outlet for their restlessness. It is natural for young children to follow their older brothers or sisters; they are often instructed to do as the latter do. Especially if a tangible object of some kind, like a book, is given to those who accept Christ, or if salvation is presented as getting something for nothing, children will imitate others, for they don't want to miss anything.

We should like to make each second birthday a more special occasion than the first birthday. If only the gates of heaven might be opened to hear the angels sing as each new soul is born into the heavenly family! If material things were used, literal-minded children would profess to accept Christ merely for the celebration. Even when kept on a lofty spiritual plane it is difficult not to give too much attention to the child and too little to the Saviour.

Every child must feel the need of definitely and personally reaching out in faith to take the gift of salvation for himself. Jacob worshiped the God of his fathers, yet needed to meet God personally. We may illustrate by holding in our hand a dollar bill or some object of value, and state that we are offering the money as a gift to whoever takes it. The child who believes what has been said, and actively comes to take the gift, is rewarded. It is not enough for him to sit passively in a chair and say, "You can give it to me if you want to."

Belief means wholehearted committal, not mere mental assent. When a child reaches out to take a gift of salvation he receives it from God's Son, who paid the enormous price that the child might have it without cost. At the sight of Him who is taking us into heaven we forget the gift, and glory in the Giver.

Individuals differ as greatly in spiritual discernment as in other respects, and must be treated individually. Some are ready for regeneration very young; other natures, with less care, are slower to respond. Our responsibility as parents and teachers is to lift up the crucified and risen Lord, and to kneel with new followers at the foot of the cross. It is easy to detect individuals who have been drawn to Christ, for children do not believe in faith not shown by works.

Instead of giving a group invitation to young children, we may suggest that any who want to accept Christ may tell you after the class or meeting. Those who are in earnest will come, while others will forget about it.

The following testimonies of teachers and children show the difference between active committal and imitation of forms:

When I was around eight or nine years old and in a Primary Sunday School class, the time of year came round when the church accepted new members. I remember that all the classes went into the church and up close to the front. We were asked if we wanted to give our hearts to the Lord. That was the first time I remember hearing such an expression. The other children one by one said they did, and so I did too. I think I did it because I knew that we should please God and because others were doing it. I didn't know the meaning of it, though, and was scared at the words, "Give your heart to God." I thought it meant taking your heart out and giving it to God.

When various evangelists would visit the church and give a plea for salvation or consecration, I went forward five or six times without knowing what it all meant. I can well remember the reason—I didn't want the church people and my friends and my mother to think that I didn't agree with everything that went on in the church, and I didn't want to be the only one remaining in my seat while others went forward. I can also remember the first time I was asked to pray. I didn't know how, but was forced by the pastor without any help as to how to begin. For many years I had a fear of prayer because of that experience.

As a child attending Sunday School I was impressed by the prayers of adults, and determined to be a Christian when I grew up. I never knew that salvation was for children. One day I thought to myself, "If God hears the older people, why won't He hear me?" I prayed to God and He heard me, and I had a wonderful experience of knowing that my name was written in heaven. The Lord was very real to me.

Eight-year-old Billy was a ringleader of all kinds of mischief. He did all the "ornery" things he could think of, arriving early to get started with his capers. At first, he knew nothing of spiritual things. After attending for almost two years, he gradually showed curiosity and interest. Then for several weeks he became quiet and concerned. One morning he came to the superintendent with these words, "All week long I've been sorry for my sins. Last night I asked Jesus to come into my heart and to wash it clean of all the sin that was there and to make me the kind of boy I should be." Looking up at the teacher, he added, "And Miss Eileen, He saved me!" Now he's an entirely different boy.

This next testimony is from a teacher who for years worked with young people, and at first doubted the reality of the regeneration of Primary children.

Our greatest problem in the fall was that of discipline. Right up until Christmas we had behavior of the kind that had this poor superintendent wondering if those boys were demon-possessed. We made it a matter of real prayer and, as usual, God answered in a way that left us speechless with delight.

Four Sundays ago Don told us how he had been saved while at home. The next Sunday Gerald came and described how he had gone home from Sunday School the previous Sunday and, in the afternoon, knelt down by himself and asked God to save him and help him be a good boy. The next week Glenn said that he had been saved quite a while ago, but hadn't told us about it, and wanted to do so. About this time, I was fairly bursting with happiness. When Kenny told us last Sunday that he had been saved and was going to be a different boy, we all said with real meaning, "Bless the Lord, O my soul!"

All of these boys are about the same age. And the wonderful part about it is that there is a change in their actions and attitudes. Not that I expect perfection from them—I was too much of a villain myself—but I do expect them to act differently from what they did before.

The part that has impressed me so much is the spontaneous way it has happened. None of the boys was saved during the school session and all of them volunteered the information. I'm convinced that our program must be making enough of an impression, therefore, to set the children thinking and praying during the week. And I'm glad—so very glad!

Do all superintendents experience this same joy in working

with children? I'm still so very green, and I'm sure I make lots of mistakes, but the Lord has been so gracious. When I think of the years of hard labor with Intermediates and Seniors, I'm more than ever determined that every Primary I have the privilege of teaching will *know* how to be saved, and I trust many of them will accept Him early in life.

The young child who is ready for rebirth is usually one who has been reared in a Christian home. Moreover, it is usually in the home that some event brings the question to bear on him personally. He then asks his parents about his own relationship to the Saviour.

Children who have been denied the privilege of a Christian home usually need a longer period of Bible training before they are ready to give themselves to the Lord. Teachers should pray fervently that each child shall confess Christ before leaving the Junior department; but pressure should always be placed on prayer rather than on urging the child to make a decision.

HEALTHY GROWTH

Any living thing must take root downward before it can bear fruit upward. Many a young person testifies that though he was saved in early years, he never knew the assurance or the joy of his salvation. Every time an invitation was given, his heart being tender, he realized his shortcomings and went forward again. Regenerated children need to distinguish clearly between once-for-all salvation and daily cleansing for sin. Although the standard set for conduct should be kept high, they should grow familiar with the message in I John and God's provision for all emergencies. Because they are not inclined to hold grudges and delay their reactions, they can form the habit of immediate forgiveness as soon as sin is detected.

A change, but not perfection, is to be expected of the young Christian. How discouraging it is for children if the esteemed "pillars of the church" catch them running through the church building, and say, "I told people you were too young to know what you were doing." If the elders of the church cannot believe in them, can they be expected to keep up their own confidence?

Spiritual Struggles. A child who has felt the saving power of Christ has discernment to appreciate the struggle of the two natures within himself. He feels the strong pull of the two forces and concretely calls them God and Satan. It encourages him to know that all Christians have temptations, but that God always gives victory if one is trying to obey Him. Conceiving of difficulties as warfare between the great powers of right and wrong in the universe, he is challenged as a Christian soldier to choose the Lord's side in each encounter.

Confession is a natural accompaniment of genuine rebirth. Just as the child desires to share his joys and sorrows with others, he wants to tell them of his new Friend and Saviour and Lord.

If a child goes home to unsaved parents he should have an opportunity to confess to several people at church and receive their glowing delight before he gets chilly disapproval at home. He can confess to the other children, the department superintendent, the pastor, or anyone else who is particularly concerned about him.

The struggles of childhood are often kept secret in the inner life, to be related only in later years.

> The incident in my childhood which made the most lasting impression on my life was when I first confessed Christ as my Saviour. My mother was not interested in spiritual things, and always *sent* us children to Sunday School instead of *taking*

us. On this particular morning the Sunday School held a decision service. When the invitation was given for those who wanted the Lord Jesus to come into their hearts, I was eager to respond. I was only in the Primary department, but as my friend and I knelt at the altar I knew that something real had happened. When the minister asked me to pray, I didn't know how. I had always "said my prayer" before going to bed, but Mother had told me what to say. I still remember the words I mumbled, "I'm saved! I know I am, and I'm glad I am!"

Truly, I was glad to be saved! I ran all the way home to tell Mother, imagining how happy she would be to find out. She was peeling potatoes in the kitchen, when I burst in with, "Mother, do you know what I did?" "No; what did you do?" asked Mother.

Here words failed me. Somehow, it was a lot harder to tell Mother than I had expected. I stumbled around, but finally got out the crux of the matter. Instead of being overjoyed as I had expected, she said, without looking up from her potatoes, "I think you better know what you are doing before you try anything like that."

Young as I was, those words pierced my heart, and I decided never to tell another soul of my experience. I went on living the life of an average child without Christ. Yes, I had accepted Him, but how healthy would a newborn infant be if practically smothered when only one-half hour old! Neither the pastor nor the Sunday School teacher ever helped me, and it was not until I was fourteen years old that I again received the assurance of salvation. Even then I couldn't tell Mother about it, and although I gave my life to Christ I tried to keep it a secret at home.

It was years before I could mention the things of the Lord at home. My father, sister, and two brothers are now saved but to this day I have not had the courage to speak with Mother concerning her soul. I write the story of Christ in my letters to her, and by His grace some day I will speak with her. Every time I want to approach the subject, this childhood scene in the kitchen appears before my mind, and I draw back into my "shell."

Church Membership. Why shouldn't church membership be granted children on the same basis as other believers? Of course, this step should not be urged until they are ready for it. But many children expect that this will be the natural corollary of believing in Christ. If a Junior (or Primary) exhibits genuine love for the Saviour and wants to use his exuberant energy for Him, could he do it better outside the body of God's people, or inside? If he lays on the altar all that he now has to give, and Christ accepts the gift, should not the church accept the giver? Is the attitude of the church to be that of leaving a child on the cold doorstep so that the wintry blasts may test him to prove whether or not he is alive?

Those who have been fitted for Christ's church above should be fit for its fellowship here below. Juniors aren't interested in the church of tomorrow unless they can do something to help today. If church membership is denied, children often feel that the church is questioning the reality of their experience, perplexities arise, and coldness may ensue.

Mrs. Annie Wittenmyer testifies:

> I was converted before I was eight years old. I was not allowed to join the church until I was thirteen, but I was just as well prepared to join at eight as at thirteen; better, for the delay dampened my zeal.

Once or twice a year the boys and girls who have recently received Christ may form the pastor's class in preparation for church membership. A pastor who understands children has here a choice opportunity to win their friendship and to cement their loyalties to the church. The class will discuss the symbols of the church, the meaning of baptism and the Lord's Supper, and the responsibility of church membership.

FRUIT BEARING

Most of us, no doubt, have seen boys and girls in their own naïve, winsome ways win to Christ those whom adults have tried in vain to reach. There is nothing so simple as children just telling what they have seen and heard, or showing in their daily conduct that Christ makes a difference in their lives. The Spirit is a witness who works in every obedient born-again soul. The only thing which limits Him is sin. He hides Himself in the weak things that God hath chosen, that no flesh may glory in His presence. "Out of the mouth of babes and sucklings hast thou ordained strength because of thine enemies, that thou mightest still the enemy and the avenger" (Ps. 8:2).

Children themselves furnish the best example of the fact that salvation is by grace through faith without merit of one's own. If children received their rightful heritage of a healthy grounding in the fundamentals, and knew for sure whom they believed and why, they would make the world's best missionaries. The sooner they act as His witnesses in their own Jerusalem, the sooner will they be ready for Judea and Samaria, and the uttermost parts of the earth.

Not only for the lost world, but also for their own growth in grace, children need the activity of vital service. They need the outworking of the salvation which has been worked in them. The Saviour works so gently, approaches so softly, penetrates so deeply, and adapts Himself so perfectly to each individual's peculiarities that the evidence of His work is in the outward results. As the new believer progresses and acts on the little discernment he has, more is given him. He then knows from experience that the same Person who renewed his life must now sustain it and empower it. Once he finds the thrill of leading others to Christ, nothing else will satisfy.

1. Why might a Junior child go through the normal steps in salvation quicker than a Beginner?
2. Explain how a child's spiritual birthday can be effectively celebrated in a way which exalts Christ, yet does not give undue attention to the child or to material things.
3. After careful study of thought content and wording, select ten salvation Bible verses which you think would mean most to the literal-minded child. Choose five which show Christ's part, and five which show our part in salvation.
4. List twelve definite avenues of service for saved children which will be profitable to both them and the church.
5. Write an original tract for Junior, Primary, or Beginner children. Make it a real story with the application woven closely into the plot, not merely tacked on the end. Develop thoroughly one or two Scripture verses rather than mentioning several. Use an approach which immediately attracts and appeals to children. Assume no previous Scripture knowledge. Keep the thought content concrete rather than symbolic. Keep the vocabulary at the level of one department. Keep the story short, from 300 to 600 words, making every sentence count.

home observance [illegible] Christ[illegible] between [illegible]
[illegible]
[illegible]

C. TEACHING METHODS

CHAPTER IX

HOW CHILDREN LEARN OR GROW

1. What usually happens to the person who is drifting along through life without compelling aims? Can you cite an example of the dynamic of a driving motive in some person's life?
2. In your life at present, what are the five most potent motives which prompt you to spend your time as you do? Are any of these the motives which regulate the lives of children?
3. Can you recall something you learned so superficially that you soon forgot it? Can you recall something else which you learned in such a vital manner that it has made a difference in your subsequent life? Analyze the motives and methods which account for the difference in results.
4. Do you enjoy review lessons? Have you ever experienced a fascinating review lesson? If not, try to find some other teacher who has. What made that review lesson interesting?
5. What is the Lord's purpose in disciplining you as one of His erring children? When boys and girls are troublesome, why is it sometimes more the teacher's fault than the children's?

"Jimmy doesn't seem to be learning anything," sighs his teacher. Can a normal child with life in his veins remain inert mentally or physically without learning anything? The very activity of his God-given nature necessitates growth and change, and this new experience is learning. But the learning may be positive or negative. When he is in contact with the things of God, he is learning either to love them or to wish he could get away from them.

When the momentous questions of spiritual life and death are at stake, teachers cannot be satisfied with methods which may work sometimes, or which work *in spite of us;* we must have methods which will work always *because of us.* It is our responsibility so to teach that no child can miss the issue.

AIMS EXPRESSING NEEDS

"Why spend time discussing aims?" asks a young teacher. "There's no question about them. Why not simply teach the Bible?" We shall teach the Bible, of course, but not so "simply." Just as a path may be so broad as to lead nowhere, so a general aim fails to get results. The ineffective, haphazard teaching so prevalent in our day is the result of good intentions to teach the Bible without knowing exactly what and why.

When the mother of a child plans his physical food, she says, not merely, "I'm going to get dinner." She says, "There was meat left over from yesterday; Jimmy needs potatoes for energy, spinach for minerals; he especially likes ice cream, and it isn't too heavy for him."

Likewise, the true teacher formulates definite, specific aims to meet his spiritual needs. At present Jimmy's chief spiritual need may be prompt obedience. It is that need which determines the Bible story, the Bible verse, the songs, the discussion, and expressional activities.

A specific need calls for a specific aim which suggests a certain type of program, method and materials, organization and administration. After these have been employed, the procedure is evaluated by testing to see what has been accomplished. Is the same need still present; does Jimmy now have a related need, or an entirely different one? This system-

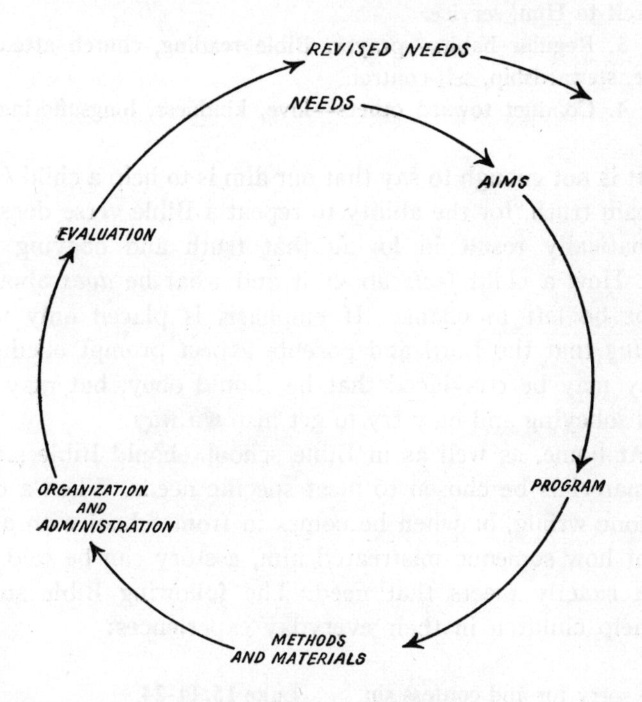

atic, efficient type of teaching is a challenge, for teaching has something definite to accomplish and measure, and spiritual growth is inevitable.

Bible teaching is allowing the Bible, empowered by the Spirit, to change pupils according to God's standards. The test of teaching is growth and progress in the line of the great spiritual goals: to lead children *to* Christ, build them up ***in*** Christ, and send them out *for* Christ.

The broad types of aims are, mainly:

1. Appreciation—of God Himself, His gifts, His mercies.
2. Response to God—salvation, personal fellowship, giving oneself to Him, service.
3. Regular habits—prayer, Bible reading, church attendance, stewardship, self-control.
4. Conduct toward others—love, kindness, longsuffering.

It is not enough to say that our aim is to help a child ***know*** a certain truth, for the ability to repeat a Bible verse does not automatically result in loving that truth and obeying that truth. How a child *feels* about it and what he *does* about it cannot be left to chance. If emphasis is placed only upon ***knowing*** that the Lord and parents expect prompt obedience Jimmy may be convinced that he should obey, but may *feel* like disobeying and may try to get his own way.

At home, as well as in Bible school, should Bible stories and materials be chosen to meet specific needs. When a child has done wrong, or when he comes in from school with a sad tale of how someone mistreated him, a story can be told him which exactly meets that need. The following Bible stories will help children in their everyday experiences:

To be sorry for and confess sin	Luke 15:11-24
Accept Christ as personal Saviour	Acts 16:16-40
Listen for God's voice	I Samuel 1; 2:18, 19, 26; 3
Talk to God	Acts 12:1-17
Feel that He is ever near	Genesis 28
Ask the Lord to help them	John 4:46-53; Luke 5:1-11
Read God's Word	II Kings 22:1-13; 23: 1-4
Speak a word for the Lord	II Kings 5:1-15

Give their money to the Lord	Mark 12:41-44
Obey God	Judges 7
Be kind	Luke 10:30-37
Feel like saying "Thank you"	Luke 17:11-19
Tell the truth	II Kings 5:15-27
Keep from quarreling	Genesis 13:2, 5-13; 14:2, 10-16
Return good for evil	I Samuel 26
Appreciate water	Exodus 17:1-7
Choose healthy food	Daniel 1

Teachers and parents and friends all realize Jimmy's need for prompt obedience, but is Jimmy conscious of that need? He may be, or he may not be. Suppose he feels no need of conforming to the wishes of adults. Shall his teachers nevertheless, give him what he needs, even against his will, trusting that eventually he will appreciate their efforts? How much interest and effort can be expected from Jimmy in that case? Jimmy needs his own aims, his own motives in the line of his own interests and values.

CHILDREN'S INTERESTS AND VALUES

A great deal of so-called learning is like the tying of artificial apples onto a tree instead of nourishing the tree in order that it may bring forth real fruit by its own creative self-activity. Teachers sometimes are satisfied when children memorize the words of truth without taking time and effort to lead them through the longer, natural process of inner assimilation of this truth. The Lord Himself as a teacher is not too busy with the stupendous affairs of the universe to see that *each* of His children takes for himself *each* step in salvation and sanctification. His concern is for fruit that shall endure for all eternity. There is no ready-made shortcut to real learning.

Artificial Motivation. Time spent in stimulating real growth is never wasted, but teachers do waste time when they begin with aims in terms of adult interests and values. When that is the case, artificial motivation is necessary, such as was common in the past: children pretending to pick apples from a tree or to pull fish out of a pond to furnish the interest needed for the repetition of Bible verses for which the children saw no need.

Formerly, when children began to read, they spent half their time on phonics, sounding out certain parts of words, as "at," "sat," "cat," "hat," "mat." For months they could read only the kind of words they had studied. They read, "see the cat. See the hat. See the mat. The cat sat on the mat. The hat sat on the cat. The hat sat on the mat. The mat sat on the cat". . . until they were thoroughly bored with cats, hats, mats, and sats. They wanted to read about the things that interested them, not the words that contained "at." Now they begin from the start to read for meaning, often using their own experiences which they themselves have first composed under the teacher's guidance. Thus they learn to read in half the time and with twice the interest and efficiency. Later they study phonics when they want to spell words for the stories they are writing.

The teacher who expects his group to *pay* attention will have to bargain for it. Children will give it spasmodically to escape punishment or to gain approval or some extrinsic object which they do want. But that kind of attention is forced; it requires a great output of effort and energy, with the child chafing to be rid of the pressure. How different is spontaneous attention, when the pupils enthusiastically bend all their powers from sheer interest, when their faces glow with excitement, when curiosity arouses wholehearted absorption in the subject at hand!

Children's Problems. Teachers' and children's aims need not conflict. After you have diagnosed the child's problem from your viewpoint, find the place where that same problem touches his life and makes a difference in the things he wants to do. Then arrange a situation to make him conscious of it in terms of his interests and values.

If possible, teach the lesson on obedience at the time when Jimmy has failed to obey, and thereby forfeited some kind of treat as the natural result. Such a problem may lead into the whole subject of rules, and why they are necessary. Children may evaluate their Bible school and home and community rules to find out why they have been made. They may re-form those for the Bible school if they find them to be inadequate or outmoded. In relation to their pets, children are the makers of the laws, and from that angle should be able to sight the viewpoint of the lawmaker. This new insight based on their own values will carry over into habits of prompt obedience.

Even more vital than starting with adult aims and translating them into the children's motives is starting with the children's own problems and interests which are already present. Being ever on the alert to detect their daily problems, the times when they feel frustrated and helpless, the points of friction when they sense the need of acting differently, the teacher can help children to live happily with others. Then they will be ready for a discussion or a Bible story or a question which makes them consider why they had trouble and what can be done about it.

What are the basic needs and interests which daily motivate the lives of children? What are the realities in their present lives? What things matter to them here and now? Why not start with these realities rather than vague future values which take no grip on their lives? Christ seeks to enter each life in its present low estate, to permeate each aspect of being, to give spiritual interpretation to the activities of head, heart, and hand. It is in connection with the incidental trifles in children's lives that He will manifest Himself to them.

The Chief Motives of Childhood. In their own actual world children act as they do chiefly because their bodies crave action, their minds seek to make sense out of this big jumbled world, they want to do things with people they like, and they want the people they think important to like them. Their present level of development impels them to skip when their muscles are ready for skipping and to write when their muscles are ready for writing, not before.

A child's learning experience may be compared to a path bordered on one side by his needs and interests, and on the other by his abilities. Beginning on his own immature level of experience does not imply leaving him there. As each present interest is satisfied, it soon leads to other advanced interests. When the child makes the oriental house that he wants to make now, the experience leads him into related knowledge of many other customs of the Holy Land.

Whatever is satisfying tends to be repeated; whatever is annoying tends to be avoided. A word of encouragement and trust is more effective than much censure. Nothing succeeds like success. Satisfaction should never follow an undesirable act. If we want children to tell the truth, even when the truth involves a misdeed that will be followed by punishment, telling the truth must be made more satisfying to them than the punishment is dissatisfying. As soon as possible they should be weaned away from the desire for human approval and be led to seek the dependable approval of the Lord.

Having been created with social natures, children soon desire the presence of others, and prefer a person's smile to material objects. They want to belong and feel at home in groups of people who understand and sympathize with them. They want to be a part of family gatherings, although they may not appreciate all that goes on. A child would much rather have a few pans on a certain shelf in the kitchen where Mother spends so much time than the most expensive of toys in a playroom by himself. He wants to feel that he is a part of whatever activities are important to those about him.

Because of limited experience, children's perspective is distorted, their outlook on the world confused, the mysteries of life many, and their evaluation of material things quite different from the values of adults! Yet they continually seek to bring order out of chaos as they fit together the pieces of a bewildering world. Since it is essentially an adult world, they make many mistakes and miscalculations to the adult way of thinking, learning only gradually adult terms and interpretations and values.

CHILDHOOD VALUES

A little three-year-old girl liked to ask the blessing at the table. She enjoyed it so much that she would prolong it as much as possible. On one occasion she was thanking the Lord for the various parts of her body—for her feet to walk with, for her hands to eat with, for her head to—then there was a long pause, as she tried to decide what her head was good for Finally, she added, "to turn somersaults on"!

If teachers arbitrarily initiate an interest too soon, they may kill that interest for the children later when they would naturally be ready for it. If the young child is taught to memorize the Twenty-third Psalm before he has any knowledge of shepherd life, or hears of the "meat" of the Word when he needs the "milk" for growth, he is not likely to be thrilled with those same words a little later, when they would be full of meaning for him. "A word spoken in due season, how good is it!" (Prov. 15:23).

An excellent teacher who specialized in work with young people, married and had two children of her own. She told them Bible stories very accurately, for she was a real student of Scripture. But she soon was aware that the children were not profiting by her teaching; in fact, they were giving extremely queer reactions instead of developing love and trust in the Lord. She went to a children's specialist for help. The latter suggested that she use for the children stories which had been written for their particular age group with their special interests and needs in mind. The mother found that the emphasis in Bible stories for Nursery children was quite different from the Bible study for Seniors, and also that spiritual results were in proportion as she was careful to meet Nursery needs and interests.

CHILDREN'S QUESTIONS

Teachers would not need to ask so many artificial questions if they would encourage and stimulate the pupils to ask more vital ones. Questions are a supreme opportunity to discover the boys' and girls' present attitude and interests. Questions make for readiness and attention.

The Bible recognizes that children will and should ask questions. "Ask thy father, and he will show thee; thine elders, and they will tell thee" (Deut. 32:7). "When your children shall say unto you, What mean ye by this service? ye shall say . . ." (Exod. 12:26). "When your children ask . . . in time to come, saying, What mean ye by these stones? Then ye shall answer them . . ." (Josh. 4:67). Questions naturally arise when God's people conduct themselves differently from others. Hebrew education was planned to provoke questions from the learners. God loves inquirers.

The Underlying Need. Why is it that the child's questions are so often irritating, especially at the Beginner age, when he asks "Why?" fifty times a day? The Beginner does not actually want to know "why" this or that happens. He is more interested in "what" happens, later in "how" a thing is done, and later still in "why." But to him the word "why" is the handiest word to give him what he does want to know.

The secret of answering all questions is to discern the need underlying the question. In the majority of cases children themselves are not aware of their definite need, but the vague searching for meaning in their world prompts them to ask "why." When a child's need is not met, regardless of the form of the question, he will simply return another "why" or another question, to the annoyance of many adults.

"How should questions be treated?" a teacher wonders. Here are the principles: Take time to give an honest answer to every honest question. If not, you will repress thought rather than stimulate further reasoning. If a young child asks a question the answer to which even he should know, be slow about scorning him until you find out what he is seeking. If he asks, "Does Jesus love me?" after you have repeated the thought several times during an hour, he probably wants assurance that though he is often conscious of failure, yet, in spite of all, Jesus loves him and wants to help him do better. Never ridicule a sincere question, no matter how ridiculous it sounds, lest you forfeit the child's confidence. The only way his mistakes can be rectified is for him to reveal what they are.

Often a child's deepest questions are read only in his eyes; they find no expression on his lips. Questions about death and other mysteries may be muffled by fear, but the understanding teacher will sense the need and delicately dispel the fear. If a child wants attention rather than information from his questions, help him get the desired attention and approval in more acceptable ways.

Answering the Need. The earnest teacher who realizes how essential it is to answer children's questions sometimes overdoes a good thing by overwhelming the group with words and lengthy explanations. When children ask about something, they do not want to know *all* about it.

> The son of a noted scientist is said to have asked his mother a question in regard to some phenomenon. His mother said, "Walter, why don't you ask your father? You know he is a scientist." "I don't want to know that much about it!" exclaimed Walter, wary from past experience.[12]

Answers given to children should be simple yet accurate. Teachers must have their own ideas clearly formulated if they are to cull the exact truth that is needed without distortion of emphasis and oversimplification to the point of error. Children should certainly be told nothing which gives the wrong connotation, to be unlearned later when they understand more about it. Whenever possible, children should be directed to sources where they can find the answers to their own questions. They enjoy the activity. The answer will be more real to them, and they will remember it longer if they discover it themselves.

ACQUIRING MEANINGS

The Principle of Apperception. An idea absolutely new is either ignored, or distorted by conceptions already held. According to the principle of apperception, learning is from the known to the unknown. New experiences are interpreted in terms of the familiar. Nothing has meaning unless it can be fitted into past experience and related to similar ideas.

When teachers do not help children interpret words, the pupils themselves grasp at anything from their past which they can bring to bear on the sounds. Many of children's so-called "cute sayings" are merely ideas which they themselves have supplied to put some meaning into sounds which otherwise say nothing to them; for example, "Eat carrots (He careth) for you," and "Good Mrs. Murphy (goodness and mercy) shall follow me all the days of my life."

The person of God is difficult to explain because He is beyond comparison with similar ideas. How can children with cruel, unjust fathers comprehend God as the loving heavenly Father? African tribes think of Him as the great warrior chief. Children naturally think of Him as a huge man because they have never conceived of a person without a body. Though they imagine unseen playmates and fairies and brownies, all of these have definite shape or form in their minds.

When the Bible speaks of the eyes and ears and hands and arm of the Lord, it is merely to help frail mortals understand His qualities and attributes as a person. The Biblical illustration of wind (John 3:8) as something whose force we feel but cannot see, is no doubt the best way to explain to children the reality of the unseen Lord.

Meanings are first acquired through activity and firsthand experience. Unless children have had experience with Bibles and churches and teachers, these terms would mean nothing at all, nothing more than would colors and sunsets and smiling faces to blind children. No word has adequate meaning until the experience behind it is adequate, for a word is only a symbol. Symbols are necessary to communicate ideas and to crystallize ideas, but words may be empty sounds conveying no meaning. Because spiritual realities are immaterial and not concrete, it is easy to insulate children from firsthand experience by secondhand information.

In one of the native languages of Australia the Lord's prayer reads as follows: "Our Father on top sky, Thy name is feared. Thou art our boss. Men-women will listen to Thee on this place earth as the good souls of men-women listen to Thee on top sky. Give us tucker till the sun goes down. We did wrong; make us good. Watch us against the bad place. Thy hands are stretched out to guard us from bad."

Present Personal Experience. Making a few spiritual concepts real and vital to children is much more valuable than trying to stuff their minds with many words which merely bore them. If they see the need of a few basic concepts which give meaning to life at present, they will acquire a taste for the things of the Lord and later will seek them for themselves. Teachers will beware of too many short cuts to learning and of relying heavily on the vicarious experience of others to teach the truth of God. He seeks personal relationship and dealings with each individual.

When teachers have done what they can to lead children through a spiritual experience, they can then rely on the Holy Spirit to do the inner work in each heart and life. They need to know what reactions to expect on the natural plane, but so to teach that the Spirit can change these into supernatural reactions. Only when teachers know what are natural responses can they fully appreciate and rejoice in spiritual responses.

When hundreds of children were asked, "What does it mean to be holy?" unsatisfactory answers were given by churched children as follows: 60 per cent of Beginners, 40 per cent of Primaries, and 25 per cent of Juniors; by unchurched children: 73 per cent of Beginners, 45 per cent of Primaries, and 45 per cent of Juniors. A few boys and girls fumbled around in their minds to find something in the sound of the word "holy" to connect it with, and answered: "holding something," "not to hold kids," "full of holes," "holy smokes," "holes in clothes," "holes in candy." One Primary asked if it were a bad word. Some answered that it meant "to be quiet," "to go to church and not be noisy," and "not to run around in church." Only a few gave gratifying answers, as "to be perfect," "to be right in the sight of the Lord," "not to have any sin on your soul," and "something precious belonging to God."

Of course, one may have a feeling for a word which he cannot express, but why cannot such a basic Scriptural term have clear-cut meaning for children? "Holy" is no subtle word difficult to visualize. In its white light it contrasts sharply with the blackness of sin.

Primary children sometimes show the meaning of the two terms by using paper and scissors. From silver paper they very carefully and evenly cut the letters *h o l y,* and paste them on gold paper without soiling in any way the lovely effect. From ugly dark paper they unevenly cut the letters ***s i n,*** and paste them askew on black paper, with paste smeared around, and the background paper crumpled and torn.

Then they associate Bible verses and the conduct of children and various related ideas with one or the other of the two words. The verse, "Every good gift and every perfect gift . . . ," belongs with the word "holy." The verse, "All have sinned and come short of the glory of God," belongs with the word "sin." When children share the Lord's good gifts with others, that conduct is good, like the word "holy." When children say bad words, that is "sin." How many things can they think of that are holy? God and the Bible and God's people in heaven and the angels. How many things can they think of that are sinful? Lying, disobeying, stealing, being selfish, and not believing God.

Natural Situations. The more natural the pupil's situation, the more direct and thorough will be the learning. Suppose Jimmy comes in from school with an apple which he took without permission. If he does not enjoy eating it and confides to Mother that he wishes he had not taken it, that is the natural situation for discussing sin, its consequences, and remedy.

If his Sunday School teacher sees Jimmy only on Sunday, but knows about this incident, he can talk with Jimmy about it; yet the intervening time will have removed much of the reality and personal element from the situation for the boy. If his teacher does not know Jimmy's personal needs, but discusses with the group typical conduct of typical children his age, the situation is another step removed. The most remote approach is talking about sin in general, for in that case it may fail entirely to be associated with anything in Jimmy's own life.

Though all situations which children need to face cannot be brought into the Bible school, teachers can at least use those situations which do occur in church. They will not be content to teach children to memorize by rote the words, "Let us love one another," and then overlook a situation when the boys and girls are quarreling over sitting beside the teacher or using the longest pencil with the eraser.

Teachers who really "teach" are ever on the alert to make full use of every natural situation, such as prayer for Johnny, who is sick; or running out to give the ice cream man a tract when he interrupts their session; calling wrongdoing "sin" and discovering what can be done about it; assuming responsibility in the room and department; planning activities for special days and events.

The Test of Learning. The chief test of learning is whether or not a child gains insight into new relationships, or uses what he has been taught in new situations. If of his own accord his behavior is changed at church or at home or at play the next time the Bible principle is involved, he has actually fitted the experience into his living in a way that now makes it a part of himself. And if he continues to use it, it will no doubt become a habit of doing and thinking, and will belong to him permanently.

ACTIVITY

"You can lead a horse to water, but you can't make him drink." You can place food before a child, but he must do the eating. You can show a child the way, but he must take the journey. You can introduce a child to Christ, but he must accept Him as his own personal Saviour.

Inner Assimilation. "It is not what we tell children, but what they think as a result of our words; it is not what we do for them, but what they do for themselves determines their development." "I have told you over and over again," says the despairing mother, but telling does not always involve receiving. [13]

> Nothing can become a part of the life until it has been acted upon; when it has been acted upon it cannot be taken out of the life. . . . When the idea has been thought in or acted upon, it has by that process become a part of the life, and though it may fade from memory, its influence is abiding. . . . The heavenly vision must be obeyed before Christian experience is enlarged by it.[14]

The Word of God must be received by the inner life. If mere external application were sufficient in itself,

> the most admonished child would be the best, the most talked to pupil the wisest, but the reverse is usually true. That which simply adheres to the surface . . . is veneer, which testing circumstances will rub off. Only that which is assimilated is of any value to the life.[15]

Formerly children were considered as empty receptacles into which knowledge was poured for future use. They were regarded as small editions of grown-ups, were dressed as adults, and taught to copy adult behavior. But a normal childhood affords the young opportunity to investigate and play as children. When they are too early pressed into an adult mold they tend to imitate the outward forms, but miss the inner meanings.

Formerly children were valued for what they would eventually become, but Christ valued them for what they were at that moment. He gave them love and assurance, and met their present needs, which would be their best protection against the future. If He meets their needs today, and if now they are strong spiritually, they will return to the same source of strength for their needs tomorrow.

Work and Play. One reason many adults fail to understand the viewpoint of childhood is the ambiguity of the words "work" and "play." Without stopping to analyze their feelings, some adults think of work as serious, profitable activity, but play as silly, senseless activity. They reason that because children spend so much of their time in play it must be worthless and wasteful.

Whether an activity is work or play depends entirely on the attitude of the person toward the activity. One man hates his daily occupation; it is work. Another enjoys his; it is play. Play may be defined as what we do when we are free to do what we will. Or it is the "joyous release of energy and spontaneous interest."

Much of the behavior of the infant is motivated only by his enjoyment of the physical activity necessary for physical growth. He learns by playing. Toys and objects are to him what textbooks and school materials are to the child in school. He discovers his world with his fingers and eyes and ears; he uses large muscles; he makes social contacts; he is continuously active. We call it play. What possibilities in every direction lie in the child's reaction to the world about him!

The child with the integrated, well-balanced personality is fearless, investigative, and experimental in attitude; he uses a problem-solving technique as the basis for satisfactory adjustment to this complex modern world.

Children take their play seriously, and often work harder at it than do their fathers at their occupations. Their play is important to them, and often leaves them thoroughly exhausted. It is play to them because it meets their interests and needs, and they develop it along the line of their capacities. Instead of making our Bible school work a chore, why not do it more in the spirit of play? A great deal more would be accomplished.

This is not to imply that every discipline in life can be enjoyed. There will ever be duties which are anything but pleasurable, which entail self-control and sacrifice. Yet these are incidental to a larger purpose which is challenging. Life in the Lord is not drudgery, but joy and peace. The native urges and drives which He has put within the child need to be "renewed in knowledge after the image of him that created him" (Col. 3:10), and then to be directed into wholesome and profitable activities.

Expression for Spiritual Impulses. If a new bit of knowledge conveys meaning to a child it will change or intensify his feelings as a result, and that emotion will end in his doing something about it. If emotions are allowed to evaporate they get into the habit of evaporating. Rather, spiritual impulses can be expressed and built into life tissue. If the children cannot do something immediately in the class session, they can at least discuss what they are going to do during the week.

In almost every session teachers are found doing things

which the children themselves should be doing. The children grow not by what the teacher does, but by what they do. Every plan should be checked for maximum effort on the part of the pupils, minimum effort on the part of the teachers.

Boys and girls are not interested in spectator sports. It is the energetic, growing children who need the activity programs, not tired, busy teachers! The pupils, not the teachers, should be preparing visual-aid materials, searching their Bibles to find what backgrounds and figures are needed, what the characters say and do. They should be memorizing the Scripture for the vital purpose of presenting the story or lesson, rather than memorizing it for no practical purpose, after the teacher has performed the active part which is fun.

Handwork may be either profitable experience or "busy work" to fill in time. The criterion is not so much what is happening to paper or clay as what is happening to children. George may make a very excellent model of a chariot without much spiritual growth. But if he decides to make a chariot to take to the home of a sick friend to tell him the Bible story, his time is not wasted. Many spiritual problems may be raised and settled in connection with something the child wants to make—a map, or a mural, or objects to use in playing stories, or objects for exhibit, or a bookcase to help him learn the books of the Bible. When young children play Bible stories they project themselves into the experiences of the characters, and relive their problems with them.

If children are allowed the attitude of discovering the truth of God for themselves in His Word and in His world, instead of being passively informed, they will be ready to do a great deal along creative lines. After discovering how David wrote his psalms, they will like to compose some praise verses of their own, expressing the particular blessings for which they feel thankful. They will enjoy setting their words to simple tunes and singing them.

They will have ideas as to how they can help in their church and in their homes and in their communities, instead of listening to other people's ideas, which may leave them cold. They will be actively enlisted in a cause which they wholeheartedly espouse.

REPETITION WITH VARIETY

Every hour of the child's life contributes to the formation of character traits and habits. Any act makes it easier to repeat that act than to do something different. Acts repeated become tendencies, then compulsions, and soon we are in the grip of a habit.

If you were saved during childhood, what did the good habits built then do for your later life? If you were saved in later life, what did the bad habits formed early do to your Christian life?

Habits either bind a person to inferior ways of acting, or they free him for service to mankind by eliminating time and thought on the routine duties of mundane existence. Christian leaders need strong habits of denying self, keeping their inner motives Christlike, avoiding self-pity, and developing the attitude of complete abandon to God. Habits formed in childhood set the direction of the life, either toward God or away from God. In salvation the Lord cuts sharply through some of these habits, but the scars of sin and self-will remain to vex, and require constant overcoming.

Eternal Vigilance for Habits. "Eternal vigilance is the price of good habits." Until a habit is securely rooted, no exception should be allowed. "Each lapse is like letting fall a ball of string which one is carefully winding up; a single slip undoes more than a great many turns will wind up again."

A story is told of a small boy whose mother sent him from the table one night to wash his hands. "James," she said, "why do you come to the table with dirty hands, when I always send you to wash them?"

"Once you didn't, Mother!" was the boy's quick reply.

The diligence of Susanna Wesley in training her children explains their service for Christ.

One night of each week Susanna devoted such a proportion of time as she could afford to discourse with each child by himself upon the duties and hopes of Christianity. . . . The children were always put into a regular method of living in such things as they were capable of from their birth, as in dressing, undressing, etc. . . . To prevent cowardice and fear of punishment often leading to lying, whoever were charged with a fault of which they were guilty, if they would ingenuously confess it and promise to amend, should not be beaten.

If a child performed an act of obedience, or did anything with an intention to please, though the performance was not well, yet the obedience and intention should be kindly accepted, and the child with sweetness directed to do better for the future.

Each lesson was studied until it was quite mastered, an instance of perseverance on the part of the teacher which is remarkable. Her husband even complained of this line-upon-line system. "I wonder at your patience," he said. "You have told that child twenty times that same thing." "Had I been satisfied with mentioning the matter only nineteen times," said Mrs. Wesley, "I should have lost all my labors. You see it was the twentieth time that crowned the whole." Which saying deserves to be written in letters of gold upon every heart, for it is the twentieth time of doing it that makes all the difference between success and failure.[16]

Such perseverance is not easy for busy parents and teachers. Eternal vigilance requires more self-discipline than most of us possess. But the reward of faithfulness is sure: "Let us not be weary in well doing: for in due season we shall reap, if we faint not" (Gal. 6:9).

The younger the child, the more necessary is repetition. The Nursery child enjoys the very same activities week after week. Older children, however, need a fresh approach each time.

How smooth the sea-beach pebbles are,
  But—do you know
The ocean worked a hundred years
  To make them so?
And once I saw a little girl
  Sit down and cry
Because she could not cure a fault
  With one small try.

The Spice of Variety. Boring repetition will not lead to the formation of spiritual habits, but rather, will lead the pupils to discover for themselves something more interesting. They need the same principle again and again from a fresh approach, from some other angle in life, and from some other problem that they feel.

A wide-awake teacher who is sensitive to the needs of the pupils and to the changing circumstances of world events will have a broad, flexible attitude toward life, and will bring a great deal of variety to his teaching. He will cultivate variety of thought, attitude, and expression.

How refreshing is nature with its novelties and changes! How stimulating is the course of the four seasons with their endless varieties! Not all is rain or snow or wind or even sunshine, for growing things need each in its season. God's revelation in Scripture is also in "divers manners" according to the needs of the people, yet always with the central message of redemption. He speaks in terms of conscience, human government, promise, law, grace, kingdom, dreams, visions, symbols, types, gradually unfolding prophecies, theophanies, and, as a culmination, in the man Christ Jesus.

The Greeks of old had a motto, "Nothing too much." Any good thing soon becomes too much of a good thing. The attention of children is easy to get, but hard to keep. The flannelgraph or any other good method loses its effectiveness if used exclusively. The pupils also should play stories, pose pictures, take charge of their own rooms and programs, discuss problems, and engage in many other meaningful activities.

Origin of General Habits. Specialized rather than general habits are formed. The Nursery child learns to remove and hang up his own wraps in church, but it is the church environment which prompts the habit once a week. It seldom occurs to him to help himself at home, where someone is always ready to do things for him. Older children may be trained to pass quietly to and from classes in the public school building, but may be very disturbing in church if their attention is not called to this habit. Broad generalized habits which function regularly whenever needed must be built by discussing each specific situation and giving opportunity for practice.

Suggestion. Most habits are suggested to children by the environment of people and things to which they constantly react. Human nature resents bossing, but suggestion is a most powerful regulating force. Because force of example is much stronger than precept, children are daily being fashioned according to the models they see around them. The only escape from their environment is to be found in the suggestion of Christ, "Come unto me."

Instead of saying to them, "Don't do that," look for a good example to commend. Instead of asking Polly to stop playing with her purse or Testament, remark that Joan looks as if she is really thinking of the words of the song. Beware of giving children wrong ideas by mentioning an undesirable response. By your warnings, you may suggest wrong conduct that the boys and girls have never thought of. By the tone and words of your commands expect them to be obeyed rather than suggest that they might not be obeyed.

DISCIPLINE

What is discipline but the making of disciples, as fine an art as any of the other aspects of teaching? If it is not regarded as the building of positive inner controls, it will have to be dealt with as negative punishment.

A Positive Technique. How may discipline be made a positive technique? By arranging teaching situations that call forth genuine attention and effort on the part of the pupils, and therefore, self-control, for the "rules of the game" are inherent in group work. Spend your time concentrating on interest and activity, and you will be saved most of the distress of correcting failures. Put the emphasis on preventing rather than punishing misdeeds.

"Provoke not your children to wrath: but bring them up in the nurture and admonition of the Lord" (Eph. 6:4). Nurture is nourishing and training to promote healthy spiritual growth. Admonition is helping children understand reasons for doing right, warning them in the face of temptation, and gently reproving the young feet that are prone to wander.

"Children are rough diamonds; they need to be polished, not struck unskillfully, not left uncut." As a rule, children like rather than dislike to be disciplined, for they are not able to be obedient until training has made them so. When they talk among themselves, one will say proudly, "My mother always makes me wash before I eat," while another will say regretfully, "My mother doesn't care what I do."

A small boy was playing in his yard, which was enclosed by a fence. When interest in his toys waned, he began to swing on the gate, then to call to people outside the gate. Though he knew perfectly well that he had been forbidden to go outside, he worked at the lock to see if he could get it open. Surprised when it did come unfastened, he first held it open, then slipped outside a short distance, and was starting down the road when his mother came after him. "I saw you, my son," she said, "when you tried to open the gate and then when you started outside."

"Well, if you saw me," he answered, "why didn't you help a feller?"

The demands made on a child should be as few as possible, be clearly understood by him, and be consistently enforced. The more demands on him, the more opportunities for friction. Like the fundamental laws of the land, they should be made by people who understand human nature, its capacities and limitations.

Legitimate rules are inherent in the very nature of things. The child expects to obey until deviation from the standards reveals to him adult weakness. When parent and teacher show loss of control and poise, he takes advantage of the situation and goes as far as he can. He should never get a hint that teasing produces results. Nagging or bossing have no place. The child who forms the habit of whining grows into the nagging adult, both reactions usually being so continual that they are disregarded.

Much of the trouble which children get into might have been prevented by parents and teachers with discernment and foresight. Neither teacher nor child can be expected to work happily with others when he is physically ill or weary. Attention to effective routine will forestall many difficulties.

Know the children well enough to visualize new experiences and foresee conflicts. Guard against danger points by leading the children into accomplishing purposes that require a measure of self-control but not more than they can muster. Give them time to adjust to commands which have not become habitual. Be sensitive to individual reactions, to the beginnings of inattention and lack of interest, and thus prevent more serious difficulties.

Use of Punishment. To be effective, punishment should be immediate, invariable, impersonal, reasonable, closely associated with the wrong-doing, and definitely disagreeable. In many cases, inevitable consequences naturally follow sin. A child reaches for the fire, and it burns his hand; he falls from a platform where he has been told not to go, and he is hurt; he disturbs a group which is listening to a story, and he has the stern disapproval of all concerned; he is careless with his handwork materials, and cannot finish the model with the rest of his friends.

When punishment does not naturally follow wrongdoing, the parent or teacher supplies the dissatisfaction. The child may be isolated from the group, he may be denied the attention he seeks, or the rod may be applied. "The rod and reproof give wisdom; but a child left to himself bringeth his mother to shame" (Prov. 29:15). "He that spareth his rod, hateth his son: but he that loveth him chasteneth him betimes" (Prov. 13:24). "Foolishness is bound in the heart of a child; but the rod of correction shall drive it far from him" (Prov. 22:15).

Mild physical punishment forms an emotional blocking toward sin, for the child feels punished when spanked. It seems natural to him, for he slaps when he is displeased.

Of course, the rod is no magic wand which works simply because it is a rod. The many references in proverbs presuppose a wise father who uses punishment as the omniscient heavenly Father uses punishment—to improve behavior. If an adult punishes in anger, or the child feels that the punishment is unjust, he connects the rod with the person rather than with the wrong act, and his confidence in that person may be destroyed. Too often punishment becomes a matter of personal contest, the adult winning only by reason of his superior strength. Something is wrong with the mode of punishment if it makes the child trust us less implicitly.

If the penalty closely fits the misdemeanor, the child's sense of justice will work on our side, and there will be remarkable co-operation even on the part of the very young.

During the whole course of punishment care should be taken to preserve the child's self-respect, lest he feel too defeated to try again. His sin should be discussed with him privately. An avenue should be left open by which he may return to the adult's good graces. Some individuals are so sensitive to disapproval that all they ever need is a word of warning.

Resentment is prevented by helping the child feel that he has sinned against the Lord. He is usually glad to pray for divine help to do better in the future. Mentioning the exact cause of trouble in prayer leaves no doubt in his mind as to where he has been at fault. When he feels that God has forgiven him, and wrongs have been remedied, the slate has been erased clean to start over again.

When a child has done wrong, we should try to put ourselves in his place and discover the root causes which lie beneath the surface symptoms. It may simply be his Adamic nature wanting his own way, or it may be that one of his basic needs is not being met. In the latter case it is more the fault of parent or teacher than of the child. If we are to help immature children develop self-control we must be sure of our own control of teaching-learning situations.

FREEDOM AND AUTHORITY

Many people think of freedom and authority as opposites rather than as two necessary aspects of Christian training. Formerly authority was abused, and more recently freedom has had its turn. In an attempt to break away from harsh severity, the pendulum has swung to the other extreme of indulging and spoiling.

Happy indeed are the teachers who exercise enough authority for the child's emotional support and enough freedom for the development of self-discipline. In a democratic atmosphere authority is neither glorified nor disparaged. Authority is necessary and welcomed not to make the child conform passively through fear, but to use our wisdom in his behalf until he develops a sense of values and inner controls.

The child wants us to be firm and to save him from his worst impulses, to ease his guilt by preventing him from doing harm, and to strengthen his better impulses to do right. He wants to feel that we are stronger than he, *and yet* loving and kind.

The reins need to be kept fairly tight at first, until the child proves himself ready to take them. It is almost impossible to regain control once it has been handed over.

The more creative, impulsive, and energetic the child, the more his own well-being demands that he be directed and restrained. He sometimes needs a firm "No" exactly as much as he needs help and encouragement. No one is deceived but ourselves when we pretend to give the child his choice and put essential demands in the form of questions; he sees through our scheme and leaves us feeling very insecure. Our responsibility to protect and guide the child implies certain arbitrary authorities, and we cannot free him by disclaiming that authority.

None of us objects to *rule,* but to misrule. Whether the child grows up a spineless creature or a stalwart Christian depends on the *quality* of our authority. We cannot acquire it by forcing children to do our will, but by becoming fit to exercise it. Of course, it is easier to demand blind obedience than to take time for the prayer and ingenuity required for intelligent control, but the child senses the deficiency of the former method.

Disciplined Expression. What is true freedom? "If the Son [of God] therefore shall make you free, ye shall be free indeed" (John 8:36). The child who is allowed to do as he pleases is neither free nor happy. He is a slave to himself, to his own innate sinful tendencies. But when through prayer in his behalf and through the teaching of the Word of God, he chooses to hand over his will to the One who made it and therefore the only One able to control it rightly, his upward tendencies rather than his downward tendencies are in the ascendency. As he exercises the good impulses and learns to deny the bad impulses, the latter tend to die away, leaving him free from the enslaving habits of the natural man. This exercise of the new nature demands expression—disciplined expression.

What children need today is not soft coddling, which increases lawlessness, but a real challenge to give of the strength of their youth, without reserve and without delay, to their Captain. They suffer for want of practical Christian enterprises which they feel are worthy of their sanguine energies. They need enough freedom to practice inner restraint and to work out the salvation that Christ has worked in them. This kind of freedom is disciplined expression. This kind of expression will build up for them assurance of victory in the Lord. In small matters they find out for themselves that "the way of the transgressor is hard."

Personal Integration. Unless our focus is centered on the

whole personality there may be dangers ahead, for a child may outwardly conform to what is expected of him, but be inwardly fearful and anxious.

So widespread is the general insecurity in our world that we wonder that nervous tension is not more acute than it is. In the first place, parents themselves are not disciplined. They do not understand themselves before they are married. Partnership with another personality aggravates the maladjustment, and then the arrival of baby adds another source of friction. To get their own way with the helpless infant, they know only authority by force, and they find that is not reliable. The child is thrown into an uncertain world that has few absolutes, his narrow environment is haphazard, and his family is inconsistent. All this is more threatening because he cannot understand.

Courageous and fearful attitudes are contagious. Courageous adults know "whom they have believed, and are persuaded that he is able to keep." They are not fussy, or severe, or high-strung. They diligently train up the child in the way he should go, and yet allow him practice in making and abiding by his own choices in small matters, and gradually in larger ones.

When from his earliest days the child is surrounded with the love of God he does not live in terror of God's punishment, because he is relaxing in God's love and not straining to get away and disobey. Even if some may rebel at times they still know God as a loving Father, always ready to forgive.

1. Note some undesirable behavior on the part of a child of your acquaintance or in your neighborhood *outside Bible class*. What is his immediate need? What will be your aim in helping him change his behavior? How can you help him feel his need of this change? What can he and you do to effect this change?

What materials and methods will you use? Afterward evaluate your procedure to see if the behavior is improved, and revise your aims.

2. Mention six vital interests or values of childhood, and explain how you could lead from these interests to spiritual habits, attitudes, or conduct.

3. Make a list of the habits you want a certain child or class to cultivate. Does the pupil see the need for these habits? What is his motive for them? When is he given opportunity to practice these habits? Are any lapses in practice allowed? How narrow or broad are the habits?

4. Where are the danger spots in your school or home which are likely to produce friction? What can be done to remedy these places? What is the underlying cause of each? If a certain child insists on causing trouble in spite of all you can do to prevent it, what will be the most effective means of associating dissatisfaction with that behavior?

5. In what ways are the children in your school or home learning to assume responsibility and learn inner control? Does firm, loving authority give them a feeling of security and protection? Does a degree of freedom give them opportunity to exercise some choices of their own?

CHAPTER X

MEMORIZATION OF SCRIPTURE

1. What *events* in the past can you remember most clearly? What *words* from the past can you remember most clearly? Analyze carefully why you remember these rather than many other experiences.
2. Why have you forgotten much of what you "learned" in your school days?
3. What Scripture words have had the greatest influence on your life? Can you explain why?
4. Bible comics present Bible facts to children in a crude, garish form on the level of Superman. At the same time that children are learning Bible facts by this means, what else, even more important, are they learning?

WHY A WRITTEN REVELATION?

In what form did God give mankind the written revelation of Himself? Not in the form of systematic theology, but in the form of human-interest narratives, of episodes of conflict and success and failure, of songs of confidence and prayers of hope, in letters with very personal elements. The whole is but a letter from God Himself. Who will be content with letters when he might meet the Person Himself? Through the Book God is waiting to show Himself. Just as He gave it in personal form, so He means it to speak personally and to reveal the person of His Son.

It is the person of Christ who is the way, the truth, and the life. It is He who is the beginning, the embodiment, and the end of life. God's plan is that the Spirit and the Word shall take men by the hands and lead them to Christ. The Spirit has been given to illuminate the Word. It is the peculiar work of the Spirit to turn the outer Word into an inner experience. The Spirit works in co-operation with human teachers who present the Living Word by means of the written Word.

The figures used by Scripture to describe itself are means to ends: it is seed to yield, rain to refresh, food to nourish, a mirror to reflect, a lamp to illumine, a laver to cleanse, fire to consume, gold to buy, a hammer to break, and a sword to pierce. Words themselves are merely symbols, the end being life in Christ. As a sharp, two-edged sword, it is meant to cut with both edges, piercing even to the joints and marrow, making men discerners of their own hearts, even to the inmost thoughts and intents (Heb. 4:12). But how often this keen weapon is made dull by constant crude handling!

The Word of God is most often likened to seed, life-giving seed. But the Pharisees of old and many religionists today know only the hard shell on the outside. That shell has to be broken before the enormous potentiality that resides in the message can be released. As seed, the Word is packed with possibilities for growth and change, to be realized when it is placed in soil which has been plowed and made soft and receptive. Then the life force sprouts forth, and the world feels the quickening power of springtime. But the seed must be taken out of the hard, dry shell in which it is received. It must find lodging in the dark earth—it must be hidden in the heart, where the forces there can play on it.

Moreover, after the seed has brought forth life, the first

need of life is nutrition—in the spiritual realm, nurture. Young growing things must have the type of food they can assimilate by their own creative self-activity. Food cannot remain in the same form in which it was received; it must be transformed into living, growing tissue.

WHY MEMORIZE?

An earnest mother presents this problem with her young son: "If I say the first few words of a Bible verse the boy can finish it. But I always have to start it for him. Should I continue to do this, or is there a better way?"

Why is this boy learning Scripture? Apparently, to please his mother. Although he should find joy in giving her pleasure, is there not a higher motive that should prompt him? Sometimes letters of the alphabet are used to organize and prompt the learning and reciting of Scripture. Often it is the Scripture reference which calls forth the response.

In each of these instances a child has only one handle for the sword of the Spirit—and that an artificial one. When does he most need this spiritual weapon? When his mother or teacher formally gives him the first few words, or a letter of the alphabet, or a Scripture reference? What soldier would know how to use his weapon against a foe if he had not received combat training? Any training situation should approximate as nearly as possible the actual life situation.

The Question of Motives. The question of ***why*** a child memorizes Scripture is even more basic than ***what*** he learns, especially in the early years when habits are being formed and life patterns are being established. Unworthy motives now will soon lead to the discarding of all memorizing as soon as outside pressure is released. Worthy motives now will mold such strong sentiments toward the Word that Christian character is insured.

What is the true, high motive which should prompt young or old to memorize Scripture? It may be expressed in a verse which the children themselves appreciate, "Thy word have I hid in mine *heart* [a word that means the whole personality], that I might not sin against thee" (Ps. 119:11). Many an unfortunate child is taught to hide the Word in his *mind,* and when prodded by an intellectual stimulus, is able to bring it forth, not for the purpose of keeping him from sin, but for the sake of satisfying some questioner. Many adults of this generation who repeated the Apostles' Creed in church as children, can quote it today "if they go fast enough and don't think about it." "Learning by heart" often degenerates into "learning by rote."

Higher motives must suggest Scripture memorization if boys and girls are to hide the Word in their *hearts.* Parents and teachers are very careful to provide children the physical food they need at each stage of development; how negligent they are in helping them meet their spiritual needs, which are of even greater importance.

Behavior problems are evident very early and very early children need to feel the heavenly Father's help. The test of memorizing is not how fluently the words can be rattled off. Mere *forms* of the truth are not enough. The test is its actual use in daily life.

Many a child receives approval when he can answer the question, "How much did the Lord Jesus tell us to love one another?" with the verse, "Love one another as I have loved you." Yet the next minute he is grabbing for the best pencil in the box, or scrambling to sit beside his teacher, or pushing to get ahead of his neighbor, with no connection made in his mind between the verse and his conduct.

Contrast with the above the following incident of true memorization.

When a mother makes a legitimate request of her young daughter, the command meets with instant rebellion on the part of the child. The mother is bewildered as to how to proceed. Before she has decided on a course of action, the girl all at once completely changes her attitude, and starts obediently to comply with the request, to the surprise of the mother, who asks the reason for the sudden change. The child replies, "I heard the still, small Voice say to me, 'Children, obey your parents in the Lord.'" That part of the Word had been hidden in the heart with such close connections with the desired response in conduct that it was used to do the work of God and keep from sin.

When Bible verses are taught in close connection with daily spiritual problems, life situations will prompt the recollection of them.

Artificial Rewards. Artificial motives necessitate artificial rewards. If a child feels no need of memorizing an answer to a Scripture reference or a letter of the alphabet, he must have extrinsic interest stimulated or he refuses to put forth the required effort. The situation is similar to the one in the home where a child forms the habit of expecting to be paid for every small task he performs. Unless superficially taught to expect bribes, he requires none. The very method of bribing teaches the child that the activity is not worth while in itself, but essentially distasteful.

If a group of children have grown accustomed to low motives because of poor teaching and low standards of life in general, the higher motives may not at first appeal to them. It may sometimes be necessary to work gradually to raise the standards, but prayer and wise methods can effect a loftier driving power.

Several problems usually accompany the use of rewards. Prizes and contests do spur on to a knowledge of words, but often fail to promote growth in grace. If pupils focus their eyes on a prize their interest in memorizing wanes as soon as it is awarded. The diligent pupils always win the prizes, while the slower ones grow discouraged. There is often criticism from parents because the basis on which the reward is given is considered unfair. Whatever effort is stimulated in sporadic and transient, not permanent.

> In one school where no prizes or contests were used, but where intrinsic interest was created by effective teaching, the general Sunday School superintendent, one autumn, suggested that Christmas gifts be given all pupils who had perfect attendance from the first of September until the holidays. As a result, one Primary girl who had to walk several blocks alone to church remained home the next few weeks after she had received her present. Though she had never before considered staying home, yet after the prize had been received, with no further reward held out before her, she stopped coming in spite of challenging teaching. A boy in the same school asked, "Isn't there anything more to come for now?"

Some leaders may comment, "But are not we as Christians working for heavenly rewards? Are not we encouraged to win crowns?" Yes, all of us are surely interested in any crowns that we may deserve. But why do we want them? Certainly not to strut around heaven in them! When we see our blessed Saviour face to face, shall we not be eternally grateful to have something to cast at His feet? Are we working for rewards, or are we working to show Him some little thanks for saving us by His grace?

Concerning her work with children in South India, Amy Wilson Carmichael writes:

> We never had prizes. The children would have been (and still would be) astonished if anyone suggested that they should

> be given something for receiving what their patient givers had given them. Reward for any kind of service never came into our scheme of things, except the reward of giving pleasure or help. The great reward, this was always made clear, was to be trusted with harder, more responsible work.[17]

Recognition. Recognition differs from rewards in principle more than in substance. Recognition adds pleasure which is deserved after the memorization has been done for its own sake. Children may be working for the reward of a badge if they have their eye on it from the beginning; or they may decide to wear badges to distinguish themselves as having completed a passage.

Both teachers and pupils can see at a glance the present status of any child's memorization if each one records in some way the verses he has memorized on a large, attractive chart. The children may color spaces after their names with different colors of crayon, or draw small objects to suggest the thought of the verses, or punch holes in the spaces.

Children should be recognized when they have obeyed as well as quoted Scripture. While some children memorize slowly, all are able to show evidence of spiritual growth. It is often true that children with the keenest minds and readiest flow of words are the very ones who most need the Word in their daily lives.

THE WORD OF GOD DOING THE WORK OF GOD

When Scripture verses for children are chosen without considering their present spiritual needs, it is, of course, very difficult for God's Word to do God's work in their lives. A list of the most select and vital verses from the adult viewpoint does not comprise the best memory course for children. The first step in Scripture memorizing is the choice of a memory course carefully graded according to the needs and comprehension of each age group.

A child is not interested in storing his room at home with objects which he will cherish in old age; he collects treasures which hold a present appeal. Neither is he interested in storing his heart with Scripture which will hold meaning for him through the years to come; he needs verses which will prove a source of present help.

He will not grow spiritually on strong meat which he cannot digest. He needs now the nourishing milk of the Word that he can assimilate and appropriate for spiritual tissue. The best way to be assured of a healthy adult in the future is to build a sturdy normal child today. We feel toward the children as Christ felt toward His disciples, "I have yet many things to say unto you, but ye cannot bear them now" (John 16:12).

Love and Obedience to the Truth. The Lord Jesus said, "Ye shall know the truth, and the truth shall make you free" (John 8:32). Why is it, then, that we meet people who know the truth and yet are slaves to sin? They can quote Scripture as readily as we, but are atheists and worldlings, whom we find very difficult to deal with. "The devils also believe, and tremble" (James 2:19). Examining John 8:32 in context, we shall find the condition for this statement in the preceding verse, "If ye *continue* in my word, then are ye my disciples indeed; *and* ye shall know the truth, and the truth shall make you free."

Is there not danger for that soul who does not live up to the light which has been given him? The heathen are without excuse because they have not obeyed the measure of light that they see around them in nature and perceive in conscience. If they do obey the light they have, further light in Christ Jesus is revealed.

Though teachers and parents of children are, of course,

striving for knowledge of the truth in the young lives entrusted to their care, knowledge of the truth is not enough. What emotional attitude is being taught as the children are learning to say the words of Scripture? At the same time, they are learning to love or to hate or to be indifferent to the blessed habit which we yearn for them to form. If there is true love for the Word knowledge is sure to follow, but, oh, how often we find knowledge of the truth without love of the truth! How does our group *feel* about the verses they are learning?

If a sweet taste of Scripture is given to children they will return for more, but not after a bitter mouthful.

> A missionary, in speaking to a group of boys and girls, remarked, "I know you don't like to memorize Scripture, but you need to do it." It had never before occurred to the group that anyone did not enjoy hiding the Word of God in his heart, for they had been taught to love the activity.
>
> In a certain children's home naughty children are punished by being sent upstairs to the library to learn a number of Scripture verses.
>
> Sometimes, as penalties in games, the last person to catch on to a trick is required to say a Bible verse.

In these cases Scripture is learned, but the accompanying attitude is likely to undo all the good that has been accomplished.

Moreover, knowledge of the truth and love of the truth must be accompanied by obedience to the truth. What are the boys and girls *doing* about the verses they are learning? They will be free only as they "continue" in the Word. Would that we could record objectively on a chart not only the words that the children can say, but also the outworking of those words in daily life!

Obedience to the truth does not imply that the children

will want to learn only specific conduct verses. There are times when problems are solved by remembering what kind of person the Lord God is, by remembering that He has provided eternal redemption, that He knows all, sees all, can do anything, and is everywhere. Children, as well as adults, need to lift up their eyes to the Lord of the hills and appreciate what He is waiting to do for them. Even to this type of Scripture, however, some response is natural, for we tend to thank God, or return His love, or seek His help.

The Vital Use of Scripture. Early in life boys and girls should experience the help of the Lord and His Word in their daily lives. It is the teacher's business to find out what are their real needs, to challenge them with these needs, and to train them to use Scripture to meet these needs.

Children love to feel that the Lord is looking for them as well as for adults to whom He can entrust the sword of the Spirit to do His work. Of course, the first work must be done in the child himself. If a child understands the import of Scripture words, if his own life corroborates the message, and if the message is given out clearly and expressively, a child's use of Scripture can be more winsome and forceful than on adults. Yet how seldom is this the case, for neither teachers nor children expect the Lord to use a child.

The following are practical instances in which children should use the Word of God to do the work of God:

1. *Scripture shows them their need of a Saviour, and how to become a child of God.* They should learn salvation verses, not for conversion when older, but for present acceptance. A child expects to act on the truths taught him. The man of tomorrow needs the Saviour today. And he needs the verses which tie in with his own experience, so far as possible in his own words. Why use a verse including the difficult word "propi-

tiation" when we might use the simple statement, "Christ died for our sins"? It is often wise to ask a child to select from several salvation verses the one which means the most to him; in this way he is hearing several and memorizing the one which means most to him personally.

In the figure of James 1:21, children will receive with meekness the engrafted Word. In grafting a fruitful shoot onto wild natural stock, the two must fit together exactly. When a verse from the Word exactly fits the heart of a child the result is union and new life.

2. *To grow in grace children must listen to God as well as speak to Him.* They are not yet ready for the concept of abiding in Him, but Juniors can realize that just as their body will not grow without food, so their new spiritual life in Christ will not grow without spiritual food. In simpler terms, just as Christ is the only One who can save them from sin, so He is the only One who can keep them from sin. They need Him every day, for every day there are hard things that they cannot manage by themselves.

3. *Scripture can help children overcome temptation and make right decisions in daily conduct.* When the issue is faced frankly, boys and girls will feel the need of hiding the Word where they can get it at a moment's notice, whenever occasion arises. They can discuss the times when it is easy for them to sin—not always in the protection of Bible school or at bedtime when Mother asks for verses, but with playmates at school or at play, when it would be impossible to get a Bible and find just the part they need.

What verse that they know will remind them of God's way when they are called names, when they are tempted to cheat, when they would like something which belongs to someone else? If actual problems which arise at church are referred to

A carload of happy vacationers were riding along the highway toward the lake at which they would spend a month. Some of the group, including the children, had never seen the lake, for their home was inland. Before they quite expected it, a blue line across the horizon made them almost gasp for joy. The sight was beautiful. One of the women was speechless. A couple of adults exclaimed, "My, my!" But the boy who had recently used the first verses of Psalm 95 in his vacation school was the only one who had words to express what he felt. He quoted reverently,

> The sea is his, and he made it:
> And his hands formed the dry land.
> O come, let us worship and bow down:
> Let us kneel before the Lord our Maker.
> For he is our God.

He went on to say, "I can't kneel right here in the car, but I feel the same as if I were kneeling." Every person in that car felt a worship experience that moment, guided by the Scripture which the boy had quoted.

If verses of appreciation are used to crystallize the beauty of God's world and love and kindness, these Scriptures will be more than mere words.

9. *Children can use Scripture to witness to the unsaved.* Of their own accord children often play Sunday School with their neighbors, and re-enact at home what goes on in Bible school. Moreover, we may definitely encourage them to tell others a verse which already means a great deal to them. Even of Primaries we may ask, "Do you suppose your playmate ever read in the Bible that Christ died for our sins? Doesn't he ever read the Bible? Then you can be God's messenger to him today, and read him God's words. Put your marker in the place, and draw a line under the words so that you can turn to them

quickly. Whose sins are 'our' sins? Christ died for my sins, He died for your sins, He died for the pastor's sins, and for your playmate's sins, for 'all have sinned.' Isn't it wonderful to know that Christ died to take the punishment that we deserve for our sins!"

THE BOOKS OF THE BIBLE AND LOCATION OF VERSES

A practical question at this point is, "At what age do children feel the need of memorizing the names of the books of the Bible and the locations of verses?"

This is not a question of when *can* children memorize them, for they can learn to say any words which are drilled into them with extrinsic motives. Though it is possible for Nursery tots to try to lisp, "Genesis, Exodus, Leviticus, Numbers, Deuteronomy," that type of learning is not meeting their needs.

When is sufficient skill in reading developed so that the child can recognize the names of the books? When can the general organization of the books be comprehended? Not until the Junior period. Juniors should be making a Bible town or a Bible bookcase to get the overall picture, and enjoy the activity of searching their Bibles. They can use various colors of narrow ribbon to mark the divisions in their own Bibles until they grow familiar with them. They themselves should study the relation of the colors to the nature of the contents, and arrange the colors as meaningfully as possible.

5 books	Law	Orange
12 books	History	Purple
6 books	Poetry	Yellow
4 books	Major Prophets	Bright blue
12 books	Minor Prophets	Light blue
4 books	Gospels	Red
1 book	History (Acts)	Purple

14 books	Paul's Epistles	Bright green
7 books	Other Epistles	Light green
1 book	Revelation	Gold

Though Primary children have little appreciation for the composition of Scripture, and can read very little, can they not begin to find their way in their own New Testaments? Shall they not begin to use these precious books when interest is natural? But how can they begin to use them without being overwhelmed and confused with too much detail?

In what part of their New Testaments can they begin to feel at home? In the first five books, with the familiar stories of Jesus and His friends. Even the names of the first five books can have meaning for them: Matthew was the tax collector, Mark was a young man in whose home the Christians held prayer meetings, Luke was the good doctor who also wrote the "Acts" of Jesus' friends, and John was the beloved friend of Jesus. For each book they should have a large poster with the name of the book, a verse with appeal for them, and a picture of that verse.

Why should young children learn the location, or the "street and housenumber," for every verse they learn? The answer usually given to this question is, "Because it is so much easier for them to learn the reference now than later." No doubt this is true if Scripture memorization becomes a wearisome process, divorced from children's needs. So often the first-year Primary group is much interested in memorizing because it is new to them; the third year is thoroughly bored.

Is our purpose to stuff children with as much as possible before they revolt against it, or to help them memorize what they truly need? When a reference is always attached to a verse and emphasized, are they more or less likely to use that verse to guard against sin? Both for their own satisfaction and for the sake of sharing God's Word, Primaries need to be able to find a few verses, but only a few choice ones.

HOW MEMORIZE?

"Obey the laws of memory, and memory will obey you." Form the habit of centering attention sharply on what vitally interests you, and you will not forget it. What are the general principles for memorizing?

1. *Learn and overlearn the passage.* If we as teachers can say that we find real delight in hiding God's Word in our own hearts, where it will be ready for use at a moment's bidding, we have solved the first problem in Scripture memorizing. If our own memory does not obey us, how can we expect to teach the children to inscribe the Word on the "fleshy tables" of their hearts (II Cor. 3:3)? Do we know by experience how quick the Spirit of the living God is to write the golden words on the heart when it is softened to a heart of flesh as contrasted with the old-time table of stone, but how quick the tempter is also to smooth over the inscribed surface of the soft heart unless the precepts are constantly used and worn deep by repetition?

The reverence and accuracy with which we say the words, and the operation of the truths in our own lives, are essentials without which none of the other general principles of memorization can be used effectively.

One chief reason why so many teachers get into ruts and refuse to get a fresh lease on teaching is that they know the joy and freedom of working with materials which are second nature to them, and are unwilling to pay the price of learning new ones. Many a lesson fails because the teacher himself stumbles over the Scripture which he seeks to teach. He may think he has fixed it very well in mind when he repeats it in the solitude of his own room to the books on the shelves and the pictures on the wall. There are then no distractions to divert attention. But the situation is entirely different when he uses it with active, unpredictable children. If he needs to concentrate on the words he cannot be free to watch the reactions of the children.

2. *Study to make the initial presentation spiritual and vital.* Is the first impression such as will challenge interest and make a deep association with life; or will the next mention of the Scripture be regarded with indifference?

> After the Bible story of Daniel and his friends refusing the king's wine, a Primary teacher looked her group squarely in the eyes, pointed her finger at them and spoke each word forcefully with a pause between, "Do-not-drink-wine-or-strong-drink." In the discussion which ensued, the phrase was used three times more, with the same emphasis. The following week when mention was made of the review lesson, one of the boys assumed exactly the position of the teacher, pointed his finger at the group, and in great seriousness with the very same intonation said, "Do-not-drink-wine-nor-strong-drink."

A forceful first impression requires very little drill.

How careful mothers are when they introduce young children to some new type of food for their physical bodies! In spring, when mother first sees fresh asparagus in the market, she comments on it within the child's hearing, "Oh, how good that asparagus looks! Wouldn't I like some of it, but it costs too much money this early!" A week later, she says again, "That asparagus looks so fresh. But the price is still too high." Later she uses a special occasion, such as someone's birthday, to buy the pretty green asparagus as a treat. She serves the child only a small portion, on a special plate, beside something else he is fond of, and in a total situation which is pleasant and inviting. Mother knows perfectly well that once the child pushes the asparagus away from him, it is going to be hard to get him to try it again. But once he has enjoyed it, the battle is over.

If parents are so careful to see that a child acquires a taste for the food which he needs for his body, how much more careful should teachers be who serve him spiritual food for his eternal soul!

3. *Teach the meaning and beauty of the whole before analyzing the parts.* Any whole is not merely the addition of separate parts, but interaction of parts one with another. A part seems like an entirely different thing outside its own setting.

The first time children hear a Scripture passage it should, in its totality, fulfill its purpose of doing the work of God. It may be introduced in a story; it may be repeated as the children enjoy a lovely picture; it may be quoted to help one solve a difficult problem. The occasion should be one of heightened feeling and sublimated atmosphere. Then, later, when each part is plucked out of its setting for the sake of more detailed analysis and study, it still retains the original background, and is not distorted in meaning.

Just as adults will memorize a short chapter of the Bible in less time, with less effort, and with longer retention, if they repeat the whole once or twice each day than if they spend the same amount of time at one stretch on any one day, so children need to repeat often the whole passage. If not, there is necessary a whole extra step of learning, the process of connecting the end of each line with the beginning of the text. This is the most difficult part of the process, yet it is acquired naturally if the whole is visualized.

4. *Surround each phrase of the passage with many associations from daily life.* Instead of one artificial handle for the sword of the Spirit, the child should be able to pick it up by any hand. The Scripture should have so many roots in his

vital interests that many daily activities will bring it to mind. He should visualize it in connection with his home, his school, his play; in connection with his parents, brothers, and playmates; in connection with morning, noon, and night.

We may be sure that the more sing-songy a child repeats words, the less meaning they have for him. Are we more concerned with exact wording, or with correct concepts?

> When a new boy had attended a Primary department for three Sundays, a New Testament was given him, with John 3:16 marked in it for him. The next week he proudly showed the superintendent that he could say it alone. At a point in the worship service when the thought centered on what God gave because He loved the world, the superintendent asked this new boy to quote God's own words. He started out bravely, "God so loved the world that he gave his only Son"; but at this point, feeling the pressure of the attention of so many people, he grew a bit bashful. He forgot the exact words, but hurriedly blurted out the thought of the rest of the verse—" and if we believe in Him we won't go to hell, but will go to heaven."

Isn't that kind of response preferable to the exact words without meaning behind them?

A memory verse or passage is not an appendage tacked on to a lesson for the sake of mental discipline. It is an essential part of the structure of any lesson; in a sense, it is the very center of a lesson. It answers the pupil's problem which formed the approach to the lesson; it is the terse generalization of the Bible story or discussion; it is the means of carrying the aim over into actual living. All the other activities serve to point up the memory verse, but it has little meaning and usefulness without a background of concrete associations.

A memory course for Primaries and Juniors is a well-balanced selection of Scripture which forms the nucleus of the units for the year. Some lessons directly teach these truths and give them a background of Biblical setting as well as practical outworking. These scriptures are then carried along through the year and used as familiar material in worship whenever appropriate.

5. *See that a spirit of play pervades each drill period.* If the pupils see a genuine reason for fixing Scripture firmly in mind they will repeat it again and again of their own accord. Yet some drill is often necessary to establish accurate wording. Even this drill should be as closely related as possible to the actual way in which it will be used. Before the children grow tired of one kind of drill "game," another should be suggested. Usually the simpler it is, the better. Teachers should keep a list of all the various kinds which are valuable.

Assiduous care in memory work carries with it its own reward. To have the children discover as they "play" with a passage that they can say it alone is a thrill both to them and to the teacher. To have the children come to a teacher requesting the next memory passage even before it is introduced, because they have finished all the previous passages, is to know the joy of directing eager pupils instead of dragging indifferent ones.

The following use of Psalm 100 with Primaries shows the integration of a Scripture passage with the entire curriculum:

> In a worship service early in November the superintendent introduces the passage by means of a story of the Old Testament Feast of Tabernacles, while another teacher draws on the blackboard with colored chalk a large sketch of an outdoor booth with its bright natural ornaments. The children read from an attractive large poster the words of the psalm, and decide which words would make the best song. Each child tells why he praises the Lord, and they all sing a praise song.
>
> For the next three weeks the Bible stories build up back-

ground for the expression of thanksgiving. The memory verses for these three lessons are appropriate parts of the psalm. The expressional work on the backs of the pupils' papers help enrich the meaning of the words.

Psalm 100 is then used to outline a whole worship service. How can the children make a joyful noise unto the Lord? Probably the best way is to play on toy musical instruments. How can they show that God wants all lands to praise Him? Children of foreign descent may stand together, or American children may hold pictures of children of many lands. These foreign representatives may praise Him with a song.

The Primaries then look around their room to find something to do to serve Him with gladness—something to make the room more beautiful or orderly. Not until they get to heaven can they come before God's *throne* with singing, but even now they can come before His *presence* with singing. What song helps them to feel that He is right there with them?

Verse 3 may be called a short sermon for some young "preacher" who truly loves the Lord. To make sure everyone understands, he may also explain why God's people are called "the sheep of his pasture." If the boys and girls are to "enter into his gates," they must first go outside. Before they start to enter, a child sings the new song composed of verses 4 and 5a.

What do the words, "be thankful unto him," call His people to do? Individuals thank Him for good gifts which He has recently given them. The next phrase reads, "Bless his name. For the Lord is good." Several children use that part of the psalm to testify for Him, substituting different names of the Lord, as "Bless *God,* for He is good," and "Bless *Jesus,* for He is good." The last part of the psalm is another sermon for someone who knows what the words mean.

The next Sunday the children select pictures to make a picture folder or arrange subjects for a picture walk.

The following Sunday a teacher stands at the door as the

children enter, and asks them what they are thinking about as they come to church. Verse 4 is used to commend those who are entering with thanksgiving and to remind those who are not. When a small group gathers they sing that verse together. When a new pupil is enrolled in the department the children enjoy doing for him what the psalm says to do and telling him what the psalm wants him to know in verses 3 and 5.

Such joyous teaching *is* possible, and it *is* being done. And when it is, the child's mind is being conditioned in favor of Scripture memorizing. What an asset this mind-set will be throughout his life! How delighted were one teacher and one mother when a second-year Primary boy gave his mother for Christmas a gift which he himself had made with much painstaking effort—a little booklet in which he had laboriously copied many of the Scripture passages that he had been learning at church. No gift could have been prized more highly.

Many teachers, we regret to say, are not willing to pay the price of seeing that joy and success accompany the child's first memorization. It means spending time in the collection and preparation of correlated stories and pictures and handwork and methods of drill; it means analyzing each thought unit to discover the particular inherent possibilities for teaching; it means taking pencil and crayons and colored paper and cardboard, and making drill cards, games, and charts for drill, and for the recording of progress; it means the providing of concrete objects mentioned in the passage. The teacher must excel in the number of sidelights that he can throw on a passage until the children have heard it and worked with it enough to know it.

Children should not even try to repeat Bible words until they have heard them again and again in meaningful situations. If a mistake is made once, that mistake rather than the right phrasing is more likely to be repeated. Mistakes may be prevented from being practiced once.

How long should a teacher continue to drill a group of children? Until the slowest one has acquired the words without any effort? The others would have lost interest long before that. The group should be directed until the average pupil is able to complete the memorization with a little conscious effort. All their lives they will need to memorize Scripture, and should not form the habit of thinking that it requires no effort. It does; but, at the beginning, it should not require too much. When the average child can say the passage, the group may go on to something else, but the passage should be used again and again in practical life until it is overlearned, and becomes a part of them. At odd times, and in presession, those who know it can give special help to those who do not yet know it.

6. *Watch individual reactions to insure success for all.* It is always a problem to maintain high standards of work and at the same time to recognize individual differences in ability and background. It is well to have a standard memory course for each year of Primary and Junior age, but this course must, of necessity, be gauged to the average child. The superior pupil may be given extra Scripture to memorize for worship services. It is very easy for the new member without the background of the rest of the group to grow discouraged and drop out of Bible class because he cannot keep up with the others. This child needs special help and consideration. He is not expected to make up back work, but receives extra help and leniency in quoting the verses. Each individual must be challenged to put forth his best efforts and to experience success from his memorization.

1. Study Psalm 119 (or half of it) as a representative Scripture portion dealing with the use of God's Word. Find the

relative emphasis on *knowing, feeling,* and *doing,* with reference to the Bible. Tabulate each relevant thought under the three headings, "know," "feel," and "do." When finished, total the number of ideas under each heading. Then evaluate your own use of the Bible to see if you are making the same proportionate emphasis. If not, what changes will you make in your teaching? The following is a sample of the tabulation of the first eight verses:

KNOW	FEEL	DO
Have *learned* thy righteous judgments (7)	*Blessed* are they (2) Have *respect* unto all thy commandments (6)	*Walk* in the law of the Lord (1) *Keep* his testimonies (2) *Walk in* his ways (3) *Keep* thy precepts diligently (4) *Keep* thy statutes (5) I will *praise* thee (7) I will *keep* thy statutes (8)

2. Show how one Bible verse that meets a child's spiritual needs has ten roots in his daily life, and how you would help him make these associations in the Bible class.
3. For your permanent file start a list of six drill games for your age group. Which one of the six would you *think* would be most valuable? Why? Then try those six games and compare actual results with your previous supposition.
4. If the Word of God is memorized in order to do the work of God what emphasis should be placed on the *quantity* of Scripture memorized? How many verses shall we try to teach a child?
5. Should a child who reaches the Junior age learn the location reference with each verse he learns? Why?

CHAPTER XI

STORYTELLING

1. Have you experienced the thrill of holding a young audience spellbound by means of a story? What seemed to contribute to your success?
2. What storyteller (of your childhood if possible) do you remember with most pleasure? Can you analyze why? Do you remember any instance when a story was poorly told?
3. Notice the part stories play in the next sermon or address you hear. Is there any noticeable difference in audience interest when the illustrations are being given?
4. Can you trace the cause of some action or attitude on the part of a child or yourself to a story?

WHY A STORY?

When the Master Teacher explained the different kinds of reception which would be given the gospel, He did not say, "There are four kinds of men who hear the Word." In true storytelling fashion, the record begins, "Behold, a sower went forth to sow" (Matt. 13:3). God gave His written Word in the form of a story of sin and salvation, showing the great conflict of the universe and its solution. It is hard to imagine the Book with the story element eliminated, leaving a formal listing of God's attributes and precepts.

Janie had early been taught to say "Thank you" for favors. Of course, her parents intended the habit to instill in her a feeling of gratitude. But constant reminders continued to be necessary, and the words came with the dullness of necessity or duty. The story of the ten lepers who were healed, and the one who returned to express his thanks to Jesus, was told Janie one day with warmth and color. Shortly afterward the teacher handed her the Sunday School paper to take home. Her usual perfunctory "Thank you" was said. But immediately a new gleam of understanding came into her eyes. "*Thank you,*" she cried a second time, with a voice that held gratitude. The teacher felt assured that a new element had entered Janie's "Thank you."

Effective Daily Vacation Bible School advertising drew into the church not only its own constituency of children from the homes of moderate means and culture, but a number of children from a near-by slum district which had been untouched except by missions. Leaders were pleased, but there was noticeable at once a different disposition on the part of the children. Even in the Beginner department, the poorly clad children were left sitting in isolation while the others congregated, Pharisaically, apart from them. Here was the first and most pressing need for Christian teaching. Most of the churched children could repeat the words, "Let us love one another," but very apparently the full application as yet had not been made.

In three days there was complete amalgamation of the two groups; they were playing together in utmost friendliness of spirit. How was it done? By stories. Stories made up to fit this situation, stories to parallel in the children's world those which Jesus told of the Good Samaritan, the Pharisee, and the publican, His words about the "other sheep," and His action in eating with publicans and sinners.[18]

WHAT IS A STORY?

If Æsop's fables, Joseph in the Bible, and many of today's best sellers are all stories, what is a story?

Looking first to the basic construction, there may be found a skeletal framework on which every story is built, even though it is not always well done. Even the simplest of stories will be found to fall into certain divisions.

But beyond this outward form is the truth which every good story carries. The fairy tale is no exception. Stories which have lasted will be found, on analysis, to carry a universal message, based on unchanging human nature. This message is clothed with color and action and embedded in a problem which works up to the climax. The hearer's interest and feeling are stirred as he sees pictured in words a dramatic resolution of the conflict.

CHOOSING A STORY

One of the marks of the growth of the experienced teacher is his (or her) increasing fund of stories. This month he adds one that meets Johnny's fear, next month he adds one that leads Marjie to share her doll with the other little girls. Over the years he accumulates a reserve from which he can draw without hesitation exactly the one which wisdom dictates will meet the need of the hour, or the emergency which has arisen. The list will include stories for instruction, for recreation, for character building. But each is a story which measures up to the highest standards and is thus worth learning and repeating.

In addition to meeting a definite need, a story also must have certain other qualifications. Does it fit the age group? The length of time allowed for it? The exact need of this particular group? Does it have familiar elements which will give it meaning to those who hear it? Does it duplicate something recently heard? Is it appropriate for the Bible school, or for a picnic?

Additional questions arise regarding the use of Biblical

narratives adapted for children. First, is it true to the Bible story? Are the added details true to time, place, custom, probability? Does it serve the purpose, and yet remain true to the Bible purpose? Is it well constructed, and adequately written to represent the Book of books?

For the Nursery. Those who work with two- and three-year-olds quickly discover what kind of stories must be chosen if the audience is not to walk away at the end of the first sentence to find more interesting activities. The subject must be one which is familiar to the child and personally touches his life. Shoes are of great importance to him, of enduring interest, it seems, while the story of a boy who had a bicycle may not be worth listening to, because the child has no bicycle and no interest in one. But if the first words mention an object or an activity in which the child engages, his attention momentarily won.

If the shoes go "step, step, step" very loudly or very softly, or with a combination of the two, the child continues to listen. He likes sensory words that make him taste the "sweet" honey, hold the "hard" nut, feel the "pushing" wind. He likes sound words like "splash," "ding-dong," "cock-a-doodle-doo." He likes words of familiar action, such as "ran," "jumped," "hopped," and "hit," and he grows impatient if the action is delayed.

The Nursery story is often a simple addition of incidents, each carrying a definite idea, and uncomplicated. Sentences should be short and direct. If description is included, the child is likely to wander away, though he appreciates colorful words like "hot" sun, "red" blanket, or "fat" baby. He likes rhythm and rhyme, patterned movement in which there is repetition of phrases or ideas.

Above all, the Nursery story must be short. Teachers

should be aware of the results of investigations which give the average two-year-olds' attention span as two and a half minutes, and the three-year-olds' as four and a half minutes.[19]

SAMUEL GOES TO GOD'S HOUSE

Baby Samuel grew and grew. "When you are old enough, you shall go to live in God's house," his mother told him.

"See, Mother," he cried, "I am getting taller." And he would stretch on tiptoe to show her.

"Yes," she would say, nodding her head at him, "yes, you are getting to be a bit taller."

The next morning little Samuel would stretch on tiptoe and say, "Look, Mother, I am getting taller."

"Yes," she would say, "yes, you are getting to be a big boy. One of these days you will be big enough to be a helper in God's house."

The next morning little Samuel would stretch on tiptoe and ask, "Am I big enough yet? Am I big enough yet?"

One morning his mother smiled and answered, "Yes, now you are big enough. Let us get ready to go to God's house." Samuel jumped up and down. He ran after his mother all around the house as she made everything ready to go. At last it was time!

Away they started down the street. Samuel was very happy because he was going to be a helper in God's house.

For the Beginner. Beginners are pushing out the walls of the narrow world of their home, and hence their stories will show a broadening scope. They will still enjoy sensory words, repetition, rhyme, and action. But plots may contain more suspense and climax, and kindergarten attendance aids in increasing the number of subjects that are familiar. A lengthening interest span will admit of longer stories. Many Bible stories may now be adapted to the child's understanding.

THE KIND STRANGER

A man who had been hurt lay by the side of the road. Poor man, his body ached and pained so badly that he could not move. He could not get up to walk far enough to lie under the shade of the trees. The hot sun beat down upon his bare skin. His clothes had been taken away from him. Everything he had, had been taken away from him. "What shall I do?" he cried. "I cannot help myself. If only someone would come along and help me!"

Trot, trot. The poor, hurt man opened his eyes. Did he hear someone coming? Oh, if only he did! He listened. Trot, trot, trot—a little louder. Those were surely the feet of a donkey. Then TROT, TROT, TROT—a little nearer. "Surely the man on the donkey will see me," he thought, raising his head. "Surely the man will help me. Yes, there he is on the other side of the road. He sees me."

But the man did not stop. He kept on riding down the road. TROT, TROT, TROT—going on, without helping at all. Trot, trot, trot—going on, leaving the poor, hurt man alone. *Trot, trot*—going on, farther away, farther away.

The poor, hurt man laid down his head and closed his eyes again.

Step, step. Was that someone else coming along? He listened. Yes, step, step, step—sounded a man's feet this time. Would this person go by, as the other had done, or would this person stop to help? STEP, STEP, STEP. The feet were crossing the road to where the hurt man lay, to his side of the road. Now the feet were close to him. He felt better already, to think that help was so near. What would the traveler do to help him?

But STEP, STEP, STEP. The feet started away again! Was this traveler, like the first man, going on his way once more without helping at all? Step, step, step—going on, leaving the poor, hurt man alone. *Step, step*—going on, farther away, farther away.

The poor, hurt man laid down his head and closed his eyes again. The sun beat down upon his aching body. He thought of his wife and children who would be waiting and waiting at home for him.

Trot, trot. What sound was that he heard? He listened. Yes, trot, trot, trot—sounded a donkey's feet again. Would the man on this donkey look, and go on by, as the other two travelers had done? TROT, TROT, TROT—came the donkey nearer and nearer. Then it stopped, and yes, the rider was stepping to the ground. STEP, STEP, STEP. The man crossed the road, and came near to the hurt man.

Then he saw a kind face bending over him, and a strong arm gently lifted his shoulders. Was this traveler one of his friends, that he should be treated with such loving care? No, he had never seen the traveler before.

First, the stranger gave him a cool drink. How good it felt to his hot throat! From the pack on the donkey's back the stranger brought medicine and soft cloth. He gently washed the dirt from the bleeding cuts, poured on healing oil to make them feel better, and bound the soft, clean cloth around them. Taking off his own cloak, he wrapped it around the hurt man, and carefully helped him onto the back of his donkey. When the donkey started off down the road again—clop, clop, clop, because he was walking slowly now,—the hurt man was on his back while the stranger walked alongside.

As soon as they reached the first large house, the kind stranger helped the hurt man to get inside, where they found a room and a bed for him. All night the stranger sat by him and cared for him. In the morning, though the poor man was much better, still he was not strong enough to travel. The stranger went to the owner of the house. "Here is some money," he said. "Take good care of the sick man till he can go home. If you need more money I will pay you when I come back."

For the Primary. The law and order of the world have made sufficient impression on the Primary child so that he is readily filled with wonder and awe as its marvels are pointed out to him. Creation stories supply answers to some of his questions. He listens with bated breath to the stories of the miracles of the Bible, and readily accepts them with that faith which Jesus pointed out as exemplary.

At Primary level, imagination is ready to assist the teacher as she paints scenes of the past or the present. Heaven may be made very real, as well as the Bible characters. The children of the Bible hold special appeal because of the interest which all children feel for other children. Stories of helping, sharing, giving, of bravery and of goodness, may be used as strong factors to set up ideals which Primaries will follow and by which they will shape their developing ideas of right and wrong.

For the Junior. "Is that true?" the Junior asks. Let the answer often be "Yes," if the storyteller would take this realist with her. Not that every story must be an actual occurrence, but it must ring true to life in spirit, if not in fact. The Junior has an insatiable appetite for adventure, for action, for speed. He enjoys the heroes of history and biography, the missionaries whose vivid experiences are as yet beyond his reach.

Down-to-earth is the character of the Junior's theology. He likes to have the Christian life made practical, to see problems solved, to know of reality and causality, to set up his ideals in terms of action. For him, to believe is to do. He has a keen sense of law, which divides between right and wrong scrupulously. To satisfy his sense of justice, characters must illustrate that it pays to do right. Though Scripture is not now taught to him primarily in story form, for he needs the activity of searching his own Bible, it will be translated frequently into life through the hero or missionary story which puts its truth into action.

HOW TO WRITE A STORY FOR TELLING

All the books of stories ever printed for storytellers may not furnish just the story needed by your group of children in the situation in which you may find them tomorrow or next week. Nor does finding a story with a plot which carries out your aim mean that the story is ready to tell, for many a story would fail miserably to fulfill its purpose if told as it is written. After a careful study has been made of how to prepare a story for telling, experience will enable the teacher to make adaptations quickly. Some stories must have large sections cut, some must be enlarged, others must be rearranged. A good plot will be worth every effort to make it accomplish a worthy purpose.

Condensation and Elaboration. The storyteller will do well to precede her own efforts to prepare stories for telling by studying the great stories which have survived the years because of sheer merit. Not only do they embody the principles of good storytelling; they have by their enduring qualities themselves set the standards for construction.

Writing stories for telling has its own techniques which invite thought. First, study the story elements. Get the plot in mind, the mood and message; see the characters, and visualize the scenes. Is it too long? Does it have descriptive portions, unnecessary incidents, and minor characters? How much of it can be cut out without losing the pulse of the story? Cut out all that may be so described. Condense until there remains only such vital material as will present to the imagination a series of warm, living pictures in a smooth flow. Take thought for unity; let no extraneous material remain. Make the story move, not stand still on one foot for descriptions or incidentals.

Most Bible stories are models of terse condensation, and, therefore, often need elaboration when we present them to children today. They cannot, like the hearers to whom the stories were first told, picture the incident in its setting. In like manner we do not need to describe a schoolroom to a Primary child today if a story has its setting there. The manner and extent of filling in details of Bible stories have aroused discussion and differing opinions.

Let us first look at the Bible story from the child's viewpoint. To what ideas and experiences of his can it be related? Too many new ideas cannot be introduced into the compass of one story. If he is to make this story his own, the child must be able to tie it up with what he already knows; it must touch his life. This viewpoint will send us searching for the contact points which will make it vital to him.

For children we may often want to supply justifiable background details that will show how the characters or experiences were like those of the group who listen. We may want to strengthen the imagery by adding more sensory elements than the Bible account gives. It may be desirable to add facts or customs gleaned from other parts of the Bible or from history.

Whatever is added needs to conform to the laws of logic and to the implications of the text. Descriptive elements must be based on knowledge of Bible lands and times so that the scenes are accurately pictured. No unwarranted fictitious details or irrelevant matter should be added.

The Beginning. In the first paragraph, perhaps even the first sentence, the characters enter, the plot begins, the action is under way. There is a hint of what is to follow, a stirring of interest, a catching of the attention. Conversation or narrative, not description, is used to introduce a vivid picture of the characters or the setting. A straight line of action forbids rambling efforts to get under way.

"There was once a boy who grew dreadfully thin because he would not eat," illustrates the direct entrance into the story which characterizes favorite tales of children. One can almost feel a hurry in such opening sentences, as though there must be no time spent in getting started. And so it is. Wasted time is wasted interest. Especially at the beginning should descriptive words be eliminated. How long is it before something happens? Let it be soon.

The Succession of Events. Once the action has begun, its course needs to be direct, not zigzag. In an ascending series of events the listener is led onward in growing suspense. Each incident or picture which fits into the total should be arranged in order of relative interest appeal, so that every part of the sequence leads to the crisis. For a very young child repetition of sounds and phrases furnishes sufficient suspense.

The Climax. Straight to the highest point in the story the series of events leads. Here the secret is revealed, the surprise to listeners and characters occurs, the discovery is made. In simple language the thread of the narrative is knotted. Anything that would weaken this highest point is eliminated.

The Ending. Nothing is now left but to set the mind at rest by disposing of the characters in a way satisfactory to the listeners. Therefore the end will be short and pleasing. It will not need padding; it will not suggest another story; it will not detract from the climax.

Above all, it will not moralize. A story is not well constructed if a moral is needed to bring out the lesson. "And so, you see, children, if you tell a lie, you will be very sorry." If the story has not convincingly and artistically already pointed out that fact in more palatable form, the tacking on of such a preachment will also fail to accomplish the purpose. Instead of winning agreeable compliance, we are likely to stir antagonism. The very force of a story is to make that kind of teaching unnecessary.

TELLING A STORY

Reading a story is never a substitute for telling it, no matter how arduously lazy teachers try to equate the two in their own minds. It requires eyes and face and voice to share a story fully with another; a book held between the teller and the listeners is a barrier which forbids close comradeship. Especially when the story is one from the Bible or concerning Christian truths should the teacher feel her responsibility to take time to learn it well, for these lessons of tremendous importance should pass directly from her soul to the souls of the children.

Preparation of the Teacher. "Miss Experienced" had been told that she was a born storyteller. So she lost her sense of need for preparation. Her rambling introduction was followed by a mere outlining of several incidents, which should have been vibrant with colorful words to bring glowing pictures before the mind's eye. In the middle there was a moment of uncertainty as her memory faltered, and then the tale limped on to the end. When the response she received at the end of the story was not enthusiastic, she concluded that modern children were spoiled and sophisticated.

"Miss Beginner" *was* a beginner in the art, and she knew it. She was awed to realize that the Bible story was to be the center of the hour, the high point of the teaching period. So early in the week she began to read and learn to love the story she was going to tell. She read and reread it till she could visualize the different scenes in a rapid succession of mental pictures. The background formed by the oriental streets, the homes of Bible days, and the clothing worn by the people, became vivid and real in her imagination. She made no effort to learn the story word for word. She wanted to avoid sounding artificial and stiff. She could not be tied down to a mechanical memorization of words. If one were forgotten, the whole trend would be lost. The written story needed to be personalized and adapted to her own mode of expression.

The pillows on the davenport were her first audience. It was a good thing they were quiet listeners and not lively eight-year-olds, for she discovered that one of the incidents was still hazy, and that appropriate words failed to come in several places. She found that she needed to have certain key phrases definitely learned. A second time, so intent was she on the mimicry, the direct discourse, and the movement of the tale, that the audience were as unnoticed as *pillows* should be. But since it still seemed difficult to make a concise beginning and ending, the storyteller learned the first and last sentences as the written story had so expertly phrased them.

A day later, an adult was persuaded to join the pillows to lend life to the scene. Effort was still required to remember the sequence, but when the storyteller left out an important detail, she found secret delight in doing quick thinking which enabled her to slip it into the narrative without making her audience aware of the correction. The adult was lavish in praise for Miss Beginner's noble efforts. Should she stop there?

No, she knew that she needed yet more practice before the story was learned so well that she could be free to watch the faces of the children as they lit up with appreciation, or showed by the slightest trace of puzzled expression that a synonym needed to be inserted or a phrase of explanation added. She still did not know it so thoroughly that it flowed forth spontaneously and thus gave her freedom in interpretation. The price to be paid for that skill was yet more practice.

Worth it? The storyteller thinks so. The efficiency with which she afterward told stories required much less effort because they were built on a foundation of solid and thorough preparation.

Preparation of the Children. A successful story requires preparation of the audience as well as preparation of the storyteller. It is asking too much of healthy children who have already been sitting through a quiet worship service that they continue to sit quietly through a story—even a very delightful story. After each quiet period they need a change of posture and movement to release the tension of muscles which cry out for activity. Physically, the group should be ready to settle down to the story in relaxed comfort.

A group who come in after an outdoor walk or game may need another type of preparation. Their scattered thoughts or excited talk may need focusing on a picture (which does not give away the plot), or conversation about something which will be prominent, or the explanation of an unfamiliar element in the story to follow. Sometimes the physical activity which relieves cramped muscles may be at the same time a form of play which will turn thought toward the truth the story is to emphasize.

The preparation of the children to listen should be varied, carefully planned, and generally brief. It is an economic safeguard to make sure that the time spent on the story is not wasted, but that the tale receives a maximum of attention.

The Storyteller's Attitude. "Out of the abundance of the heart the mouth speaketh" (Matt. 12:34). Therefore the story must be in the heart of the storyteller, be reflected in her enjoyment and appreciation of it herself, in her respect for its message, in her serious approach to its presentation. The children will relax and drink in the message from the storyteller who comes to them with an air of confidence. They will quickly discern whether she is being natural. They will feel her appreciation of them and their attitude, their viewpoint, their enjoyment. They will catch from the attitude of the storyteller something which she cannot put into words.

Voice and Gesture. What a powerful instrument the voice can be! What shades of meaning, what contrast, and what characterizations its variations can give! The storyteller wants her voice to be polished, but not affected; clear and distinct, but not exaggerated. She will practice the conversational elements to make each character's speech so befit him as to bring up a mental picture of him. She will make her voice an instrument of righteousness as she uses it to speak reverently of the things of God, seriously of those things which should be solemn, joyously to reflect the joy of the Lord, with all the weight of her personality behind the truths she utters.

Since stories lie chiefly in the realm of words, the unnatural or studied gesture diverts attention from the story. Only the pointing, or wave of the hand which insists on being made, should be allowed. Then it will be an integral part of the thought, and merely add emphasis. Some storytellers may need to curb a tendency to use gesture too much, but few will need to take thought to add it.

Illustrations. Little children, for whom words are an uncertain medium of communication, may be helped to follow the thought by the skillful use of pictures to back up each concrete idea. Stories usually go better if pictures are not used with older children, since the manipulations are not likely to be smooth enough to coincide with the flow of word pictures. Attention should not be diverted from the story to objects or pictures, even though an excellent illustration of some part of the story is available. It may be shown before the story if it will help to insure understanding without giving away the plot, or afterward, to add appreciation and emphasis, and to review.

Interruptions. If the story is an artistic whole it should not be interrupted. Young children can be taught early that it is their turn to listen during the story, if the length of the story is carefully adapted to their ability to concentrate. In beginning to build the habit a very short story should be told, with commendation for quietness. Sometimes a special chair at home, or the story rug in church, may be used to fix the idea that a certain form of behavior is expected and required if the child chooses to come to the story time. Some children will learn more readily if their remarks are ignored. Personalizing a story by using the child's name or saying of an action, "just as you do," or of a character, "like you," may help a child concentrate who is easily distracted.

On the other hand, when a child is following the story and his remark is a spontaneous reaction to it, the teacher will usually welcome its suggestion, weave it into the story, and thus encourage mental participation. For young children she will often repeat rhymes or phrases which recur several times during the story, and the children should be encouraged to join in these parts with her. As they repeat, "step, step, step," they will enter into the story with increased enjoyment.

FOLLOWING THE STORY

To stir emotion or desire without guiding it into an outlet of expression is not only dangerous but wasteful. Sometimes prayer will be the first natural response. Then the children will want to change their conduct accordingly. A song may serve to emphasize the theme of the story or express its emotion. Drawing may be a physical release for stimulated thought. Pantomime puts into active physical postures what many children will be quite unable to express in words or drawing.

Thus the Nursery child who has heard about the dear little Baby Jesus may be in the mood to make "I love You" a real prayer. Or he may be ready to stand in front of the picture of the Baby to sing a Christmas song, or to rock a "pretend" baby in his arms as the pianist plays a lullaby. If the story was intended to arouse love for Baby Jesus, it should be followed by some type of activity which will express that emotion.

The Beginner child will enjoy all these activities of the Nursery child, with additional ones, such as modeling clay, for which better physical co-ordination has prepared him. Acts of service and giving for the Lord's work may become meaningful activities after a story. After he has discovered how he can please the Lord in his conduct, immediate opportunity should be given him to practice that conduct.

Primaries and Juniors offer a wider variety of objective means of expressing the feelings and carrying out the purposes for which a story is told. Their own questions and conversation afterward may bring home forcefully to them what they ought to do. Retelling the story in parts, or playing it, may serve to heighten the emphasis. This is not to say that there will be review, drill, or handwork merely to recall the incidents. A well-told and worthy story needs no repetition; it does invite expression. Instead of having its moral pointed out, the children will be ready to work it out, guided by the teacher. Perhaps it leads to creative work—the writing of a song, poetry, or a litany for the worship service.

Some stories will lead directly into Scripture memorizing and give meaning and purpose to persistent effort by the children which no amount of urging could accomplish. Stories may be used to launch a service project, to lead into picture study, and often for Primaries and Juniors to open the door to an invitation to heed the Saviour's call to come to Him.

1. To influence a child to the action or attitude you wish

him to take, watch for an opportunity to test the efficiency of a story compared with mere precept or command.

2. Has the average teacher any legitimate excuse for limping through a story? If she does, what do the children infer is her attitude toward the Lord, the Bible, the church, and themselves? How much time does it take to properly learn a story if it is practiced twice each day for a week? Would such spacing require more or less time than massed practice on one day? Why?

3. Is it the good storyteller or the poor one who is inclined to moralize at the end? Why? If a well-told story fails to effect the desired results, what would you suppose to be the reason?

4. Suggest several activities which would be profitable for each of the three age groups following the story of the Good Samaritan.

CHAPTER XII

VISUAL AIDS

1. Do you recall any picture from your own childhood or from that of another person which has made a lasting impression?
2. In teaching children, what has been the most effective use of visual aids which has come to your attention? What specific aims did this method of teaching accomplish?
3. Have you known any teachers to neglect visual aids? Have you known any others to overuse them? When teachers have overused them, what other helpful methods have they failed to make the most of? What happens when any one method is used exclusively?
4. Study some of the outstanding uses of visual aids in Scripture. Note what materials were used, why, how, and the results (Ex. 30-38; Josh. 4:5-9; Jer. 13-11, 24; Ezek. 1:27, 28; Amos 7:1, 7,8; 8:1-3; 9:1; Matt. 6:26-30; 17:1-13).

VALUE OF PICTURES

Pictures are no longer considered a luxury, but rather a necessity in the Bible school. They help teachers "adorn the doctrine of God" and dispel any erroneous ideas that goodness and dullness go together. What a child looks on, that he becomes. We live in an era of visual education. As teachers of the Book of books, are we vainly struggling to gain entrance for the gospel of our Lord and Saviour Jesus Christ through only one channel, the eargate, or are we seizing every opportunity to enlist the whole personality? What goes in through the eye is more likely to find lodgment in the inner recesses of the being than what goes in through the ear. According to a Chinese proverb, "One picture is worth a thousand words."

> In a certain family there were five sons, all of whom became sailors. As one after another of the growing boys showed a decided preference for the life of the sea, the mother was perplexed and somewhat disappointed. One day a visitor in the home pointed at a picture on the wall and exclaimed, "What a beautiful picture you have there!" The painting showed a sailing vessel riding the waves, the sun's rays reflected on her silver sheets. Then came the realization of the truth that the picture had been responsible for the sons' decisions.

1. *Pictures center attention and build atmosphere.* Is the attention of the group easily distracted by interruptions beyond control? Pictures may become an ally to center attention. The teacher who offers himself as the only center of attention during the whole period often discovers to his dismay that he is not appreciated. He will have a much greater influence if he keeps himself in the background while guiding and supervising the children's activities, especially if one of these activities is their own use of pictures.

For example, an effective background for worship on Easter Sunday may be arranged by selecting a lovely scene of the angel and women, and in front of it an open Bible. If the picture is printed on thin paper and pasted on glass, a lighted candle behind it can be focused on the shining angel to further show his brightness.

Raymond Frame, of the China Inland Mission in Honan,

describes a difficulty which pictures may help to solve when used by the Spirit of God to combat the forces of evil:

> To preach intelligibly is not the greatest difficulty; far greater is the difficulty of keeping the people's attention fixed on the message when you are speaking intelligibly. I have known it often to happen that just at the point in his sermon where the speaker would begin to deal with vital things—Christ shedding His precious blood on the cross, and the necessity of our exercising faith in Him in order to be saved from the final punishment we all so richly deserve—that at this point some disturbance would occur which would completely take the listeners' minds off what was being said. We have met with this so frequently we have learned to expect it. They miss the most vital truth of all.[20]

2. *Pictures clarify new ideas*. A multitude of words will not serve so well to clarify mental images in the child's mind as will one carefully chosen picture. Of course, models and objects make an unfamiliar idea even more concrete, but we are not always able to find or construct models.

Bible manners and customs seem very strange and remote to children of today. If we try to compress our imagination to their extremely narrow world, we shall not take it for granted that they can visualize an oriental house when we merely tell them that it had stairs on the outside, or a well, when they have drawn water only from a faucet. They may need to see several pictures of women and children carrying water on their heads from the village well before they can feel that the characters are not circus performers, but merely ordinary mothers and children getting their daily supply of water.

3. *Pictures stimulate new interests and recall past experiences*. If we wish our children to initiate a new project, we surround them with pertinent pictures that will arouse their

curiosity, conversation, and thought. Requests will soon come for materials to work out creative activities as an outgrowth of the new interests stimulated by the pictures.

How difficult it is for children to recall what has happened to them in the past! Yet if they can see a picture of an experience which they have enjoyed, the delight in both the picture and the event is heightened. "I did that once," the child exclaims with joy. We transport him into a past event in order that we may lead from the familiar to larger and richer concepts.

4. *Pictures furnish incentives for right conduct.* Although we watch for patterns of Christian conduct in the classroom itself, and prize especially good examples in life situations, many types of behavior are difficult to see at church. We must provide for the transition from church to home, where the children are forming habits every day in the week. Pictures can show a boy in the early morning telling God he loves Him, even before he runs out and says, "Good morning," to Mother and Father.

5. *Pictures make impressions vivid and therefore lasting.* The following is the testimony of Mrs. Harvey J. King, of the Africa Inland Mission in the Belgian Congo:

> The feltographs and the little folding organ have become real missionaries, as I have them with me on every *safari.* Such remarks as this have been overheard in the villages after hearing and *seeing* a message with the use of the feltographs: "Even though one had not believed before, one could not help but believe after *seeing* that message." And from those on the mission station who have heard the message over and over again, "I am hearing the gospel now as though I had never heard it before!" . . . Roman Catholics were drawn to the meetings by the feltographs and organ [though] they were warned not to enter our churches.[21]

PICTURES OF JESUS

A growing interest in the use of pictures has accompanied the church's awakening to the needs and glorious possibilities of leading the younger generation to Christ. A few who testify that they were cautious in beginning to incorporate pictures into their programs would now feel greatly cramped if they were to be denied them.

Is there any indication in the gospel records that God's Son as true man as well as true God was immediately singled out in a crowd because of different outward appearance? Since we are not able to keep all pictures of Christ out of the sight of our children, why not provide them the best which the ages have produced?

Is it easier to show children that every figure designated as Jesus is only an artist's conception, or is it easier to make their best Friend become increasingly real to them without the use of pictures? We may display several artists' portrayals of the same Bible event, such as Christ blessing little children, and encourage the children to compare and contrast the scenes. The settings are different, and especially is His face different in each, although in all He is shown with such a noble combination of strength and tenderness that, though He may have been a stranger, no little one hesitated to seek His embrace. Most of the artists felt utterly unqualified to undertake a representation of God made flesh, and yet they wanted to give to the world, as an evidence of their personal devotion, the most wonderful and loving face that brush was able to place on canvas. The children may select the picture of Him they prefer.

Then they may close their eyes and imagine what they think He looked like—the matchless One who is truly God and yet who became truly man to show us what God is like. Our mental image of Him is much more wonderful than could be put on paper, yet He is brought down to the level of our infinite sphere when pictures help us visualize a human form. Beauty of color, form, line, and composition aid in appreciation of all that is holy.

The test of any material and any method is whether or not God has consistently blessed and used it in the hands of His servants. There is little question as to the seal of divine approval on this phase of the expression of the love of Christ.

What other one character has figured so largely in the world's treasures of art through the ages? There has been no period in the history of the church without its distinct representation of Christ in art. Being the universal Man, the "desire of all nations" (Hag. 2:7), all races see Him through their own eyes, and paint Him as one of them. This is their devoted testimony, and, like our own in word and deed, though it be imperfect, the Lord is pleased to use it.

CHOICE OF PICTURES FOR CHILDREN

Artistic Beauty. Why are children universally attracted by the "funny" papers? Is it because their appreciation of beauty and line and color is no further developed than this low type of picture? Other things being equal, would the average child choose a crude picture in preference to a lovely work of art? No, if the other criteria for selecting their subjects could be made equal, they would not. Although untrained in the subtle nuances of beauty, they instinctively are drawn to what is pleasing in appearance, unless other elements supersede that of beauty. The innate feeling for the beautiful may either be expanded by guidance, or repressed until it is no longer in evidence.

One element to seek, then, is artistic beauty, and if possible a good color print. It is the color of the comic strip that first attracts. Ours is an age of color; we have all become color conscious. Inexpensive magazines offer large colored advertisements such as would have been rare and costly not many years ago.

Action Rather Than Still Life. The garishness of the comic strip is not in its favor. But though its color attracts, it must have more than that to hold the attention of children. And it does hold them by the element which is by far the most essential in the choice of pictures for children—action. In the "funnies" someone is always going somewhere. And he is not going slowly, he is immediately there; and at once something else is in the offing. The remarks of the characters are almost unnecessary, for the action pictures tell the story.

From their youngest years children learn to read pictures that tell them stories. But it is much harder for them to get a message from a picture without action. They are especially interested in children, yes; yet a child merely posed is not a picture for children, since nothing is happening. An exquisite scene of awakening spring flowers will pass unnoticed in favor of a picture of a child gathering or smelling or discovering early flowers, which will speak to them of the heavenly Father's care.

A Positive Message. All pictures with genuine action are not equally helpful. Let us seek to have a positive message in the picture and avoid the negative, lest we either distress the child or put unworthy ideas into his mind. The purpose of a conduct picture is to hold before the child an ideal for him to emulate.

Size Suitable to the Purpose. Although small pictures should be collected for picture maps and scrapbooks and illustrations, those displayed before a group need to be large enough to be enjoyed without strain. When small children complain that they cannot see a picture unless it is practically in their hands, it is true they cannot see it in a way that is at all satisfying.

Experiences within Comprehension. The experiences suggested by the picture must be within the child's comprehension. An example of a picture containing symbolism and therefore unintelligible to most children, is Holman Hunt's "Light of the World," which portrays Christ with a lantern knocking on a door overgrown with weeds. This picture makes a fascinating study for adolescents, but it should be left for that age which can see beyond the literal and matter-of-fact.

If teachers are doubtful whether or not a picture has a childlike message they can try it with several children, and note their responses. Pictures furnish one of the best backgrounds for revealing to a teacher the interests and characteristics of different ages. If one selects a picture with a good underlying narrative, and shows it in turn to several ages, he can analyze which parts of the picture were enjoyed and which overlooked.

Details True to the Incident. When choosing Bible pictures for children, it is important to examine the details to determine whether they are true to the incident and to life. Why should it be generally believed that there were only three Wise Men, since the Bible gives no intimation of their number? Songs have helped to ingrain this impression, but pictures are also responsible. Every year we receive Christmas cards picturing the Wise Men and the shepherds together worshiping the Christ Child at the manger, although it took the Wise Men so long to travel from the East that Mary and Joseph with the Babe had moved to a house by the time they arrived.

Few of the artists who have painted "The Last Supper" show the disciples reclining at the table, as was the custom in those days. Why are many people surprised to learn that the

Bible nowhere implies that angels have wings? Through the years most adults have absorbed more Bible facts and doctrine from pictures than they have gained from conscious means of instruction. What a delightful method of teaching if only the pictures are accurate and emphasize the truth of Scripture!

If one is constantly alert to true and untrue details, pictures with discrepancies may be used with great profit with Juniors. They may seriously search their Bibles to decide which pictures are accurate and which are not. This exercise provides motivation for thorough investigation, not only of happenings, but also of manners and customs. The pupils will become justly critical of pictures, and will grow to love certain pictures which stand the test of their keen discernment.

Outlines Clear. Another element to avoid in the use of Bible pictures with children is too much detail. Their pictures should be very clear in outline, for then they cut a faithful stencil on the mind. Since many of Jesus' miracles were performed in the midst of throngs of people, the picture to be accurate must show the multitude. Yet the picture may be so cluttered with people that small children are unable to find the center of interest and tell what is happening. One picture of the triumphal entry is so confusing with crowds of people and palm branches that even adults look at it and fail to see the figure of Christ riding on the donkey. Some artists who understand the children's viewpoint have succeeded remarkably well in giving a suggestion of a multitude without clouding the effect.

Part of the heritage of every young child should be a beautiful picture of the Lord Jesus Christ with one child—only one. If this picture is in his room at home or in his Nursery or Beginner room at church, he will day after day put himself in that child's place and come to feel the personal concern of the Saviour for him.

USE OF PICTURES

In how many different ways have you been using the pictures which you have collected and purchased? There are as many ways of using them as there are types of pictures, and the value of those you have may be greatly increased if you use them to full advantage.

Choose a picture wisely and you will have little difficulty discovering how to use it, for the child himself will direct the discussion. The greater the story element in a picture, the greater are its possibilities with children. All pictures of the Lord Jesus calling the children to come to Him after the disciples had rebuked them for disturbing the Master hold a personal message for children. Some artists have added even more meaning to the scene by making each individual child also tell a story.

Give your group time to project themselves into the characters. Some teachers are inclined to spoil pictures for children by plying them with obvious questions, and advancing their own interpretations before the picture has had an opportunity to speak for itself. Tact and restraint will keep the study from becoming a mechanical exercise when it might be a spiritual experience. God seems very near and real as the children quietly gaze and open further vistas by their own comments. The teacher can add her comments unobtrusively to guide their thoughts.

After the Bible story of Paul and Barnabas going out as missionaries, a teacher showed a group of Primaries the picture of Copping's "Hope of the World" as she sang "Jesus loves the little children, all the children of the world." For a few seconds the group silently drank in the message of the artist. "I like it," said Harry. "That's the way it should be," added Donald. Then they spoke of the clothing and the color of skin of the various foreign children, and why they dressed that way in their country. Joan answered Mary's question whether or not the Chinese now wear braids of hair down their backs.

Suddenly Joan frowned as she noticed that only the Negro boy sitting at Jesus' feet was not touching Jesus. "No, he isn't!" marveled the others. "Why not?" "Jesus loves him just as much." "Doesn't He?" They turned to their teacher for assurance.

She helped them answer their own question. "See how lively that dear colored boy looks! What do you think he was doing just before he sat down there on the ground?"

"I bet he had been right up there on Jesus' lap," commented Nick. "Yes," agreed Mary. "Now he's looking straight up at Jesus' face so that he won't miss anything Jesus says. I bet Jesus is saying that there's nobody He loves more than the black boy."

Use with the New Story. As suggested in the chapter on storytelling, pictures have a ministry alongside stories. When shall the picture of the new Bible story be shown—before the story, during it, or afterward?

Does a real storyteller need anything to illustrate the story while he is telling it? For children above Nursery age he relies for effect solely on the power of his words, reinforced perhaps by simple dramatic motions. His appeal is eye to eye with his audience and he wants nothing between. In the faces uplifted to his he watches to see mirrored the emotions which he is describing. He desires no picture or other illustrative material to interrupt the sequence of events which he is building up to a climax. Once in a while the picture might be displayed without comment at a propitious moment during a story, but not often. It is not wise for children to form the habit of commenting, nor is it wise to allow any outside element to intrude into the telling of a Bible story.

Most pictures should be displayed after the story, for they usually portray the climax of the narrative. We certainly should not betray the plot before we begin. Afterward the picture will serve to deepen true impressions made by the story, and will correct any false concepts without limiting the child's imagination.

Pictures or objects which illustrate unfamiliar ideas should be shown before the story in order to prevent misunderstanding or confusion as the story progresses. For example, if the incident about Philip and the Ethiopian is being told, a story in which a chariot is prominent, chariots and their use should be described before the story. If the picture of that story does not give away the plot it may be shown first.

Also pictures that raise questions may be shown before the story to motivate the telling. The children enjoy guessing who the people are, where they are, and why they might feel as the people in the picture apparently feel.

Use with Review Lessons. Pictures are especially helpful for review lessons. Without them it is difficult for children to center their attention on the several stories to be recalled. With them, it is fun to play simple games to distinguish characters, to associate the memory verses, and to make personal applications. If a group decides to put on a program for another group, pictures of familiar stories will be an easy way to organize the presentation. Young children speak more readily if they are telling about a picture they are holding.

Use with Bible Verses. Picture walks and hunts are favorite activities for Beginners. Suppose the children are interested in the beautiful world which God has made. With each nature object the teacher wishes to associate the thought of God and the Bible verse, "All things were made by him." The name of each object that can be seen by the children is used in the verse instead of "all things"—"Flowers were made by Him," "Birds were made by Him." To represent objects which cannot be seen, place pictures on the wall. The children incorporate each object in the verse. At the end all God's creation is summed up in the exact words of the Bible.

Young children also like to walk around the room to find a picture which answers a certain question. Beginners cannot select pictures at a distance. They like to be close to them, and they also need the physical activity of walking to find the picture in question.

Primaries will listen to verse after verse of Scripture in order to match them with one of several pictures. Probably the most valuable set of pictures for Scripture matching are three for Holy Week—Palm Sunday, Good Friday, and Easter. The salvation verses we want our boys and girls most to hear may be selected. The children are kept alert when some of the verses apply to both the crucifixion and the resurrection.

Use in Playing and Posing. Children like to pose pictures, imitating the characters' posture, or to carry out the action in which the characters are engaged. Good Bible characters for action are the people whom the Lord Jesus helped—the fishermen, the blind man, the sick boy, etc.

An excellent picture to pose is the beloved "Angelus," by Millet. For a background, the sky and field and distant church steeple may be drawn on the blackboard by the children. Any basket and long pole and man's hat will serve for the necessary properties. Several children may compete to see which couple best assumes the postures of the man and woman in the picture and look as if they are truly thanking the loving heavenly Father for His goodness to them. As each couple takes position the pianist should play bell music, such as "L'Angelus," by

Gounod. While the best couple poses, the whole group talk silently to God.

Use in Handwork. Pictures are essential for many of the projects which the children propose. After studying a few principles for the mounting of pictures, Juniors are able to select those that are worth while for the different Sunday School rooms, and to mount them neatly. Missionaries welcome pictures in small paper frames, and picture puzzles cut into a few pieces after being pasted on construction paper.

Some songs may be illustrated by picture folders, with all the phrases of the song represented. Small pictures are useful for picture maps. Picture posters and displays have great teaching value if rightly used. An outgrowth of a lesson on the Boy Jesus in the temple at the age of twelve may be a poster entitled, "About My Father's Business," showing pictures and explanations of what a boy today may do to be about his heavenly Father's business.

DISPLAYING PICTURES

When we step into some children's rooms in churches, we observe that there are pictures—yes, many pictures—but it is evident that the same ones have been posted in the same place and left week after week, with no change. Perhaps once a season a dozen or more soiled pictures are taken down and as many others put up in their places. So many are displayed that the children notice none of them. They notice neither the old ones nor the new ones, their only impression being that the bulletin board is always covered with them.

Avoid too many pictures and too great a variety at one time. Each Sunday select, or supervise the children in selecting, a few which bear directly on the subject to be discussed. Place these few on the children's eye level, where they will be most likely to broadcast their message during the presession period, or at any other free moment in the hour. Utilize various means of display for temporary pictures—a beaver or cork board, burlap screen, chalk tray, browsing table, low easel, or wire standard on a table.

Permanent Pictures. Two or three carefully chosen permanent pictures should be included in the equipment of each department room. Even permanent pictures are appreciated more fully if given a period of rest each year. If a room lacks such pictures, or we wish a new one, a choice of a large framed picture will furnish an excellent project for the group.

We may bring in, and encourage the children to bring in, several appropriate subjects from which to choose. All of them may be studied and discussed before the vote is taken. If one child has a decided preference, he will use all his force of persuasion to influence the others. We could find no better motive for picture study. And when the large reproduction is finally purchased, it will have rich associations of meaning for the children. The pupils may collect the money themselves if no other source is available. They also will enjoy planning a special ceremony for the day when it is to be unveiled.

As the leader guides the children into the presence of the living God, will the surroundings of the room hinder thoughts of His love and holiness, or will the children's eyes rest on a lovely masterpiece of art?

The following are the best types of pictures for long-term display:

Nursery—Jesus and one child, a child listening to a bird.
Beginner—Jesus and the children of the Bible story, the boy Samuel at prayer.
Primary—Jesus with arms outstretched, Jesus and foreign children.

Junior—the Boy Jesus in the temple, General George Washington at prayer.

Mounting Pictures. Why spend time and money mounting temporary pictures? Because mounting enhances the beauty of a picture and also preserves it in handling. Do we use pictures of one size more frequently than others? A convenient form for handling all of this size is to prepare a frame with clamps on the back, so that the pictures may be readily slipped in and out of the frame.

Although some leaders advise only neutral shades of tan for mounting material, a wider variation in color is more interesting and allows freedom to bring out all the possibilities of a picture.

For pictures of greater value and usefulness, and those which will be handled by the children, use mounting board, which comes in neutral shades of brown, gray, green, and black. For pictures of less value, and for those requiring colors not obtainable in mounting board, use construction paper, which comes in all colors. For the narrow submount or edging between the picture and the mount use light-weight poster paper. Materials for mounting can be purchased to best advantage at a school supply house.

Even Juniors like to study the principles of mounting, and can give valuable assistance in preparing pictures for their own and other departments. The color of the mount should not attract attention to itself, but should bring out the picture more clearly. It is the same principle that we use in selecting our clothing. The principle of mounting is the same as that of Christ in the believer—He is the picture, we are the mount; we are to display Christ, not call attention to ourselves.

One should look in the picture when selecting the color for the mount, since it should reflect some color there. That color should be matched, for a different shade of the same color does not produce a pleasing effect. Usually dark pictures look better on light mounts, and light pictures on dark. When the picture is brightly colored—as many of them are for children—the mount should not be the dominant color, but some dark color in the picture which makes a good background for the center of interest.

The narrow submount or edging usually reflects some small feature in the picture which can well be emphasized. It is not needed unless it is a contrast both to the mount and to the outer edge of the picture. The white margin around a picture is usually removed, unless a touch of white is desirable to center something white in the picture.

In pasting the picture onto the mount the narrowest margin is left at the sides, the top is slightly wider, while the bottom is wider than the top. Subjects which are uncommon and difficult to obtain in a picture may be pasted on with rubber cement so that they may be removed later in case they are wanted for other purposes, as picture folders and posters.

Classifying and Filing. As you continue to collect and buy all kinds of pictures of all sizes, you will be confronted with the necessity of careful organization for efficiency. Classify pictures according to size and subject. Work for sets which have mounts of uniform size, for then when you select a number for a certain purpose they will look as if they belong together.

The main headings for classifying children's pictures according to subject will probably be: Old Testament, The Life of Christ, The Apostles, Worship, Special Days, Missionary Interests, Child Activities, The Four Seasons, Nature, and Animals.

Small pictures may be organized in envelopes under the above headings. Medium-sized pictures are most readily accessible when they stand upright in a box or carton. If large pictures are mounted on heavy materials, they may stand upright; otherwise they should lie flat in a large folder. If possible they should be kept dust proof.

FLANNELGRAPHS

The flannelgraph has a decided advantage over pictures in that it shows action. The children actually see what is happening as the thought progresses, instead of viewing one completed scene, as in a picture. The characters may be moved about at will, and yet be left in one spot by a mere pat, for a piece of flannel is pasted on the back of them. Cloth has the advantage over paper in that cloth sticks to cloth.

The first figures to be widely distributed were the Hollenbeck and McCall sets—outline drawings on white construction paper. Beatrice Hollenbeck tells of the origin of these figures:

> In the early winter of 1935 my sister and I were invited to conduct a Junior Church in one of the state's largest liberal churches. Some of the old timers looked very doubtful. "A Junior Church lasting an hour and a half after Sunday School with that lively group! It was tried years ago; it was stopped because the noise disturbed our service upstairs." The superintendent was willing to try again. We were willing, but a bit fearful. What could we do to hold the youngsters and win them to Christ?
>
> We began by using a flannel board, for we had previously worked out several Bible and missionary stories. Our first figures were small and crude, but were received enthusiastically by the Juniors. As the boys and girls demanded more stories, we searched for figures to buy, but found none.
>
> Each week, therefore, with Eddy and Duane and Don in mind, we worked out a set of nine-inch characters. Each week nearly a hundred Juniors rewarded us with their approval. They

have been our inspiration for one hundred sixty stories down through the years—they and their younger brothers and sisters. The flannelgraph was the only thing which kept the door of opportunity open in that liberal church. Many children there have come to Christ, and several parents, who saw the transformed lives of the children.

Other churches began asking for demonstrations of the flannelgraph, then other towns. A missionary from China visited us and took away several of our stories. Soon we were getting orders from Chicago, Texas, Tennessee, and points east—wherever the missionary went. We were surprised that others would want our figures.

We copied the patterns by hand, and sent them free to all who asked. It was hard work, especially on hot afternoons after a long day of Daily Vacation Bible School. We decided to charge a dollar a set so that people would be more apt to use them. When we made a hundred copies on the hectograph we felt that it was quite an advance, but wondered if we would ever get rid of that many. Since then our mimeographed sets have gone and are still going all over the world. Letters from other users have been as great an inspiration as the Junior Church.

The flannelgraph has been responsible for many vacation schools, and for openings in many churches which otherwise would have been closed to the gospel.

The Visual-Aid Board. The best foundation for a flannelgraph is an easel with a slanting board of plywood. It should be sturdily constructed lest it collapse at some inopportune moment. Simpler than an easel with legs is a board placed on a table to provide height, and supported by standards on the back, or otherwise braced, so that it is not straight up and down. If the board is hinged in the middle, it is easier to carry about. Black flannel is sometimes glued onto a light board, and the other flannel placed on it.

The Flannel. If the desired colors of flannel cannot be

purchased, they may be dyed. Although elaborate backgrounds may be bought, these make a scene too complicated for young children after the figures have been added. Plain colors, perhaps with a few suggestive lines, are better for them. Crayoning the flannel may add a natural touch, such as purple on gray hills, and black on gray for rocks. Old felt hats furnish a convenient source of material for small objects, as trees, bushes, and flowers.

After a few scenes have been worked out, the same background material may be used for many other stories by adding only the distinctive features of the new ones. Blue sky, green grass, hills, roads, trees, and flowers will be needed again and again in most of the scenes. Although some parts of the pictures, as trees and flowers, may be made either of cloth or of paper with cloth pasted on the back, cloth is usually preferred. Palm trees look well if two trunks are cut together from brown flannel, and the tops of the two trees also cut together from green flannel. A smaller tree behind the larger two will give a pleasing sense of distance.

The Figures. If a Bible school department buys the same type of figures for all its stories, these figures may be combined in various ways for additional purposes. For instance, to show that the Lord Jesus is on a higher plane than even the best of men, a picture of Him is placed high on the visual-aid board, while the figures of David and Moses and Daniel and Joseph and Paul are taken from their respective stories and placed on a line on the board below God's Son. If all are the same type of figure, they look as if they belong together for this new lesson.

A few other suggestions also stem from experience. Take care that the figures are pressed and kept flat, lest they curl up and keep falling off the board when used. Make the figures as sturdy as possible by pasting flannel over the entire back to prevent a small arm or other projection from getting torn off. When preparing to give a flannelgraph story, have the figures laid out in the exact order in which they will be used. Fumbling around for a certain piece interrupts the message.

For coloring figures many people prefer tempera paint to water colors if the figures are not shaded. Sometimes figures need to be outlined and colored on both sides, as in the case of Daniel when he goes up the stairs of his house and then comes down again. Both sides will stay where placed on the cloth if a piece of flannel is pasted on both sides as part of the garment that he wears.

The Children's Part. The more the children can do in connection with flannelgraph stories, the more benefit they will receive from them. Juniors and adolescents may work them out as service projects to give to the younger departments. It is they who need the activity, not the teachers. Even small children can show the action after they have seen the teacher give the story once or twice. Juniors and older Primaries are afforded valuable creative work by choosing a Bible story suitable for this medium, and planning one or two scenes with their characters and action.

The most interesting flannelgraphs are those which incorporate the most action. Outdoor scenes are easier than indoor. An artistically inclined child may do the more difficult figures without tracing them. Thinking through the scenes to picture accurate geography of the Holy Land and customs of Bible times will result in Biblical research for information.

Even children may watch the perspective of their pictures. Roads and rivers grow narrower as they run up and back on the board. The children probably would prefer to crayon rather than paint their figures. Different groups of children may each make a flannelgraph and practice presenting it until they are ready to tell their story to others. They will often feel the need of using and therefore memorizing the exact words of Scripture. Several children may have parts if each child moves one figure and talks for it.

A Warning. When time is limited—and what teacher's time is not limited when he gets a vision of the possibilities in reaching boys and girls for Christ?—he is tempted sometimes to spend what time he has in preparing visual aids and then hastily asking the Lord to bless them. The Lord does not work that way. Nothing can precede prayer nor take the place of prayer. It is in prayer that God directs what methods to use. When He directs a method requiring manual preparation, He will give time to prepare it. It is through prayer that the Spirit of God works; without His inner work no methods, no matter how attractive, will be effective in reaching the heart. It is only He who gives the sense of reality to spiritual things and charges the atmosphere with the sweet savor of Christ.

OTHER TYPES OF VISUAL AIDS

The wise teacher makes extensive use of the blackboard to make simple diagrams and sketches as well as to write words. He often asks himself, "Is there a more graphic method than mere words by which to convey this idea?" Charts and diagrams for children need be only suggestive, for they will use their imaginations to fill in details. Just as places often will be visualized on maps, so will other relationships be shown by lines and figures.

Object lessons already have been discussed in connection with symbolism in the chapter on Mental Development. They have a ministry with Juniors and less extensively with Primaries. They are useful when they are so closely tied up with the spiritual application that the children cannot miss the point. The test of their use is whether the children's minds are left on the interesting objects which were manipulated, or on the lesson intended; and whether that lesson is left as a hazy abstraction, or is brought down to the realm of practical conduct.

Observations and exhibits help to extend children's experiences. When they are studying shepherd life they may profitably visit a farm which raises sheep; when they are planning a Christmas tree for an orphanage they will want to find out the needs of the orphans; when they are studying Palestinian life they will enjoy a tour of an oriental museum. Older children may make exhibits of missionary curios and scenes, various kinds of Bibles through the ages, different types of churches, nature collections which show the minute care and wisdom of God, and Biblical models and objects, such as chariots, lamps, beds, clothing, homes, boats, occupations, and trees.

Slides, films, and movies of a spiritual character are now being produced on the level of children. They should be carefully inspected for quality of content and technique. It should be remembered that all visual materials are *aids* to good teaching, not substitutes for a Biblical curriculum or a teacher's planning. Unless they make a real contribution to the lesson, they have no place in a session. Their values need to be conserved by preparing boys and girls ahead of time, so that they will know the reason why pictures are being used, and what specifically they should be looking for. Like stories, visual aids should be followed by discussion and action which fits them into their place in the total program.

1. For the age group you teach or are most interested in find a picture to illustrate the five values of using pictures as outlined in the beginning of the chapter.
2. For your particular age group select ten pictures which measure up to all the standards for the choice of pictures.
3. Mount six pictures according to the principles outlined.

4. Look ahead to the lessons which you will be teaching in the next few months, and decide how you can use pictures in three new ways that you have never tried before. Choose the pictures, mention what aim you wish them to accomplish, and describe exactly how you will use them to effect those aims.
5. What free and inexpensive sources of pictures are available to all teachers if they but keep alert to the possibilities?

D. WORSHIP EXPERIENCES

CHAPTER XIII

WORSHIP

1. Study three worship experiences as found in Scripture, such as those in Exodus 3:1-6; I Kings 8; Job 38:1-42:6; Isaiah 6; Amos 9; Luke 17:11-19; Acts 3; Revelation 11:15-19. Note what occasioned the experience, what form it took, what its immediate and far-reaching results.
2. Analyze what happens in your own moments of worship. Mention some of the outstanding occasions or events or conditions which prompt your worship.
3. Recall the highest moment of worship which you have experienced in a children's group. What factors would you say were responsible for this feeling of nearness to the Lord? What did it do for the children?
4. Do the pupils in your class or home know for themselves the joy of giving something of their own to the Lord, or do they merely put their father's money in the church offering?

Does the Bible school session on Sunday morning begin with "opening exercises," or with a worship service? The term used to designate the first part of the hour does matter in this case, for too long have we started with a few exercises to open the session instead of genuine worship activities.

"Those who speak about "opening exercises" usually refer

to mere exercises, not of the children but of the leader, when he stirs himself for the first time that week to round up the Bible portion to be read, and the hymns to be sung, and some one to play the piano, since the regular pianist has not yet arrived. Hymns too often have been given out to those who have come on time to keep them occupied until the latecomers have straggled in. Prayer has been mostly by the teachers for the teachers. Scripture has been in the form of drills or contests, or has taken the edge off the lesson because the new passage has been read. Even if the leaders have been worshiping, very few of the children have been. Many a child has attended Sunday School for years without once feeling the presence of God. "Brethen, this ought not so to be."

MEETING GOD

Contrasting sharply with the spirit of "opening exercises" is the spirit of a grandmother's reverent worship in church, as a young woman recalls her childhood:

> There is one scene which shall never be erased from my memory. It is as vivid today as it was in the days when I sat in the little country church by my grandmother's side. For a brief two years of my childhood, I lived near my grandmother and attended the same church. For the most part it was a community of devout Christians. Some were so pious and stiff and sober that I was almost afraid of them. I had no desire to be like them. But the loving manner of my dear old grandmother was quite different.
>
> There seemed to be nothing short of death that could keep her from attending the services on Sunday. Not only was she there, but always among the very first few to arrive. She had her pew, as was the custom, and immediately on entering she went to her accustomed place. No, she didn't sit down and look around or visit with others who happened in early. She sat

with head bowed and two little old wrinkled hands over her eyes. I can see her yet. There she sat pouring out her heart to God and preparing herself for the message which was to follow. It seemed so long as I waited for her to raise her head, that I might talk to her. But even then, somehow, without words she made me understand that church was a place to worship in quietness and not to converse.

For many years my grandmother held a state record for regular church attendance. She lived to be ninety-two years old and was faithful to the little church to the last Sunday she lived. One night she slept out into eternity. How often I thank God for such an example! To this day it makes my heart ache to go into a church and see people visiting as though it were a social gathering intead of a calling together of worshipers.

The Meaning of Worship. The root meaning of the word "worship" signifies "worth ship," the reverent acknowledgment in thought, word, and deed of the "worthship" of God. Worship is the culmination of spiritual experience, when self reaches out for God, feels Him near, and adores Him.

To worship is man's highest prerogative, because in it God is all. It is submissive adoration of the King of kings and Lord of lords. The other exercises of the spiritual life all tend toward worship—reading the Word, prayer, love, faith, surrender, and obedience. In an attitude of worship the spiritual life is in control over the mental and physical, as God intended it to be, but sin often perverts the spiritual and brings it into subjection, with its voice of conscience dulled.

A Bible school session fails to accomplish its highest function unless the pupils meet God. Knowing about Him should lead to knowing Him.

Why is it that there is so little genuine worship when God is waiting to meet with His people and show Himself real to that soul who is "devoted to the extolling of his glorious attributes" (Eph. 1:12, 1930 Weymouth Version)? "Draw nigh to God, and he will draw high to you" (James 4:8). "Seek, and ye shall find" (Matt. 7:7). Worship must be each individual's own personal act, even in the experience of children, for only those whose hearts reach out to God feel Him near.

"More than servants to work for Him, God wants sons to fellowship with Him." It is recorded of Enoch, one of the noblest characters in Scripture, that he walked with God. Nothing but God's presence truly satisfies the longing of the saved or unsaved. Nothing else will counteract the gaudy attractions of the world.

How the overstimulated child of today needs the calm and quiet of the divine presence! Only by looking at life from the divine viewpoint can he get a sense of eternal values. Only by adoring surrender can man give unto God the glory due unto His name.

The head and the heart are of equal significance in spiritual welfare; neither is sufficient in itself. The head must know the way of salvation; the heart must appropriate that knowledge with affection. The Bible lesson appeals primarily to the head; the worship service appropriates that revelation. The Bible lesson teaches what is God's will; the worship service establishes personal adjustment to God's will. Psychologically, therefore, the Bible lesson should precede worship, on the same principle that we adults each morning in our private devotions first let God speak to us through the Word, and afterward we speak to Him, prompted many times by the reading.

In worship, emotion predominates, but is based on knowledge. Children are especially sensitive to feelings. They often understand feelings in an adult worship service although they may comprehend little of the terms used and the underlying facts. They absorb the pastor's love of Christ and his concern for souls from his tone of voice, from the way he says the name of the Lord Jesus Christ. When facts as well as feelings can be comprehended in their own worship service in terms of their own interests and needs, when fact and feeling can reinforce one another, what great things can be accomplished by the Spirit of God!

The deepest experience in worship often occurs during moments of silence. The phrase, "They bowed their heads and worshiped," is found in Exodus 4:31, 12:27, and Nehemiah 8:6. As the piano played a lovely quiet selection to prepare a certain group of Primaries for prayer, a six-year-old in the front row leaned over to the boy sitting next to him and whispered, "Isn't it just like heaven!"

An Atmosphere of Silence and Expectancy. The atmosphere that is conducive to worship is not one of repressed silence, but of active anticipation. Children are much more sensitive to atmosphere than to words. As they enter the door of their Bible school room they should feel that something of a spiritual nature has always happened in the past, something worth waiting for, something they could not predict, for it was always different, and today also something will happen.

Great things happen only when adequate provision is made. The leader who expects something to happen and provides for spiritual growth by making the children expectant will not be disappointed. Worship services which bring boys and girls into the presence of God do not just happen; they are the result of careful and prayerful planning and preparation.

If the children feel God's presence, restlessness will cease and the Spirit of God can work. Restlessness will not cease by the tapping of a desk bell, or by pleading exhortations to be polite. The atmosphere should be such that the leader could say at intervals in the service, "Surely the Lord is in this place."

If the children are not quiet, bad habits result in actual spiritual harm. They must not learn by practice that they can do something else during prayer, when all eyes are closed.

Don't look for God to come only in one particular way in a worship service, but look for Him. Expect Him to come. Don't overlook this element of surprise, for it is God's way. Be always in a state of expectancy, and leave room for God to come in as He likes.

The Relation of Form to Experience. If the children are quiet but feel no softened fullness of heart, going through the elements of worship becomes mere form; the activities become "substitutes instead of channels, weights instead of wings." It is sad but true that we sometimes actually train our children to be formalists, for the doing of things becomes like the law of old; the heart soon vanishes, leaving the doers barren and cold. Who is content with the cool, respectable conventional type of Christianity?

"Too often we inoculate young children with a very mild type of *religion*—the word is used advisedly—which renders them practically immune to *Christianity* in its original and dynamic form." Satan wishes children to be inoculated with religion lest they be converted to Christ. God forbid that we should teach a "form of godliness, denying the power thereof," when we have in our midst the living reality of Christ and the unfeigned faith of childhood!

Form may express experience and it may induce and intensify experience, but form alone cannot be depended on. Children, being very suggestible, may catch the spirit of a song or prayer, or they may instead learn that Christianity means going through certain motions. "The deadliest Pharisaism today is not hypocrisy, but unconscious unreality." It seems to be easy and natural for the unsaved person to get the impression that there is merit in going through the forms of religious devotion.

One Bible school teacher testifies that the most real experience of worship that he ever witnessed took place not in a church building or in a home, but in a public school. Contrary to the general rule, the uniqueness of the form of worship in this case played a part in its impressiveness.

> It was Armistice Day in 1928, and taps were to be sounded in the corridor outside the elementary schoolroom. The first grade children discussed with the teacher the waste and crime of war, and were emotionally ready to ask God for a peaceful world. At the moment the trumpet sounded, one child in the group—recognized by the children as well as by the teacher as a natural leader both in social life and in school lessons—spoke up with reverence and determination, "I am going to kneel to talk to God." She dropped down beside her seat. Immediately every child in that schoolroom followed her example. The teacher, herself not a Christian at that time, felt that God was very near as she beheld thirty first graders bowed before God of their own accord.

Experiences of this type should not be extraordinary but ordinary in the Bible school.

Confident Leadership. What gives a teacher confidence as she guides her group in worship? First, there must be consecration, then training, and finally experience. Manifestly the cloud of the Lord's glory must fill His temple—whose temple we are. Of course, consecration without training will accomplish much, but genuine consecration is never content to remain untrained. Experience too is as essential for growth of teachers as it is for growth of children.

A young teacher, though she saw the Lord working in

her class, was nevertheless dissatisfied with the response of the pupils. She came to her superintendent for the reason. Because she unstintingly gave herself each week to prayer and study of the children and the preparation of materials, she expected to secure the same response as did the superintendent after many years of experience.

"But how can I lead children with confidence?" asks a teacher who works in a church where the other leaders do not appreciate her aims and methods, where even the environment seems to militate against a spirit of worship. No matter how far away one may be from his goal, he can lead with confidence if he is taking legitimate steps in the direction of that goal. If we do all we can to guide the pupils toward Christ, He will do what we cannot do. That is all He asks of us. We can still be confident and courageous.

Some teachers make elaborate plans ahead and are held bound as slaves to those plans. Others make no plans, desiring to be unbound and plastic in the hands of the Lord. Those who are truly borne along by the Spirit have made full preparation by prayer and materials, but are quick to adapt and modify and change their ready-made plans if a better situation arises. When we have considered more than one way of reaching a desired objective, it will be easier to abandon our own plans if the children offer a suggestion which will accomplish the same purpose. Though we make all our plans in accordance with what we know of Joan and Billy and George from the past, yet we cannot foresee what each one is going to do today.

A word of warning about planning worship materials in the flesh, which is constantly clamoring to intrude into spiritual activities. When time is limited, as it so often is, the temptation is first to get together materials and then, if time remains, ask God to bless them. God does not work through plans schemed by self, but He will be ready to guide ahead of time as well as during the session. "Not by might, nor by power, but by my Spirit, saith the Lord"—not by might of winsome personality, not by the power of psychology, but "by my Spirit, saith the Lord."

VARIOUS TYPES OF WORSHIP

Since worship is an attitude of heart rather than a particular outward form, the inner attitude finds many kinds of outward expression.

1. *Objective and subjective worship.* Objective worship centers in God, subjective in the individual's inward response to God. These two types should be properly balanced in the program. Unless we continually lift our eyes unto the Lord of the hills from whence cometh our strength, we shall have a distorted perspective of the value of earthly things.

Most worship services begin with such thoughts of God as "Holy, holy, holy," "Great is Thy faithfulness," and "O worship the King, all glorious above." After we have caught a fresh vision of the Lord God, we are ready to adjust our lives and activities to His will. The subjective response to His objective existence and attributes will be expressed in such thoughts as, "Believe on the Lord Jesus Christ," "I give myself to Thee," and "Go ye into all the world."

2. *Informal and formal worship.* Most children's worship services are informal, directed by their immediate interests and needs. Occasionally, however, the whole group or a worship committee enjoys planning with a leader a formal service in which every part is prescribed beforehand. The boys and girls decide the order of the parts, and who is to perform each part. The participants practice their parts to assure smooth procedure. The children may like dignified services of this type so well that they ask to have them repeated, yet formal services should not have too prominent a place.

3. *Spontaneous or unplanned worship.* Informal worship has a great deal of planning behind it, but spontaneous worship is unforeseen and unpredicted. It springs from the heart during moments of joy and wonder and gratitude. It may last only a fleeting moment, but often it is the most real kind of worship. It is common in a Christian home where a child acts naturally and freely without the presence of a group of people and the bustle of a school situation.

But if the Bible school room has a homelike atmosphere and sympathetic leadership, spontaneous worship is likely to occur whenever new spiritual insight is gained. When the first snow falls in winter, or the first flowers burst forth in the spring, a child may utter in real worship, "What will heaven be like when this is so beautiful?" When he realizes that God still loves him though he sins, the look in his eye may reveal how much that fact means to him. One little girl remarked to her mother, "I love God even more than you, because He gave you to me."

On Sunday morning we have not one, but a group of lively children, each with his own interests and inclinations, yet we also have the added inspiration of the Lord's day, the Lord's house, His Holy Word, and the children spick and span in their best Sunday clothes. The Lord God is waiting to reveal Himself if only His people do their part.

BUILDING A WORSHIP SERVICE

1. *Let the children's immediate interests and needs lead the activities.* During the week a teacher has been praying and planning along the line of his pupils' general home and school background; yet on Sunday morning he also wants to know what they are thinking about specifically as they enter the church. If their minds are on ordinary subjects, he can no

doubt find one of them which readily lends itself as an approach to the service.

But if they come in all excited about Susan's father who just returned from the war with his arm off, it is likely that the thought of using what one has for the Lord will be much more real and profitable than any other theme. For the Sunday before one of the teachers leaves for the mission field the children may plan a service to tell him what they are going to do for him while he is gone.

> On the Sunday after a Junior girl died, many questions were asked about death, and many incidents from her sweet life recalled. She had said to the nurse in the hospital after a blood transfusion, "This was not the only blood that has been given for me. The blood of the Lord Jesus saved me from sin."

In a children's session, the unexpected will be the usual. Children are full of surprises, never dull or monotonous. They keep the teacher young in spirit and flexible in habits of thinking and doing. A question or comment by a child is not considered an interruption, but an indication of the trend the program should take. The younger the child, the more flexible the program needs to be. As teachers mature in teaching experience they see opportunities for worship in events which formerly have seemed disastrous.

Almost every part of the program will be connected in some way with personal matters. Instead of using perfunctory calls to worship, a Primary child may look over the group and repeat calls to worship to particular individuals who look as if their minds were on themselves rather than on the Lord. The songs may be in relation to Mary's illness or John's vacation.

Whenever possible, tell actual stories which have happened to people the children know. If Helen has composed a poem the children would rather hear that than the most remarkable sonnet of a Wordsworth. If we pray for Joan's father while he is away, the boys and girls will get more feeling for God's protection than if we pray for safety in general for everyone.

If a worship service is to include and win the child's whole personality, it will be different in some vital respects from an adult worship service. It will be shorter, more active, and more unconventional. If an action rhyme is suggested to children's minds they will not regard it out of place, since it portrays a Bible story.

> Isaac Watts thought of heaven as a land where "congregations ne'er break up and Sabbaths never end." Many have seen a grim humor in this description, and have sympathized with the little girl who told her mother she wanted to go to the other place, where there was "more going on." [22]

2. *Build thought and feeling up to a climax of decision.* A worship service is a work of art to be developed toward a culminating point of challenge to the will. It will then have unity, proportion, and emphasis. All details will fit into the comprehensive aim, will work up to a decisive focus, and will result in action by the pupils. Of course, it is more difficult to make use of the pupils' suggestions than to plow straight through with one's own previous preparation. Yet if correlated materials and methods are well in mind, and the teacher is sensitive to the guidance of the Spirit of God, the steady build-up to a climax will result in new relations with the Lord.

3. *Organize familiar material in a variety of ways.* Such a happy medium may be effected between the familiar and the

unfamiliar that the children will neither go through the motions of a mechanical routine nor be so attracted by novelty that their attention is diverted from the Lord. There must be enough sameness to make them feel that they belong and are at home in the service. There must be enough newness to make them think what each part means. Though the children's repertoire of songs will not be very extensive, the ones they love need not always be used from the same approach, nor the same aspect be emphasized. Correlating the worship with the theme of the Bible lesson will usually care for the variation in the use of the familiar elements of worship.

Some unexpected feature should be planned for each session. It may not be used if the children introduce other ways of developing the idea, but in case they do not, interest will be kept on a high plane. The feature may be a story, an object lesson, a flannelgraph illustration, simple dramatization, victrola records, band instruments, etc. Make extensive use of the blackboard, pictures, and objects. Poems may serve to reinforce Scripture, but should not be substituted for Scripture. Stories make the truth attractive and challenging, and should result in something being done about the ideals stimulated. Special speakers or special musical numbers should be brought in only when they are on the pupils' level and meet the need better than more active participation by the group itself.

HINDRANCES TO REAL WORSHIP

"What hinders real worship?" repeats a distraught teacher of children in a small school. "One hundred and one things keep us from leading the children into the presence of God! What's the use of naming them all? There's so little we can do about them."

Granted that Satan seems to center his attack on this part of the Bible school hour, for he is fully aware that responses of the heart are as essential as instruction of the mind, yet many hindrances can be overcome. God does not do what we can do. Said one writer, "The man who has vision and no task is a dreamer. The man who has a task and no vision is a drudge. The man who has a task and a vision is a hero." No philanthropic undertaking is of more real use in this world, none more fascinating to watch, than the Sunday School in which children can grow spiritually in the light of the glory of God.

An Ungraded School. At the outset let us face the fact that our problems will pile up if the school is not graded departmentally. There is sufficient variation of interests and experience within a department covering pupils differing two or three years in age. Many leaders have gained new pupils and proved the need of an extension to the present church building by holding one or more departments in a home or a store near by, or even on the church lawn in summer. Often disciplinary problems are caused by failure to meet the needs and interests of each age on its own level.

Until the time when a small church is able to grade its school, it will consider the needs of all in its program:

1. Worship often may be based on common experiences, such as a building project or a missionary responsibility, and on seasonal interests, as special days or world conditions. Each class may assume responsibility for a certain part of a new building or a missionary's outfit; then the offerings are dedicated together. An inspirational service may challenge all ages for the next special need, which may feature the destitute of war-ravaged countries or a Christmas tree for an orphanage.

2. Elements for worship may be chosen with all the groups in mind. There are both songs and Scripture which deal with the vital problems of life in simple, concrete language. Such materials will be discussed subsequently.

3. Some parts of a service may be planned particularly for children, some for young people, and some for adults.

4. Members of the various age groups can co-operate in planning and leading worship services. This will help to give each group a sympathetic understanding of the viewpoints of the others.

5. After children have studied Scripture, songs, and stories in their class sessions, these materials may be incorporated in the worship when they enrich the theme. Psalm 100 is often appropriate for the opening of a service; salvation verses should be used instead of one's own words, and Matthew 28: 18-20 when service projects are being initiated.

Interruptions. Interruptions proceed from many sources —from lack of organization, from outsiders, from pupils, and even from teachers. Smooth procedure is impossible without co-operation by all officers and teachers, with regular planning and preparation before each session.

One hindrance which can be eliminated in nearly all cases is that of outsiders disturbing the worship service. The adult who walks through the room seldom realizes that, like the well-meaning disciples of old, he is displeasing the Lord by keeping the children from the blessing that Christ wants to give them. A teacher can mention tactfully that an adult walking through a children's room hinders even more than would a child if he walked through an adult service, no matter how good his reason for doing so.

On the doors of some Nursery and Beginner rooms is found this verse printed on an attractive poster:

> Step softly, ye who enter here,
> These children are so small and dear;
> You would not interrupt a prayer—
> Their thoughts fly here and everywhere.

Children can understand that they not only disturb, but miss much by entering late. A wise and loving secretary can remain outside the department door, talk with latecomers about arriving on time in the future, help them remove their wraps so as to enter quietly, and converse with them until a break in the program when their entrance will disturb the least. The children themselves may plan and make attractive posters discouraging tardiness, to put outside the door for latecomers to ponder.

Leaders themselves may be guilty of letting drills and lengthy announcements to teachers intrude into the worship service. Drills have their place, perhaps after, but not during worship. A children's session and a teachers' meeting have never been successfully combined. Children cannot be expected to attend to every word that is said unless every word is for them. All adults must truly enter into the worship or the children cannot be expected to. More is no doubt *caught* from their reverent and active participation than is *taught* by the planned program.

Inadequate Environment. There is no excuse for surroundings to be disorderly and unattractive. Each room where children worship conveys a message in itself. It should say, "Worship the Lord in the beauty of holiness." Although some rooms are not light and airy as we should like them to be, all may be clean and tidy, with touches of color and objects of interest.

Beautiful pictures hung low; objects of nature, such as bright flowers and growing plants and a fish bowl; curtains decorated prettily, perhaps by the children; fresh paint on walls and furniture, are possible in almost any room, and often transform the worship service as well as the environment.

The most attractive room cannot be an orderly room unless cupboards and files have been provided for work materials, and hooks for wraps. Some children will keep on their Sunday clothes and become overheated rather than throw them on a table in a heap with many others. Chairs and tables must be of proper size. How can children who are not in physical comfort keep their thoughts on God?

Lack of Provision for Presession. Teachers have been heard to complain of the limited time for the spiritual training of children in the Bible school hour, and yet waste the valuable presession moments from the time the first child arrives until the group assembles. If left to their own devices, children learn bad habits amid noise and confusion. They often feel that there is no need of getting to Sunday School on time because they dislike to wait for things to begin. On the other hand, interesting presession activities help prevent tardiness.

A browsing table or center-of-interest table provides a background for the theme of the day. If the Bible story mentions anything strange or new to the group, models or objects or pictures or books may show it. Personal questions on the blackboard may prompt an informal discussion of a problem solved by the lesson. Certain extra correlated activities can be done in short periods. Last week's lesson may be reviewed to find out how it was applied at home during the week. Some of the children may prepare special parts for the worship service. Individual attention can be given to memory work. Children may feel responsible for certain duties in the room.

But more valuable than any of the foregoing activities is the teacher's personal interest in the individual child during the first few minutes when he can converse with him alone about his daily doings and problems. Later the child may be reminded of these things he wants to tell the teacher and will voice them even if they do not pertain to the subject at hand. Everything of interest to the pupil is of interest to his teacher if the latter fully qualifies for his position.

SCRIPTURE IN THE WORSHIP SERVICE

The major elements of any worship experience or worship service are music, prayer, Scripture, stewardship, and fellowship. Since there is a great deal to be said concerning music and prayer, a whole chapter will be devoted to each of these topics, leaving the other three elements of worship to be discussed here.

Choice and Purpose of Biblical Materials. If one thinks of building a worship service as creating a structure, such as a pyramid, it is easier to visualize how each element of worship contributes one level in raising heart and mind to the elevation of the Lord's viewpoint. Drill for the sake of drill has absolutely no place in worship; it causes the structure to crumple instead of ascend. Though using Scripture with meaning is in reality the best type of drill, yet in worship it is used solely for the purpose of providing experience with the Lord.

The Scripture brought into the worship service is already familiar, unless the pupils feel a need for something which has not been introduced previously. In that case the teacher gives it, and the children may decide to practice it outside the worship service in order to be able to give it themselves the next time.

A correlated memory course provides familiar passages on each subject of interest. The short, terse memory verses are chosen primarily to sum up the generalization of the weekly lesson and to furnish a sharp reminder to take home for daily living during the week. But longer passages on each theme furnish devotional material in beautiful language to lift thoughts heavenward.

In the back of each leader's mind should be all the familiar passages which the pupils have already lived with, and these should be woven into the texture of worship whenever they are appropriate. The teacher himself may use one informally in conversation, may suggest that the group repeat one with him, and may ask a particular pupil to give one in connection with a personal incident which has special significance for him.

If a superintendent is free to devote his attention to the children as they enter the room, they may tell him of thrilling spiritual experiences which have happened during the week. Often these experiences are tied up with some reference to Scripture; if not, the teacher may help them make an association. Later during the worship service he asks Mike or John to share with the others what the Lord did for him at home. When the children get into the habit of using the Word of God to do the work of God, everyday occurrences will remind them continually of parts of Scripture, and they will themselves offer many instances of its working in their own lives.

Variety in the Use of Scripture. If a spirit of expectancy is to reign in a room, no element of worship will always be used in the same way. Certainly the new Bible portion of the day should be saved for the lesson and not read previously.

1. Bible verses as well as songs call the group to worship.

> I was glad when they said unto me, Let us go into the house of the Lord.—Psalm 122:1.
>
> Be still, and know that I am God.—Psalm 46:10.
>
> The Lord is in his holy temple: let all the earth keep silence before him.—Habakkuk 2:20.
>
> Surely the Lord is in this place.—Genesis 28:16.
>
> O come, let us worship and bow down: let us kneel before the Lord our maker. For he is our God.—Psalm 95:6,7a.
>
> Worship the Lord in the beauty of holiness.—Psalm 96:9.

2. The children recall Bible verses and stories which already have a rich background of meaning for them, and testify as to which scriptures have helped them during the week.

3. After a passage has been repeated, a child tells in his own words what it means to him.

4. During the presession period individual children prepare to read new verses.

5. The group repeats a short response after each of several related ideas. As individuals mention specific things that the Lord has done for them, they may all repeat, "O give thanks unto the Lord, for he is good."

In the Primary department the teacher may cite brief instances in which a person tried to please God in his own way, as by trying to be good, going to church, giving money, helping people, etc. After each incident she may say, "But that is not the Lord's way of saving people," whereupon the group responds each time, "Believe on the Lord Jesus Christ, and thou shalt be saved."

Primaries may also choose between two responses. The teacher may write in large, clear letters on the blackboard, "I will be sorry for my sin," and "I will be glad in the Lord." As she reads several verses which pertain to one or the other of these sentiments, the group responds with the first if the verse speaks of sorrow for sin, and with the second if it speaks of joy because of what the Lord has done. She reads verses such as:

> All have sinned, and come short of the glory of God.—Romans 3:23.
>
> My help cometh from the Lord, who made heaven and earth.—Psalm 121:2.
>
> Every good gift and every perfect gift is from above, and cometh down from the Father.—James 1:17.
>
> He that committeth sin is of the devil; for the devil sinneth from the beginning.—I John 3:8.
>
> All we like sheep have gone astray; we have turned every

one to his own way; and the Lord hath laid on him the iniquity of us all.—Isaiah 53:6.

God so loved the world, that he gave his only begotten Son, that whosoever believeth in him should not perish, but have everlasting life.—John 3:16.

6. The leader tells the background of a Bible story to arouse interest and assure comprehension, and then reads the actual story from the Bible.

7. The pupils match Bible verses to pictures, or vice versa. For instance, from a group of several pictures they decide which pictures illustrate the Bible verse, "All things are possible to him that believeth."

8. The teacher paraphrases a Bible verse in terms of the children's own experience, while the children quote the exact Bible words.

9. A cumulative story may be woven around a Bible verse or passage, the story building up meaningful concepts behind the words, which are repeated often in the course of the narrative.

10. The pupils give an object lesson or flannelgraph story incorporating Scripture to give it effectiveness.

11. They word a prayer from a Bible verse and use it as the group prayer.

12. They sing Bible verses, perhaps songs which they themselves have arranged.

13. They decide on a Bible verse to quote between the stanzas of a hymn to bring out the thought of the song more forcefully.

14. They compose their own litanies. After they have studied the praise of God's people of old, as in Psalm 136, they enjoy making their own psalm of praise to commemorate their

experiences of the Lord's mercies. At first their attempts may not sound poetical, but after studying the beautiful language of the Bible, they will learn to express themselves more adequately, and will have greater appreciation of God's Word as worship material. Children cannot be expected to desire to create a litany or find words for it unless they have had a genuinely deep experience which will spontaneously spill over into expression in word and deed.

15. Juniors may work out related Scripture verses in the form of the devotional material of "Daily Light." They select correlated verses which mean the most to them, arrange them into an effective whole, and prepare to read them during the worship service, perhaps with a background of soft music.

16. Juniors and sometimes Primaries can use the method of choral reading or a reading choir. After they have studied in detail the story of the bringing of the ark to God to Jerusalem, they can plan three choirs and a keeper of the gate to read Psalm 24. Choir one may quote verses 1 and 2, a singing choir may render verses 3 and 4, choir three, verses 4b, 5, and 6, and all the choirs unite on the rest of the psalm, with the exception of the two questions in verses 8 and 10, which are asked by the keeper of the gate.

The activity of preparing this Biblical material for use in worship necessitates careful study of its meaning. The mode of expression in each case is dependent on the import of the thought itself, and must be rendered "in spirit and in truth." It requires insight to decide whether boys or girls should quote each part, whether it should be given fast or slow, loud or soft, calm or animated. As a group works out Scripture in these creative ways, the Word of God also works itself into their own hearts, and the Spirit of God can work it into their daily lives.

STEWARDSHIP

Although children in the Bible school often repeat the Scripture verse, "It is more blessed to give than to receive," they seldom really believe those words until they have personally enjoyed a practical experience in giving. If we are to change the natural tendency of *getting* to the transcendent attitude of *giving,* we must so arrange circumstances that the child receives more satisfaction from giving than from getting. During the early formative years most children have never been privileged to have this experience, they see very few examples of sacrificial giving in the people they know, and thus they grow up secretly questioning God's high standards of stewardship.

Christmas is the supreme opportunity for training children to give. Since the heavenly Father gave His very best, we have a real Christmas only when we give His Son our best on His birthday. People may give costly gifts to relatives and friends, but only those who give to the Saviour on His birthday have a real Christmas. At least at church the emphasis may be wholly on the active giving and wrapping of presents in Jesus' name rather than the passive anticipation of getting. At the Christmas party games may be played featuring what children give rather than what they get.

Collection or Offering? In our Sunday School departments, do we take a collection or an offering? A collection stresses the amount of money received, while an offering establishes the desire on the part of the children to share in God's work. A collection is defined as a mass, a heap, an aggregate. An offering considers the effect on the giver as well as the amount received.

"The gift without the giver is bare." When children are

urged to bring their old toys to give to orphans less fortunate than they, the toys may be a fine collection so far as the orphans are concerned, but may not be helpful so far as the pupils are concerned, for the latter are not bringing an offering, but merely getting rid of the old to make room for the new.

That kind of *collection* contrasts with the following *offering:*

> After Bible stories about giving, a group of Beginners decide to help make some orphans happy at Christmas. They visit the orphanage to ascertain what the children have and do not have, and invite them to their tree.
>
> One Beginner—let us call her Jane—sees a sad-looking little orphan and concludes that a doll will make her happy. Having no money to buy a new doll and desiring a gift of her own for Jesus on His birthday, Jane naturally goes to her nursery for a doll that can be spared. To part with any one of the family is a sacrifice. It cannot be the old one that has grown so familiar and beloved, but one of the newer ones is chosen. Her mother helps wash its clothes and freshen it as much as possible.
>
> This dolly is taken to church and held lovingly until the orphans arrive and sit with the Beginners around their tree. Then the Beginners put their gifts into the hands of these friends whom Jesus loves as well as He loves them. As Jane puts her dolly into the arms of the sad-looking little girl, the other clasps it tightly and beams all over. Jane murmurs, "You'll make her a good mother," and feels satisfied that her sacrifice is appreciated by both Jesus and the new mother.

This is real giving, rare in the experience of children, but necessary for growth in grace. The experience of giving must be made more gratifying than that of keeping or receiving.

Teachers will study individuals to make sure each one knows what it is to give of his own. Primaries and Juniors should receive allowances and be trained to tithe and spend their money wisely. Children learn the value of money by being included in the family's financial conferences, and discussing together which items shall be maintained in a limited budget and which must be curtailed.

If children contribute regularly to the Lord's work out of their own money they feel they are giving to Him much more personally than when the money is their father's carried by proxy. Juniors enjoy keeping records of all money received and spent, and, looking back over past months' expenditures, can learn to judge which items were foolish and which will count for eternity.

Specific Needs. Children are never tempted to spend their church offering on the way to Sunday School if they feel an urgent need in the Lord's work. But many who bring their father's money as a peremptory duty would spend it on themselves if the opportunity presented itself. One small boy who hung behind after Bible school was found to be waiting for more Sunday School papers; he usually brought a penny to church, but this Sunday he had brought five cents and expected five papers, because he had the idea that the money was to pay for the literature given out.

Children fail to respond to general calls, but will heartily endorse definite needs which touch their hearts. Speaking to them at length about India's sinful darkness will leave them untouched, but present to them little "Preeta," who has never heard of Jesus, acquaint them with one specific Indian child who is different from them but nevertheless lovable, and they will slight their own church offering to give her every nickel and dime they can get.

The boys and girls in one church helped send their friend Tim to Japan as a missionary. Very regularly did they save their money that he might have what he needed. One summer in vacation school the leader told a story describing graphically the need of a boy in China, and at the end asked if they would not like to broaden their missionary interest to include the Chinese boy. A few of them voted for him, but most of them couldn't think of "letting Tim down," as they expressed it.

When children study a foreign country they should correspond with missionaries for pictures, curios, accurate information, and present needs. One Beginner department is building an African hut so that black children their own age can go to the Christian school that now accommodates only older children.

Nursery tots may not comprehend needs outside their own narrow world, but they can help pay for their favorite picture books, and give flowers or other tokens of appreciation to the teacher who plays the piano for them. After an appeal is made to children for a certain purpose, the happiness resulting from their gifts should be faithfully reported to them.

The offering needs to be closely associated with the Lord. There are the intangible gifts of love and trust and devotion and prayer which we can give personally to Christ, but material things go to others in His name, for He said, "Inasmuch as ye have done it unto one of the least of these my brethren, ye have done it unto me."

Depositing and Dedicating the Offering. The money may be gathered by each class, by ushers, by marching around the room to put in one's own, and by putting it in baskets by the door. The latter method prevents the dropping of money on the floor at a crucial point in the worship service, but care should be taken lest some of the boys and girls get the impression that they "pay as they enter," as they do at secular affairs.

To prevent wrong impressions an attractive offering center may be arranged not too close to the door. It might be merely a picture of children depositing their money, or it might be more elaborate with a picture of the local church beside the container for local expenses, a picture of the group's missionary undertaking beside the missionary basket, and between them a Bible verse, such as I Chronicles 16:29: "Give unto the Lord the glory due unto his name: bring an offering, and come before him: worship the Lord in the beauty of holiness."

Whether the offering is gathered before the session or not, it should be dedicated during the worship service, for it is in truth a genuine act of worship if the giver's heart is in his gift. Scripture verses, Scripture responses, song, prayer, or poem may be used. A most appropriate poem or song for Primary and Junior children is:

We bring our gifts to Thee;
Oh, may they useful be!
Help us to give the greatest gift,
Ourselves, O Lord, to Thee.

THE ELEMENT OF FELLOWSHIP

Welcomes and birthdays are justified if simple, brief, and spiritual, for an uplifting atmosphere of cordial Christian fellowship should pervade all the activities of the Bible school.

New Members and Visitors. The new member and visitor may be welcomed most warmly and made to feel at home in the group without being made too conspicuous. The timid child needs his attention drawn away from himself to interesting activities which help him forget himself. The forward child loves attention, but may act very willfully before the end of the session if he is allowed to feel too important.

When children return after illness, or when some special event takes place, emphasize God's part, to provide motivation for genuine worship.

A beloved grandmother was one Sunday visiting a Beginner child and came to church with her. When they reached the Beginner room the child could not think of leaving her grandmother, and suggested that she attend the grandmother's class. Instead, the teacher invited Grandmother to stay in the Beginner room. What fun that whole group had with Grandmother! She became the center of all they did that hour. They sang songs for her, told her Bible stories, and prayed for her. Grandmother told them how she used to go to church when she was a little girl, and the Bible story which was her favorite. The children's lavish attentions did not hurt Grandmother at all; for weeks the children talked about the good time they had had.

Celebrating Birthdays. Too often precious Bible school time is wasted by a monotonous celebration of birthdays. To children in the lower departments birthdays are red-letter days above all others, for no other day, not even Christmas, belongs solely to each child individually. As teachers we have an opportunity to show personal interest and to encourage a new step in growth.

Birthdays, however, should not too often intrude on a Sunday School period which is all too short at best. To justify their place birthday celebrations must be spiritual, and not a duplication of activities found in the home.

For Primary and Junior pupils, the Bible verse, "Jesus increased in wisdom and stature, and in favor with God and man," may be called the birthday verse, and its meaning be translated into practical terms on each birthday Sunday. The birthday children are surely growing taller—perhaps they can tell you how many inches they grew during the past year. They are growing wiser—they may recall one important thing they learned in the past year. How are they growing more pleasing to God and man?

A vegetable that has grown out of its normal shape in one

direction may be brought in as an illustration. The pupils do not want lopsided growth, with less concern for growth in grace and in the knowledge of our Lord and Saviour Jesus Christ, when the human being is composed of three parts—body, mind, and spirit. They may discuss what they want to do for the Lord this new year, now that they are a whole year older. They may like to choose what special duty they wish to assume in connection with their department, such as being responsible for the bulletin board, welcoming visitors and new members, or being secretary for a month.

The whole group rejoices with those who have acquired a second birthday within the past year, for they have been born into the family of God as well as into their earthly family. Sometimes the little tract entitled "Two Birthdays" is given children who are not yet saved.

A birthday committee of teachers may be appointed for the younger children, while a committee of Juniors likes to work out its own service under supervision. Primaries and Juniors can wait to celebrate all the birthdays of each month on the middle Sunday so as to be near the largest number possible. But a month seems like such an eternal age to Beginners that their observances are warranted every Sunday. And there is more time for them because younger children need a change of activity every few minutes.

Let the home give the child his cake and gifts, but let the church give spiritual significance to the day of his birth. One type of celebration is a birthday calendar for each month, with an attractive picture and the dates marked for each birthday child. A pretty seal is given him to paste on his date, and on the seal is his Bible verse for the new year. The teacher first reads it to him, the group discusses it, and the birthday child then reads it. Juniors can make their own calendar posters.

The lighting of candles makes an impressive ceremony. Some schools use a large candelabrum and others light small candles from a large one representing the Lord Jesus. If the symbolism of light is mentioned it should be expressly carried over into daily life. For instance, before a child blows out his candle, he may think what he is going to do this week or month to show he loves the Lord. Older pupils often consider it babyish to receive cards or bring birthday money, but truly appreciate recognition as a part of the regular worship service, as singing with the group, "Just as I am, young, strong, and free," or performing services of honor, like ushering or reading Scripture.

It has been discovered that children often believe that they are requested to bring birthday pennies to pay for the card or candle they receive. What should be their motive for bringing a special birthday offering? To say "Thank You" to God for His love and care through the years. It is rewarding to see them put in as many pennies as their years, and then a coin or two extra, saying, "This is extra for the Lord," or "He's been so good to me!"

Birthday offerings are certainly not the only offering that should be given to missions, although they may well go for that cause. Closely related to saying "Thank You" to God for love and care is the sending of birthday money to an orphan's home where live the children deprived of the homes and fathers and mothers that most children enjoy. The following prayer emphasizes the thought of God's care through the years:

We thank Thee, heavenly Father,
  For all the loving care
That Thou hast given *Donald*,
  At home and everywhere.
For *seven* years Thou hast guarded him,
  Asleep, at work, at play.

O Father, love and care for him
On this and every day.

1. Describe three or four contrasting kinds of atmosphere or emotional climate which you have experienced at some time in your life, and explain what effect they had on you. How important is the atmosphere in which any growing thing lives?
2. Describe a class session when God showed Himself real in an unexpected manner. Describe a class session when the children's needs and interests led in an unexpected manner.
3. Study your Bible school hour to see if anything seems to be done merely as a form without meaning or reality. In which part of the worship service does God seem nearest?
4. What are the hindrances to real worship that you encounter in your school? If you cannot discover how these can be overcome, keep seeking the Lord in prayer, and discuss the problems with other teachers who are interested.
5. Pretend you are a missionary. Write a letter home from the mission station to a group of boys and girls who have sent you a gift of money to share in your work. According to the age of the children, consider the length of the letter, the children's interest and vocabulary, and specific information about one phase of the work rather than general statements which mean little. Tell them how you have used their money to buy something that figures in their lives. A graphic picture with local coloring may be so vivid to them that definite missionary vision will date from such a letter.

CHAPTER XIV

MUSIC

1. What kind of music do you use when you worship spontaneously at odd moments during the day? How does this music affect your thoughts of God?
2. As a child, were you brought up on the grand old hymns of the church which constitute one of the Christian's most priceless possessions? If not, how do you feel about having missed this heritage of the people of God? If so, did you understand and appreciate all you sang? Did all of them meet your spiritual needs at the time?
3. Ask several children which Bible school songs mean the most to them. Analyze their responses as to which songs aid their spiritual experiences.
4. Have you noted any misuse of music with children?

VALUES OF MUSIC

It was by means of a children's hymn that God was pleased to save the mother of Gipsy Smith the evangelist, through whom was wrought the salvation of her husband, his brothers, and their families.

> When the family was traveling in Hertfordshire, the village doctor found that the eldest daughter had smallpox, and ordered the gipsy wagon out of town at once. He sent them to a by-lane

a mile and a half away, where the father erected their tent. The wagon was the sickroom and the father the nurse. In a few days brother Ezekiel also came down with the dreaded disease. The worst came when the mother also succumbed.

The father was in great distress. He felt that all hope was gone, and knowing that he could no longer keep the family separate, brought the wagon back to the tent. Both parents seemed to realize that the mother was dying. The father asked her if she thought of God and if she tried to pray. She answered that she was trying, but it seemed as if a black hand came before her, showed her all she had done, and something whispered, "There is no mercy for you!"

Many years before, the father had once heard the gospel faithfully proclaimed and his heart had been stirred, but there was no light. He could not read, none of his friends could read, and there was no one to whom he could go for instruction and guidance. After he had told her all he knew of the gospel, he went outside, stood behind the wagon, and wept bitterly.

While he was weeping, he heard her sing:

> I have a Father in the promised land,
> My God calls me, I must go
> To meet Him in the promised land.

He hurried back to her and said, "My dear, where did you learn that song?" She told him that when she was a little girl, her father had pitched their tents one Sunday on a village green, and seeing the people go into the chapel, she had followed them in and they sang those words.

It had been twenty years or so since she had heard the lines. Although she had forgotten them all those years, in her moments of intense seeking after God and His salvation, the Holy Spirit brought them to mind. She had lived in a religious darkness that was all but unbroken during her whole life, but a ray of light had crept into her soul when she was a little girl, by the singing of this hymn. She could not read the Bible; she had never been taught about God and His Son; but these words came back to her in her dying moments and she sang them again and again. Turning to her huband, she said, "I am not afraid to die now. I feel that it will be all right. I feel assured that God will take care of my children." [23]

Says Amy Wilson Carmichael concerning the ministry of song:

> There is something immortal in the seeds of song. One evening, after Kohila had begun her nurse's training, we were walking along the waterside when a young man came up shyly. "Do you remember me?" he asked. "I used to come to the children's meetings under the tamarind tree." He chanted text after text and sang song after song. And I marveled afresh at the power of life in the merest thistledown of song, and more and more we set words of eternal import to any simple tune we could find and committed our needs to the winds of God.[24]

Since worship is primarily a matter of heart response, and since music is the language of inner feeling, gospel hymns are one of the best means of expression in worship. Music also creates atmosphere, directs thoughts Godward, brings to mind and emphasizes spiritual truth, rouses to right action, and unites a group in bonds of Christian fellowship.

STANDARDS FOR THE CHOICE OF SONGS

Of course, not all songs used in Bible schools are equally effective in accomplishing the above purposes. Neither young nor old are ushered into the presence of God on the wave of a cheap, trashy tune. Should not a song about the Lord or addressed to Him be worthy of His transcendent attributes, with dignity suited to the maturity of the group?

In the public school pupils are being trained to interpret

the various kinds of music; some pieces tell them to run or skip or hop for relaxation and exercise of large muscles, some are soft lullabies to induce rest, while others are for appreciation, perhaps of waterfalls or fairies. Do we want the children to get the impression that their Bible school songs are the same type as music for skipping?

But children's hymns and children's choruses which meet the standards have their place, but adult hymns and adult choruses are not children's songs unless they measure up to certain requirements. Children's hymns are most appropriate for Sunday morning in the house of the Lord, children's choruses for afternoon and evening meetings, many times held in homes. Children's hymns are not necessarily solemn and sedate—they should have a decided rhythm and strong melody. We are glad to find adult hymns that are simple enough for children, for we want them to know the time-tested old classics as soon as they can appreciate them, and be able to join with the congregation in regular services.

"But the children like the catchy choruses," some teacher may answer, "and they don't like the more dignified hymns." Have the children ever had a chance to learn the more dignified hymns—children's hymns, not adult hymns? Children are born with unspoiled tastes; it is not with maturity but with training that they acquire a love for the best. If they have been brought up on a diet of candy they will not immediately be hungry for a diet of vegetables, but even so can gradually be trained to prefer what is more nourishing. Through the songs that we choose for them we are molding their tastes and characterizing the person of the Lord.

Requisites for the Words. 1. Can the pupils enter into the experience and truly mean the words? By what snatches of song do children spontaneously express themselves? What kind of songs do they compose under skillful guidance? Would that more teachers were able to help them make their own! A song should express what children feel constrained to say, but lack the ability to say. A phrase which is emphasized in Bible school, like "Believe on the Lord Jesus Christ," is likely to be chanted and sung over and over at home during the week.

Scripture clearly teaches the uselessness and vanity of singing which is not intelligent and heartfelt:

> God is the King of all the earth: sing ye praises with understanding.—Psalm 47:7.
>
> All the earth shall worship thee, and shall sing unto thee; they shall sing to thy name. Selah.—Psalm 66:4.
>
> I will sing with the spirit, and I will sing with the understanding also.—I Corinthians 14:15.
>
> Speaking to yourselves in psalms and hymns and spiritual songs, singing and making melody in your heart to the Lord.—Ephesians 5:19.
>
> Let the word of Christ dwell in you richly; in all wisdom teaching and admonishing one another with psalms and hymns and spiritual songs, singing with grace in your hearts unto God.—Colossians 3:16, R.V.

Tragic rather than humorous are the stories of children who merely sing words instead of worshiping through their songs.

> A new member of a Primary department tried to sing with the others, " 'Tis Love Brings Us Here," but she thought they were singing, "Mrs. Love brings us here." A woman named Mrs. Love lived next door to her, and she knew that Mrs. Love had not brought her to Sunday School. She looked up at her teacher and said, "Mrs. Love doesn't bring me here. My daddy does."
>
> Several years ago a certain class of Primary boys showed particular fondness for the song, "I come to the garden alone,

while the dew is still on the roses," etc. The teacher was puzzled until one of them asked, "Why don't we have a song about Amos, too? Every Sunday we sing about Andy but never say a word about Amos." Then the teacher realized that those boys were singing, "Andy walks with me, Andy talks with me, Andy tells me I am his own."

If, however, the pupils truly enter into the experience of the words, we can expect the Spirit of God to bring a song to their remembrance during the week when they need it. Testimonies such as the following by a young woman should be more common than they are:

> I remember one night during my childhood a thunderstorm woke me up. Mother and Dad were sleeping upstairs, and I was all alone downstairs. The loud claps of thunder and bright flashes of lightning frightened me. All of a sudden I began to sing to myself the song, "Be not dismayed whate'er betide, God will take care of you." It gave me the assurance that God was watching over me, and soon I fell asleep again.

2. Are the children's experiences expressed in children's language? Children's unpremeditated bursts of song are simple, direct, and concrete. Such is the following by a young shut-in, the first half being in a minor key, the last half in joyous major:

> Oh, I'll never see the sun again,
> For I'm a little shut-in.
> But since I have Christ Jesus as my Saviour,
> The sun comes in every crack!

A young girl came home from Sunday School singing, "This Little Light of Mine," and seemed to enjoy it very much. Her mother asked her what the song meant and why she liked it so much. She said she liked the motions, but didn't know what it meant. The mother suggested that since she had learned it in Sunday School it must be about the Lord, but the child disagreed. "No," she said, "it's only about my candle." The mother then proceeded to explain to her what the song really did mean. The child's answer should strike deep into the heart of every parent and teacher. There was distress on her face as she said, "Well, if that's what it means, why doesn't it say what it means?" Yes, Teacher, why don't children's songs say to them what they mean?

The children's own Bible memory verses set to music are especially valuable, for the melody enhances the beauty of a thought which should be rich in meaning for them, and which the Lord has promised to bless. The first personal pronoun is helpful, for the thought of the words is then made individual.

3. Do the words have spiritual value, with definite Bible teaching, worthy of precious Bible school time? Analyzing carefully the content of the songs in children's songbooks, one finds numbers like "Climb, Climb Up Sunshine Mountain," which have no spiritual message for literal-minded boys and girls. Even some like "One Door and Only One" are not clear and complete in themselves, but require accompanying teaching, which is often neglected.

A few songs for children are inaccurate Biblically. "Why Do Bells for Christmas Ring?" is an excellent song except that "a lovely shining star" was not "seen by shepherds from afar." If "wise men" are substituted for "shepherds," they then follow the star to the manger—which also is incorrect.

When children are taught that the Lord answers all prayers which are brought sincerely in Jesus' name, why should they then ask the Lord to hear them, and sing as a prayer response, "*Hear* our prayer, O Lord"? Rather,

We are glad that Thou *hast heard* us,
For in Jesus' name we pray;
We are glad that Thou wilt answer,
Answer in Thine own best way.

4. Do the words have literary and artistic merit? Are the words artistic poems in themselves, or must the music cover their defects? The simplest forms of art are often the hardest to achieve. Many adults who attempt to compose children's songs are unable to limit the experiences of the songs to the children's narrow world, to limit the vocabulary to their few terms, and to limit expression in general to their literal and concrete mode of thinking. If they do, the result is often insipid, whereas the children deserve character and beauty. If any teacher or parent who is poetically inclined knows children, as well as the Lord and His Word, may he yield himself to the Lord for the task of creating songs, for they are sorely needed.

5. Do the words meet the present spiritual need of the group? Do they reinforce and help the children interpret and express the activities in which they are now engaged? Do they have a natural place in whatever is the absorbing interest?

Requisites for the Music. 1. Does the music fit the words? In other words, is there what is called "truth in music"? Teacher or children should be able to tell from listening to the music alone what type it is, whether it is a joyous praise song, a quiet prayer hymn, or a challenge to vigorous Christian living. Is the general tone of the music the same as that of the words? Does the melody grow high or low, loud or soft, fast or slow, according to the thought? Is the emphasis placed on the important words, or is the thought broken by holding a word which should not be stressed? For example, "God loves you, God loves me, God loves all—things that be." In the middle of one song of thanksgiving, the phrase, "Thank You," is repeated three times. The music so fits the words that the pupils can readily pick out the places where those "Thank You's" are repeated. When they sing, "As the heavens are higher than the earth," truth in music requires that the music go up on the word "higher."

2. Is the music easy enough for the children to sing alone with joy and freedom? Many songs used in the Bible school are carried along by the piano and the song leader and the most musical pupils, with slight participation by the children who need it most. Not until a song is very familiar can one use it to worship and take it home to continue its ministry during the week when real temptations arise, and to witness to family and friends. Songs for children should not be too fast or too long, nor have many slurs or difficult intervals.

Alvin was a Beginner whose parents made it impossible for him to attend Bible school regularly. He enjoyed singing, but had not used the songs enough to know them well. One Sunday when the group was singing, "Jesus loves the little children, all the children of the world," he was disappointed because he was always too slow to sing the colors of those children whom God loves. He asked the children to sing it again so that he could get in the colors. He didn't sing at all in the first of the song in order to be ready for the part he was especially interested in. Before the others reached that point he took a deep breath and blurted out, "Red and yellow, black and white," gave a sigh of relief that he had accomplished this feat, and relaxed in comfort as the group finished the song.

3. Is the music worthy of the spiritual content of the words, and will it help the children cultivate a taste for the

best? On their own level, does the music unconsciously tell them that the things of God are above the things of earth, yet reach down to human life as it is being lived, to enrich it and lift it heavenward? Some of the simple melodies of the great masters have been set to words and are appropriate for children, as, for instance, the "Bethlehem Lullaby," arranged from Brahms' "Lullaby." If the words are distinctly spiritual, but the music is not, children may have accurate ideas about the Lord, but inadequate feelings toward them.

4. Is the melody within range of the children's voices? Is it written on the staff without tones going higher? The teacher with an alto voice finds herself in a quandary, for she realizes that the children should sing high rather than low on the staff. Sometimes a child with an ear for music can take the lead instead.

Adapting Certain Songs. Only a few songs for young children have passed the test of consistent blessing through the years, notably such as, "Jesus Loves Me, This I Know," "Praise Him, Praise Him, All Ye Little Children," and "Jesus, Friend of Little Children." Primaries as well as Beginners would profit more by these true children's hymns if only another word were substituted for the word "little." Primaries realize how fast they are growing up, and do not consider themselves "little children." They like to sing, "Praise Him, Praise Him, All Ye *Happy* Children," and "Jesus, Friend of *All* the Children."

When children sing "The B-I-B-L-E," ask them what they think is meant by the words, "I stand alone on the Word of God." Very few of them have ever thought about those words. When they do, they naturally are amazed that it seems to say to put the Book on the floor and stand on it, and either look or say, "But we don't do that!" No, of course we don't; yet if they think abut the words, that is what is conveyed to literal-minded boys and girls. This song may be adapted as follows, "The B-I-B-L-E, the Book God gave to me, to tell me of His wondrous love, the B-I-B-L-E."

A few hymns which adults regularly use are also suitable for children as young as Primaries: "Jesus Loves Even Me," "Do You Wonder Why It Is I Love Him?" and "Saviour, Like a Shepherd Lead Us," if a unit on shepherd life is being taught. When children this age worship in an assembly with adults, why not at least occasionally choose songs which both adults and children can use to worship?

Such selections may be improved by adding children's stanzas to some of the hymns in which the music and a refrain may be appreciated by children. Out of their own experiences Juniors may compose a stanza or two for "God Will Take Care of You." Primaries enjoy the following extra stanzas for the beloved song, "May Jesus Christ Be Praised":

On ev'ry holy Lord's day
I bow my head and pray,
"May Jesus Christ be praised";
At home the whole week long
These words are still my song,
"May Jesus Christ be praised."

To Him I will be true
Each day my whole life through,
May Jesus Christ be praised.
His Word I will obey,
I'll work for Him today,
May Jesus Christ be praised.

When the boys and girls get older, they will learn grown-up stanzas for this hymn, but at present they can sing a couple of stanzas written for them. When they worship with adults, they can sing their stanzas, then adults can sing the regular stanzas.

WHO LEADS THE SINGING?

In an informal session where children are free to worship and sing and pray spontaneously as their hearts are moved, the children themselves and the teacher will start songs at odd moments without thought of a piano. In many Nursery and Beginner rooms the piano is never used for singing, but only for rhythms. Young children can match human voices much better than they can match the music which drowns out their weak attempts until neither they nor the teachers can have the joy of hearing them sing.

A Song Leader? Even in a formal worship service of a large Junior or Primary department few superintendents want a song leader. A song leader who conducts a song service is usually a musician who knows more about music than he knows about children. He is accustomed to conducting music for older people, and may train the children to sing accurately and effectively as a chorus, but seldom uses the element of music to build up a progressive worship experience.

Even in a large department the children's interests and reactions should point the direction the worship service is to take. Music is woven intrinsically into the other elements whenever it contributes to the theme. The superintendent who has his finger on the pulse of the group has in mind the songs which fit into the theme of the unit, but he cannot always predict the order or moment in which they will be needed. It would be very awkward for the superintendent to step in and out of leadership whenever a song is needed in order that a song leader might lead it.

The Pianist. When a piano is used, the piano should lead the children's singing rather than the superintendent. It creates the atmosphere, regulates the tempo to a large extent, and determines the quality of the singing. Would a superintendent rather have for his pianist an expert who comes in only for the music, or one of his own teachers who plays fairly well?

What should be your qualifications, pianist?

1. *Tune your soul to the mood of the service.* Since you are one of the important leaders in the department, you will either advance or hinder the aims of the superintendent. You must be truly worshiping along with the group if you are to direct their expression of it. Even the posture of your body and the expression on your face, as well as the tone of your notes, will speak to the pupils and suggest imitation. Some musicians who might be available often lack an understanding of children. A teacher in the department is much more qualified in this respect than any outsider.

You should be at hand as soon as the first pupils arrive, in case they wish to learn a new song, or sing an old one, or practice as a choir.

2. *Play notes and time accurately and with assurance.* Is a teacher in the department satisfactory as a pianist even if he does not play well? No. Of what use is the teacher's responsive mood if she is unable to express that mood—if he limps along striking discords and missing the time? The feeling in his soul must be adequately expressed through his fingers.

3. *Subordinate the harmony so that the melody is not clouded.* The pianist need not be a fancy player; a fancy player would defeat the purpose of music. An accomplished pianist may be tempted to show off his skill, just as a soloist has the tendency to sing for the children instead of leading them. The ideal pianist plays clearly and with a light touch the octave in which the children sing.

4. *Be familiar with the leader's plans, and be ready to be led by the Spirit of God.* Be so familiar with any song which

might be needed that you can turn immediately to the page, or begin to play softly a preparation for prayer by the mere signal of a nod from the superintendent. The most valuable pianists are so in tune with the spirit of a service that they are ready with a more appropriate song than the one planned if a discussion or a speaker takes an unexpected turn.

VARIATIONS POSSIBLE WITH PARTICULAR SONGS

Study each song's distinctive nature to discover its peculiar inherent possibilities.

1. *Give the occasion of the writing of a song, or an example of the way the Lord has used it.* Incidents which have happened to children or to members of your own church are more personal and effective than those which you read.

> Years ago in Indiana lived a man who had not been inside a church for seven years. One Sunday evening he took his children to a meeting. Nothing that was said or done interested him until "Jesus Loves Even Me" was sung at the close of the service. On his way home, in bed that night, the first thing in the morning, and working in the field the next day, he could think of nothing else. Could it be possible that Jesus loved a sinner like him? His eyes were so blinded with tears that he could not see to go on with his work. Out in the lovely field, all by himself, the man accepted Christ as his Saviour.[25]

2. *Make from the words a short story using synonyms in case there are unfamiliar words.*

> Alice went home from church one Sunday so glad in the Lord that she sang as she set the table for dinner, "Oh, how I love Jesus!" She was the only Christian in her home. Her mother and sisters in the kitchen were quarreling and talking crossly to each other as they prepared the food. They heard

Alice singing happily about Jesus, and noticed how sweetly she did anything they asked her to do. One of her sisters said aloud, "I wonder why she loves Jesus so much."

Alice answered, "Do you wonder why it is I love Him? I will gladly tell you why. It's because He left His home in *heaven* to die for me. That is why I cannot help but love Him." And she went on with her work singing this song that showed how she felt: "Do you wonder why it is I love Him—"

3. *Use two or three distinct variations in tone.* When Beginner pupils graduate into the Primary department they take along with them their beloved song, "Praise Him, Praise Him," but, as Primaries, they bow their heads and sing softly when they come to the phrase, "God is love." This keeps an old song from losing the meaning of the words. Whenever a phrase of a song is repeated, the first phrase may often be sung softly, the next a bit louder, and the next with full tones. Such a song is:

O come and let us worship,
O come and let us worship,
O come and let us worship
Christ the Lord.

4. *Illustrate the thoughts by a picture folder.* When a song is expressed graphically in word pictures, collect illustrations for each phrase and bind them into a picture folder or mount them on a long strip of construction paper with folds like an accordion. Songs especially good for this use are "All Things Bright and Beautiful," "Fairest Lord Jesus," and "The Bible Is the Best Book."

5. *Adapt songs to fit special occasions.* Very flexible is a song which ends, "Thank You, God, for everything." For the final word may be substituted some of the specific blessings which are expressed in two syllables or less, as "Thank You,

God, for mothers dear," "Thank You, God, for Jesus Christ," or, omitting also the word "God," "Thank You for the Bible true." For Mother's Day, Primaries may talk about God's gift of mothers, and sing to the tune of "Jesus Loves Me, This I Know":

Mother loves me, this I know,
For she often tells me so,
With a gentle word and smile,
Mother loves me all the while.

Yes, Mother loves me,
Yes, Mother loves me,
Yes, Mother loves me,
And how I love her, too!

6. *Use simple motions if they are natural,* but they must reinforce the practical meaning of the song rather than detract from it. Most motion songs are more valuable for physical relaxation than for spiritual worship. When children make the motions of fishing for fish as they sing, "I will make you fishers of men," the motions reinforce the symbol, which they usually do not comprehend, rather than the spiritual message for which the song was written.

Contrast this type of motion song with the following that children themselves initiated:

How strong and sweet my Father's care (point upward),
That round about me like the air (turn around in place)
Is with me always, everywhere (spread arms wide to the side),
He cares for me (point to oneself).

7. *Use spiritual values to interpret instrumental music.* Juniors can study Wagner's "Pilgrim's Chorus" in connection with Psalm 121, decide when and how to quote the verses of

the psalm as the music is being rendered, and all take up the hymn of praise at the end, perhaps composing their own words.

After hearing very briefly the story of the sick boy whom Jesus made well, Nursery tots like to walk around the room showing first how sad everyone was when the boy was sick. They walk slowly with drooping heads as the music sounds a sad minor. When the teacher says joyously, "Then Jesus made the boy well!" the music changes to a happy major. The children begin to hop and run to show how happy everyone became.

To the music of "Master, the Tempest is Raging," Beginners and Primaries like to express with their hands what happened to the Sea of Galilee. The pianist marks a strong contrast between the calm, smooth water at the beginning, then the storm developing fury, and, finally, the stilling of the angry waves after Jesus' rebuke. The children stretch out their arms to represent the surface of the water, and in time with the music show how small ripples grew higher and higher and higher, until they were rolling waves. At the climax the superintendent may say, "Jesus spoke to the raging billows, 'Peace, be still.' " Immediately the great waves drop, and the children smooth out the straight surface of the water.

8. *Encourage the boys and girls to compose their own songs*. When one begins a chant, help him finish it and sing it to the group. After a group has had particularly rich experience in connection with a Scripture verse, they will be ready to interpret it musically by giving it a melody.

In composing a tune the group first decides on the general mood of the words, whether the feeling should be low and sad and slow, as for the thought of being sorry for sin; light and high and happy, as for a praise song; or soft and slow and meditative, as for a prayer song.

Praise songs are probably easiest to try first. The children suggest several tunes for each phrase until they discover one which pleases them. Each phrase is combined with the preceding ones to make sure it fits into the whole. After the entire melody is written on paper, it is well to have a person who writes harmony approve it before the children learn a tune which is incorrect musically.

TEACHING NEW SONGS

One reason for the prevalence of the modern jazzy chorus is that it can be readily *caught* by a group of children, whereas the more dignified children's hymn must be *taught* in order to be fully appreciated. Anyone who likes to sing can get a group to follow him on a catchy chorus, while a hymn requires a teacher who is willing to give himself to prayer and preparation. A truly beautiful song, whether it be hymn or chorus, only grows dearer with frequent repetition, and is destined to bring forth eternal results which will repay the teacher a thousandfold for his labor.

1. *Use few enough songs so that they will become well known and loved.* Can you worship while you are busy reading the words and music of a new hymn which you never saw before? How well must you know it before you are free to use it for a spiritual purpose? Since it takes time really to teach a new song, a teacher will carefully study the selection of a few that he feels are the best possible songs to meet the particular needs of his group. It is more valuable to choose for a year ten or twelve good songs than to expose the children to a great many which will not become familiar enough for them to take home.

Solos are advisable only when there is not time to teach a correlated song, such as a song for a particular special event or a certain Bible story. In general, children themselves need to sing rather than listen to the best of singers.

2. *Never urge children to sing louder.* Why is it that leaders are so often heard urging groups to sing louder? "Come on now," they say, "you can do better than that! Sing it out!" These leaders realize that there is a lack somewhere, but are unable to analyze the difficulty. Singing loudly will cover up the deficiency, for the singing sounds better on the surface. But what is basically wrong? The children are not "singing out" because they have nothing inside to sing out. Rich, full tones result only from overflowing hearts—no mere artificial means can be substituted. A light tone is the true musical voice for children. Worship services must build up genuine spiritual feeling, and then songs must be chosen to express that feeling.

3. *Be sure the children are emotionally ready to make the words their own.* How can we expect boys and girls to acquire the habit of worshiping God through the ministry of song if we ask them to sing words which are contrary to their experience? Yet groups consisting of individuals with all kinds of backgrounds, unsaved as well as saved, are asked to sing words which are true only of believers. Any group can truly sing of the sacrifice and love of Jesus for mankind, but they cannot all sing of their love and sacrifice to Him. To do so is to teach a "form of godliness, denying the power thereof."

When songs are taught, they are sometimes taught in this manner: "This morning we are going to learn a new song. Here is the first line. Now you try it. This is the second line. Now it's your turn," etc. Drill has a definite place in any kind of memorization, but the purpose of drill is to fix permanently what has already been comprehended.

How pathetic to lead a group of children in singing ardent words like, "I am so glad that Jesus loves me," with hearts and minds unprepared to mean those words. The children need to discuss previously what wonderful things they see in the Bible, decide what is the one dearest thought in the whole Book, perhaps choose the three or four foreign words they would first want to learn if their parents were to go as missionaries to Africa and they would have to meet black boys and girls who had never heard of God's Word. They should try to visualize our world if Jesus had not loved them enough to die for their sin. They should realize how much they have done even in the past week to displease the Saviour, and how much He still loves them! Some will enjoy testifying how much they love Jesus because He first loved them. Then they will be ready to sing, "I am so glad that Jesus loves me." After the initial preparation of heart, a reminder may be sufficient, as, "Because God *so* loved us, and Christ *so* loved us, we are *so* glad."

A song is really taught when the pupils see the need for it, feel the import of what they sing, and when every phrase is surrounded with such a rich background of meaning that every time the song is used it will recall or express vital spiritual experiences. When the children want a certain type of song, it is often wise to give them a choice of two which would meet the need. Their decision requires reflection on the meaning and insures readiness for it.

4. *Usually introduce words and music together.* A song is a unit composed of both words and music, and should be used as a unit unless there is a specific reason for not doing so. According to the principle for any type of memorization, it should be introduced in a spiritual setting in a way in which it will meet a practical need.

5. *Usually teach one stanza at a time.* The whole may be introduced for appreciation, but young children especially need to know each stanza thoroughly before proceeding with the next.

6. *Let the children listen to a song several times before they try it.* Have you ever heard a song leader urge, "Come on!

Try it! It won't matter if you make a mistake"? Won't it? It is much easier to take time to prevent errors than to root them out after they have been made. When an error is practiced once, the tendency is to repeat it. Children need to listen to the song, but they will not listen passively. Unless they are engaged in activities to which the song relates, they will need a fresh incentive each time they listen.

a. The leader sings the song as it contributes to group activities, and as he builds up a background of appreciation.

b. Worship songs may be played for quiet music at the opening of the session.

c. The pupils listen to find the answer to some question, as, "How many times do you hear the word 'holy'?"

d. The children discover how Scripture songs differ from the exact Bible words. Phrases are sometimes repeated and sometimes omitted.

e. As the pianist plays each phrase separately, the pupils try to recall the words which belong with each phrase.

f. Playing they are a soft orchestra, they hum the melody as the leader sings the words.

g. They practice one short significant part first. That is their part, while the leader or soloist sings the longer and harder part of the song.

h. They listen to correct any error in pronunciation, rhythm, or interpretation. Dividing a group into "parts" keeps them alert if they have a tendency to loose singing.

AN EXAMPLE OF THE TEACHING OF A NEW SONG

For Primaries, "Jesus, Friend of *All* the children."

In the spring Primaries often hear the story of Jesus blessing the children, along with stories of Jesus helping people. They are then ready for a fresh attack on the problem of the definite way in which He will help them. They realize anew that He can do anything, that He always has time for the concerns of children, and that He is waiting to help them if they do their part. "What is their part?" becomes a very real question. They have tried and failed by their own efforts to do what they know is right.

As the group enters the Primary room on the Sunday morning after they have heard the story of Jesus and the children, they decide to assemble, or find already assembled by the teachers, the various artists' representations of that memorable event. They compare the pictures and note how differently the artists have conceived of the scene, and pick out the one which they prefer. One boy remarks, "Weren't those lucky kids who really saw Jesus when He was here on earth!" They are reminded of the song which expresses their feelings:

> I wish that His hands had been placed on my head,
> That His arms had been thrown around me,
> And that I might have seen His kind look as He said,
> "Let the little ones come unto me."

Another member of the group agrees that those children were surely lucky, but asks, "What about the children who didn't live where Jesus was in the Holy Land?" The teacher answers that only a few of the children then living on the earth saw Him, but that since He went back to heaven, He is a spirit and can be everywhere. On that day of old, He blessed all who came to Him, but not all came. Today He will bless any child who asks Him. A couple in the group bow their heads right at that moment and ask Him. The teacher continues, "Jesus died to be the Saviour of the whole world. But does everyone ask Him to be his Saviour? He wants to be the Friend of all children, but many children have never said to Him (sing the first two phrases of the new song),

Jesus, Friend of all the children,
Be a Friend to me."

Donald then relates how he asked the Lord to help him one day in school. His teacher had said that all who did their numbers exactly right could be in a little play. He bowed his head, and asked Jesus to help him get his numbers right; Jesus did help him and Donald was in the play.

As the teacher sings again the first two phrases of the song, someone asks if that is all of it, whereupon he sings the last two phrases of the first stanza,

Take my hand and ever keep me
Close to Thee.

Primaries are not yet ready for the concept of abiding in Christ as an indwelling presence, but they do imagine Him at their side.

As the teacher sings again, he asks the children if they could sing this song about any of their other friends, and they discuss how their parents cannot always be with them, friend policeman cannot always be at every street corner to help them across, friend doctor cannot always heal their sicknesses, and even the weather man can only predict the weather, not control it.

The teacher asks which word (in that first stanza) slides on two notes just as Jimmy did when he and his father were climbing a steep, slippery hill last month. Jimmy considered himself so grown up that he could climb the hill without holding his father's hand. Twice he slipped down before he was willing to grasp his father's strong hand. Even earthly fathers need to take the hand of the almighty heavenly Father or hard things will be too much for them.

"What do you like to do with your best boy friend,

George? What do you like to do, Jane, with your best girl friend? Would you ask a girl or boy to be your friend and then forget about him? Some people ask the Lord Jesus to be their friend and then forget about Him." "I won't!" comes a warm response from several pupils with the best of intentions, but with a short attention span.

"Do you really want to talk with your best Friend and listen to Him and go where He will go with you? When might you sing these words to Him?" Marion thinks that she knows them now, but she is warned that she should never sing them to Him unless she really means them. Those who want Him for their best Friend then bow their heads and for the first time sing the song directly to Him.

Dan remarks that when we put our hand in Jesus' hand we feel there the prints of the nails where He was wounded for us, and the group sings again, much sobered by that thought.

Use any comment which the children make on the subject of growing to introduce the second stanza at some later date.

> Teach me how to grow in goodness
> Daily as I grow;
> Thou hast been a child, and surely
> Thou dost know.

In the spring everything wants to grow. Children measure on the wall how much they have grown through the winter, they notice how small their clothes are getting; the onions in the vegetable bin are beginning to sprout, and the green shoots are beginning to come up out of doors.

In what ways are children growing? In what way does God especially want them to grow? Some children not in Bible school today are actually growing in badness instead of goodness. Find the largest boy and the smallest girl in the group. It is possible that the smallest girl is growing faster in goodness than the tallest boy. The children will like to hear the story of how God rejected tall, handsome King Saul in favor of the boy David, who pleased God.

How many days a week are the children growing taller? Only on Sunday? Will they have goodness to go along with their tallness if they grow toward God only on Sunday? Some boys who are strong in their bodies are only babies in goodness. The group may want to try to figure a way to measure their growth in goodness.

They perhaps decide to make booklets to take home to remind them how they can grow in goodness during the week —read the Bible, talk to the Lord at both regular and odd times, let Him help them to be unselfish and kind whether they feel like it or not, let Him tell them what they can do to help at home and at school, etc. They may copy the song in their books.

To imagine how the Boy Jesus "was tempted in all points like we are, yet without sin" (Heb. 4:15), they examine pictures of the town in which He lived, and the sort of things He would do. They conclude that no doubt He carried water from the village well when it was very hot and He was tired, took care of younger brothers and sisters, and asked His heavenly Father for help when He was doing something difficult in the carpenter shop.

Of course, the teacher repeats the song again and again informally as the activities proceed. In the future the children use the song whenever they feel the need of the Lord's help.

1. Why is music sometimes called "the thermometer of the spiritual life of the church"? Which songs do the pupils of your department enter into most fully? Why?

2. Classify the songs used in your department as to the form of address; whether they speak to God or to oneself or to other people or to things, etc. Can these various types be made more meaningful?

3. Have you ever known hymns to be used to fill in time, to cover distractions, to use available talent, to entertain and amuse and to continue a customary routine? Join in a dialogue with the leader who thinks the above purposes are legitimate, and try to persuade him that music in the Bible school should be employed for the loftier motives of expressing and inducing spiritual experience.

4. Rate from 0 to 9 the songs which are at present being used in your department, measuring them according to the standards outlined: five requisites for the words, and four requisites for the music. List ten songs for your age group which measure up to the standards in all particulars.

CHAPTER XV

PRAYER

1. What proportion of the time you use in preparation for your Bible school teaching do you think should be spent in prayer? Why does the practice of most teachers lag far behind their theory in this respect?
2. What is the result of asking a person to pray when he does not feel ready to approach the throne of grace? Why is it that children sometimes hesitate to lead in prayer?
3. Do you remember the first time you led a group in audible prayer? How old were you? What were the circumstances? What effect did it have on you?
4. Can you call to mind some prayers of good length which you followed closely to the end? Can you think of others which you had great difficulty following? What made the difference?

Christopher Dock, a most successful schoolmaster of the early American colonies, was a born teacher; his small book will always have a place in the history of American education, though he did not want it to be published.

> He said, "I have a great love for children, a grace from God, otherwise it would be a great burden among the scholars." . . . One day in the year 1771 he failed to return to his home. People investigated. They went to the school. There they found

him kneeling as in prayer. Before him was a list of the names of all his pupils. It had been his custom each evening after he sent his children home to take the school roll, kneel before it, and pray to God. He would pray that his injustice or neglect of any child might be forgiven; that on the new day to come he might do better for each and all. He never depended on himself. He always asked God to help him teach each child.[26]

When asked to report an outstanding incident from her childhood, one young person said:

> Soon after I was saved I went to camp at Maranatha, Michigan. A group of us children went for eight days with our pastor and his wife, who were young people. While there, one night we had a bonfire down by the shore of the lake. This was quite an event for us. When we were ready to go, we could not find our pastor's wife. As it was dark, the group decided to leave her behind, knowing she could easily find the way. A few of us girls stayed to look for her. We found her in the woods kneeling on the ground praying. We did not know what had brought her there to that quiet spot, but her nearness to God left a very deep impression upon my heart.

ESSENTIALS FOR VITAL PRAYER

Prayer in a children's session is all too often *by* the teachers and even *for* the teachers. The teachers' prayer meeting should be before the children's session, not during it. Paul's exhortation against speaking in an unknown tongue in I Corinthians 14 is just as applicable today in regard to young children. Teachers use vocabulary and ideas which are wholly outside their realm of experience, truly an unknown tongue to them. Paul says:

If I pray in an unknown tongue,
my spirit prayeth, but my understanding is unfruitful.

What is it then? I will pray with the spirit,
  and I will pray with the understanding also. . . .
Else when thou shalt bless with the spirit,
  how shall he that occupieth the room of the unlearned
  say Amen at thy giving of thanks,
  seeing he understandeth not what thou sayest?
For thou verily givest thanks well,
  but the other is not edified.
I thank my God, I speak with tongues more than ye all:
Yet in the church I had rather speak five words with my understanding,
  that by my voice I might teach others also,
  than ten thousand words in an unknown tongue (I Cor. 14:14-19).

Individual Participation. Since a child cannot analyze or tell many of his needs, he must learn to meet them by imitating the adults in his environment. Fortunate is that child who daily sees his parents and teachers, whenever faced by a difficulty, turning first to the loving heavenly Father. Not by precept but by example he should first learn that God always hears and always answers His children. The child who regularly hears prayer that is deeply in earnest, that humbly desires God's best way, and that is expressed simply and briefly, unconsciously absorbs the essential elements of vital prayer. That should be his introduction to the subject—it should be "caught" very early before it is "taught."

When the child comes to the next step, that of expressing his own personal prayer, he may have some questions to be answered. For, like salvation, prayer to be real must be each individual's own personal act, whether we are considering a group at church or one child alone at home.

A four-year-old was walking along the sidewalk of a strange city in which she was visiting relatives. Seeing a dog coming toward her, her first impulse was to cry, but she had already cultivated the habit of prayer in time of need. She sent up a quick call. As the dog approached her, it turned from the sidewalk, made a wide half circle around her, then returned to the walk and ran on.

Every child should have the privilege of many of these direct answers. When you lead a group of boys and girls in prayer, don't you often wish you might see as God sees what is happening in the inner recesses of each heart; or at least be sitting in a back seat, able to watch the outward postures? How many of the group are actually praying? How many are actually having fellowship with the Holy One? Were their hearts prepared beforehand? Was the atmosphere conducive to real prayer? Although a poem like the following may be used to advantage, it alone is not sufficient preparation of heart.

"We fold our hands that we may be
From all work and play set free.
We close our eyes that we may see
Nothing to take our thoughts from Thee.
We bow our heads as we draw near
The King of kings, our Saviour dear."

The Psychological Moment. Is it always the best policy to have prayer at the beginning of a worship service? Some teachers like to begin their class periods that way, discussing the intimate problems and victories of their small groups. But when a larger number gather for the opening worship, most of the pupils may feel in no mood for prayer, and it will not be real.

Since prayer is the very heart of worship, the closest approach to God, we cannot always predict the moment when the soul will be ready to have dealings with the Almighty. We may expect it after the story or at the solution of a problem, but an unforeseen event—and what children's session is not full of them?—may have much greater personal significance for the children than anything we teachers had planned. If the heightened feeling is crystallized at that moment by suggesting prayer, it will be real.

God will seem near if a group of boys and girls bow in prayer at odd moments whenever a conscious need is felt. For instance, small Jack in the Beginner department is annoying other children by shuffling his chair back and forth. The teacher remarks, "Something in you wants to sit quietly and something else wants to make noise, doesn't it?" Jack nods. "But God can make everything in you want to please Him. Let's ask Him to help." A sentence is all that is needed and the chair is entirely forgotten.

One morning during a Primary worship service in vacation school, the leader noticed that Rodney's eyes suddenly began to fill with tears. She said nothing until his grief began to attract the attention of the other children. Then Rodney explained that he had ridden his new bicycle to church that day, had locked it and put the key in his pocket. Now as he had put his hand in his pocket, he found that the key was gone! Of course, there was no further worshipful praise when he didn't know where his key was, nor for the other boys and girls when they knew it. But prayer was very real as they asked the Lord to help Rodney find the key; God knew everything and knew exactly where it was.

After Rodney had gone out with one teacher to search and inquire for the key, the group was then content to go on with the worship service. So busily engaged in activity were they that when Rodney later returned with the key, they hardly noticed him. But at the end of the morning, when it was time to leave, they joined him in thanking the Lord for His help.

Training in the Expression of Prayer. Those of us who started to pray aloud late in life are especially cognizant of the children's need to begin early to become accustomed to hearing their own voices and to become acquainted with the form of prayer. The preschool child in the Christian home talks to God as naturally as he talks to members of his family. Often he may be heard to stop and exclaim, with eyes open or closed, "Thank You, God," or perhaps a few more words about some good gift, such as, "That was a lovely sunset you gave us tonight!" At bedtime, when a child is sleepy, he cannot be expected to recall what happened during the day. It is no wonder that expression then is often forced and mechanical.

Should children be encouraged to use the words "Thee" and "Thou" in addressing God? If they hear them constantly in the home and hear Scripture read each day, they will soon be using these terms themselves. Children from unchurched homes stumble over them in their reading, and need explanation as to the reverence and honor shown to Deity. As soon as possible we want the children to use these terms, but natural spontaneity must never be sacrificed in favor of them. Prayer is the heart's sincere desire regardless of the expression. When attention is focused on the expression it may cease to be the heart's longing. It then degenerates into a form, with the heart left barren and cold.

How sad it would be to dampen the ardent spirit of the boy whose prayer follows, by criticizing the use of "You" and "Your."

"God who art in heaven,
I like to talk to You.
Most people call it praying,
But it's talking that I do.
I talk when I'm in trouble;

I tell You when I'm glad;
For though You don't need telling,
It helps me when I'm sad.
And You are always listening,
For You never turn away,
And when I need an answer,
You know just what to say.
Your voice is very quiet,
But I know it can be found.
I hear it like a whisper,
I feel it like a sound."

Prayer for Material Things. Guiding children into intimate communion with the living God may sometimes be attended with difficulties, but always with extraordinary thrills because of the natural faith and dependency of the younger generation. They naturally and reverently approach their Maker and Redeemer.

Prayer to be real to a child must express his personal needs and interests. Why, then, is it not natural for him to ask for the everyday things that he wants? We cannot expect the young child to be burdened with the spiritual problems that are on adult hearts. As he grows in grace, his requests will also mature. If we should leave his prayer life until he is ready to plead for the souls of men, we could not establish the habit at the formative age.

Moreover, God teaches His older as well as His younger children to ask for daily bread and for other temporal needs. And He does answer this kind of prayer for the children, although they often confuse "needs" with "wants." Many times a snowfall has arrived at their request, or a thunderstorm has abated.

But we encounter problems as we pray with the children for material things. Just as we wish them to feel that "Thou,

God, seest me," and yet is not a policeman spying out their misdeeds to punish them, so we want them to feel free to ask for anything that seems good to them, and yet not picture God as a glorified Santa showering down toys. They must sense the fact that only God knows what is best for us to have. Often they are told that their mother or teacher knows best when they cannot understand the reason for some refusal. They also need to kneel with Mother for requests that concern them both, and then leave the solution to God, for He knows better than Mother. He alone understands each of us perfectly, and sees the end from the beginning.

It is often deceiving to a child to be told that God always answers prayer, unless he understands that God has three answers—that "No" and "Wait" are as truly answers as "Yes." Polite human beings do not turn away without answering our questions; certainly the heavenly Father will do no less.

We may use with the boys and girls this simple illustration of God's answers to prayer. Suppose Mother is baking cookies when you come home from school. Of course, you want one, and how good it tastes! Then you ask for another. This time Mother's answer is, "Wait until suppertime." At supper you eat two more, and when you ask for the cookies to be passed again, Mother says, "No. Three is enough for one day." Even the small child can comprehend that the Mother who loves her baby will refuse him when he cries for the bright flames or a sharp knife.

One Junior group was asked to write on paper what prayer is. Some of the answers were discouraging. "It's asking God to make hard lessons easy." "It's asking God for something your father won't buy for you." "It's asking God to do something so you won't have to."

A wise teacher will discuss with individuals probable reasons why prayers are not answered with "Yes," as well as rejoice with them when their requests are granted. God desires us to pray so that we may learn to know Him, even more than to receive His good gifts. If He made everything easy for us, we would become weak softies instead of developing into strong, noble characters on whom He can depend, even in time of temptation. Often we think we are waiting for God to work, whereas He is waiting for us to be ready to receive what He is so eager to grant.

With the best of intentions, some parents discourage prayer for material things, but try to help Sonny form the habit of asking the Lord to make him a good boy. What effect does it have as a child continually asks God to make him good when he is fully aware of his shortcomings, and his prayer is not connected with particular matters of conduct? Soon he gets the impression that prayer is a mere form, followed to please his parents.

VARIETY IN THE FORM OF PRAYER

Using prayer in different ways and at different times during the Bible school session strengthens the concept that we may pray at any time, in any place, in any posture. If only one mode is used week after week, the boys and girls fail to think of talking to God under other circumstances.

Adults Leading. A simple test of any teacher's ability to reach a group of children on their own level is his skill in leading them in prayer, for of all parts of a session this demands genuine understanding and appreciation of each particular group. If he is to *lead* and not *leave* the pupils, he must express briefly and loudly the children's needs and interests in children's language.

One Sunday an honored guest was asked to lead in prayer a Primary group that was accustomed to entering fully into the experience of talking to God. He prayed in closing, "Keep these children under the shadow of Thy wings, in the hollow of Thy hand, and as the apple of Thine eye." The literal-minded boys and girls were much relieved to hear the familiar "Amen." They looked up at the superintendent with questions and exclamations written all over their faces, "Now whatever was *that* supposed to be?"

Much of children's apparent lack of reverence is mere honesty. They do not hypocritically assume the posture of prayer when they cannot follow the thought. It is sometimes wise to ask the pupils what we should say to God today, and use their words as well as their ideas.

Words Repeated After Adults. If the children are unfamiliar with the form of prayer and reticent about expressing their own thoughts, they may occasionally repeat the leader's words after him when group attitudes are unanimous and enthusiastic and definite. It is deliberately teaching hypocrisy to ask children to repeat words which are true only of the leader. This type of prayer should be prefaced by the sincere invitation, "Because we all feel this same way," or, "Because I think you feel as I do, wouldn't you like to repeat after me each part of this prayer?"

There is also a danger inherent in the phrasing of this type of prayer. The sentences tend either to grow too long or to be broken into fragments. If they are too long, the pupils will fall by the wayside before the end. By the time they are repeating the last of a sentence they will have forgotten the thought of the first part. If that long sentence is broken up, the continuity of the idea is destroyed. Each sentence or phrase should be short and complete in itself.

Rather than saying, "We thank Thee . . . that Thou art always with us . . . to tell us what to do . . . and to keep us from harm," lead thus: "Thou art always with us. We thank Thee. Tell us what to do. Keep us from harm."

Children Leading. Children should not be asked to pray aloud unless they feel deeply a real need and have at least one concrete idea to express. Then there will be no distracted self-consciousness and stumbling over words with the result that next time they will hesitate to try.

One young person recalls dread of prayer. She says:

> I always had a fear of going to Sunday School when I had a certain teacher who insisted upon each child in the class saying a sentence prayer. I was shy and dreaded having to pray before the group. I overcame this through another teacher who was understanding and sympathetic.

Another young person had a blessed experience. She says: "The first time I prayed in front of a group I became completely oblivious of anyone else's presence; it was just the Lord and I."

Although the needs which children feel may not be the needs which adults feel, if some of their family or friends are sick or in trouble, or a saved child's parents are yet unsaved, they are eager to keep going to the Lord and sharing the burden with their group.

After children have selected a picture of something for which they are grateful, it is easy and natural for them to thank the Lord for that one thing represented by the picture they are holding. Sometimes they make wishes about a certain person, and turn those wishes into prayers. Often a teacher may ask some question, as, "Has the Lord done something special for you this week?" or, "Is there someone in your family whom you are asking the Lord to save?" After a number have testified, suggest that those who mentioned one blessing or one person come to the front of the group and tell the Lord about it. "He is the One whom we should thank," or "He is the One who saves from sin."

If the children stand or sit in a line or circle there is no question as to whose turn it is. A mature child should head the line, for those who have had little experience in prayer will be inclined to imitate his free expression and natural tone of voice.

Directed Silent Prayer. The habit of "praying without ceasing" is most often the unuttered lifting of the soul to God in gratitude or longing. Silent prayer helps form the habit of intimate fellowship with God, but in a group it needs to be directed. It is especially appropriate at moments of deep concern as an expression of personal love or devotion or stewardship. When very personal matters are to be brought to the Lord no one else can say what one's own heart feels.

The teacher may say, "Wouldn't you like to tell the Lord how you feel when you think how much He loves you?" The leader pauses for silent prayer. "Would you like to tell Him how much you love Him?" Pause. "Ask Him what you can do this week because you love Him." Pause.

> Although we cannot see God,
> We feel that He is near;
> Although He does not speak aloud,
> We hear His voice so clear,
> Whenever all is hushed and still,
> Whenever we will do His will.

A soft musical prayer response played instead of sung may encourage silent prayer after audible prayer, and it also lends dignity to a worship service.

PRAYER POEMS

To say a prayer is not to pray
Unless I mean the words I say,
Unless I think to whom I speak,
And with all my heart His blessing seek.

Prayer poems are so easy to say, and so hard to pray. The child from a Christian home should have no need for the words of someone else, because his own words should always come freely. But for the child with no spiritual background it may initiate the habit of prayer, help him form his own, and enlarge his vision of prayer. Many a child who has never prayed before has taken a poem home from church and used it every night. Families have been saved as a result of a child's insisting on saying at table a simple grace which he has learned in Bible school.

We see the danger of prayer becoming only a mechanical, perfunctory repetition of words when we discover that many older adolescents when in trouble resort to the old, "Now I lay me," that they learned in childhood as the only way they know of talking to God. If a form prayer is given a child be sure that it expresses what he feels or is able to feel, and find him another as he grows and his needs change. Along with the form, he should be learning to know the Lord and to talk to Him directly. Soon the crutch will fall away from disuse.

Group Composition. For Primaries and Juniors, composing a group prayer under supervision is a study in the form of prayer. The children discuss how they begin a letter, and write a salutation on the blackboard, such as, "Dear Sally." How do people address the Lord God? They substitute various salutations for prayer, "Dear Lord," "Our Father," or "Heavenly Father."

The prayer proper usually consists of two parts—thanking the Lord for what He has already done, and asking Him for what we need. If the children suggest two sentences of praise and two of petition, they can first read the prayer together, and then pray it to the Lord.

If they word a sentence using the familiar second person "You," discuss why we say "Thee" and "Thou" when we talk to the great and holy Lord God who made the heavens and earth and all that is in them.

How does a letter end? How does a prayer end? If the children realize why prayers need to go to the Father "in Jesus' name," those words at the close will never become mere form.

Following is a group prayer which a Primary department composed on the Sunday before Children's Day:

> Dear heavenly Father,
> We are glad that we can speak Thy Word next Sunday.
> We are glad that we can be the choir.
> May many parents come.
> May they all want Jesus to be their Saviour.
> We pray in Jesus' name. Amen.

Bible Verses and Songs. Bible verses and songs addressed to God are prayers, and should be used as such. Many times during the week children may feel the reality of verses such as, "Teach me to do Thy will; for Thou art my God" (Ps. 143: 10), and "Thou, Lord, art good, and ready to forgive" (Ps. 86:5). Songs such as "Speak, Lord, Thy Servant Heareth" and "Saviour, Like a Shepherd Lead Us" encourage communion with God at home whenever they come to mind. If Juniors practice wording prayers from Bible verses it will be easy for them to turn Scripture into personal prayer for their daily devotions.

1. Recall the time in your experience when a group of children drew nearest to the Lord in prayer. What made that prayer especially real?
2. Recall some psychological moments for prayer which came quite unexpectedly. What determines the form which a prayer should take at a moment of heightened feeling?
3. Which pupil in your class is most reticent about volunteering to lead in prayer? Study his temperament, his home background, his needs, and suggest how and when he might feel most concerned about sharing his interests with the group.
4. Find or compose a prayer poem which expresses that child's needs and interests in his language.

CHAPTER XVI

SPECIAL DAYS

1. Can you recall any special day programs which you felt definitely helped the pupils grow in grace? Why were they helpful? What effect did they have on the parents?
2. Can you recall any special day programs which you felt were not planned with the children's needs in mind? What was the effect on those children?

> There are teachers who seem to regard the Sunday School curriculum as a series of programs connected by drills and rehearsals, and consider a good year's work accomplished if their children appear well at these public performances. No sooner is Rally Day over than plans are laid and songs rehearsed for Christmas; the Christmas tree has scarcely turned brown when Easter recitations are given out; nor have Easter lilies faded before Children's Day drill has commenced.[27]

Would you prefer to celebrate all the special days in your own department? How many times should the whole school meet together during the year?

The problem of special days, like those of attendance and discipline, is solved by a vital every-week program in each department. If there is sufficient prayer and preparation behind each session, the children will move their households to get to church, they will be challenged by fascinating activities, and will have many things to share with parents and friends for special days.

VALUES TO SCHOOL

If we consider the values of these special day programs, we shall know how often to plan them. In the first place, there is value in the whole Bible school's assembling for the sake of enthusiasm and a common purpose. Even the young child needs to see the whole of which he and his friends are a part. Although each department is working on its own level, with its own corps of leaders, yet all are working to show the unbelieving world outside what the saving grace of Christ can do by the Spirit through the Word. All have one pastor and one superintendent. These shepherds of the flock should have a personal interest in each individual child, and each child should *feel* that personal interest.

Special days have value for the school itself because they serve as a means of promotion, they call attention to its accomplishments, and they educate the adults in the importance of work with children. This adult education needs to be carried on continually. In most churches adults hear few Bible messages on the child text, although it is given in all three Synoptic Gospels. In many churches the Sunday School is expected not only to be self-supporting, but also to contribute largely to other needs; it is not valued as the chief harvest field and training ground of the church.

The adults, many of them, have little appreciation of the work that is being done with the young children. Otherwise, why are they so careless about walking through the children's room when the superintendent is trying to lead the pupils into the presence of the Lord? Why do they come to a children's program ready to laugh and be entertained by what the children will say and do?

VALUES TO CHURCH

In addition to instructing church officials as to the place of children in the total program, special days afford a valuable means of reaching unchurched parents. At every season of the year the children help win their parents, but all the parents will make a special effort to attend on Children's Day to see their Joan and Harry participate. Of course, if the program consists of pretty little nothings we cannot expect God to work in the children's hearts. But if the children speak the Word of God with understanding, God can bless His Word when *they* speak it exactly as much as He can when the pastor speaks it.

EFFECT ON CHILDREN

If special programs are to merit their place in the curriculum, however, their greatest benefit should be to the children themselves. It is a deplorable fact that in the past they often have had a harmful effect on the pupils instead of impressing on their minds the things of God. The results in their lives will depend entirely on the teacher's aim, what he is striving to attain by the program.

Is he trying to do something *for* the children, or is he trying to do something *with* the children? Is he trying to show off the little darlings, or is he trying to provide further spiritual experiences for them? If he is trying to show them off, he may work hard to secure a good presentation of pieces and songs which will entertain the adults. No matter how the children feel about the performance, no matter how tired and confused they become, they must be drilled and perhaps even exploited to show off to best advantage.

What is the effect of this kind of program on the forward

child? On the shy child? The aggressive child is in his element. He is smart enough to repeat whatever brings the comment, "How cute!" He learns selfishness and pride *in the Bible school.* The timid and plain child, on the other hand, shrinks farther back into his feeling of inferiority. It is to the praise of self and not to the glory of the Lord when children are trained to say words they do not understand, but which are intended only for the audience.

Special day programs will count in the lives of the boys and girls as well as in the curriculum of the school if they are made the culminating activity of their regular sessions.

THE CHILD'S CALENDAR

A child's year is marked not by months, but by special occasions which have a personal bearing on his life. It is our privilege to see that the child senses the Lord's part in these events. On his birthday we may well emphasize the fact that some people have only one birthday, while others have two! Some have been born into God's family as well as into their earthly homes.

Thanksgiving, Christmas, and Easter form the basis for the Bible school curriculum for young children, and cannot receive too great stress if we are to counteract the commercial attractions of the world. We can depend on the public school to lay a foundation of the historical significance of the first Thanksgiving. Building on that a sense of deeper gratitude, we can help the pupils find satisfying means of expressing their praise. In spite of the thrill of material gifts and the tinsel and glitter of Christmas—and a child naturally loves the concrete—yet the celebrations of Jesus' birthday can be made so attractive in the Bible school that seldom will Santa be mentioned, even by the children from the most worldly homes. Likewise, neither bunnies and eggs nor the awakening world can vie with the glory of the risen Saviour at Easter.

On Valentine's Day the red heart can be made the basis for very effective teaching. We can use paper hearts on which are written the greatest of all the messages of love, "God so loved the world that he gave his only begotten Son," and "Christ also hath loved us and hath given himself for us." All other ideas of love grow pale compared with such a sacrifice.

Though the birthdays of Washington and Lincoln are adequately celebrated in the public school, in the lives of both these statesmen we can bring out a spiritual note quite neglected in the public school.

PLANNING THE PROGRAM

The teacher who is thinking of the spiritual results in the lives of the pupils will celebrate many informal occasions in his own room, where they occur naturally and can be appreciated at each age level. Yet he will be glad to assemble with the rest of the Bible school a few times each year, on Children's Day, Rally and Promotion Day, and perhaps at Christmas. He realizes that these few times may afford motivation for growth in grace if rightly approached.

The children will readily appropriate his purpose when he explains to them that "many of the big people do not know how much we are learning about the Lord; many of our parents would like to visit our room, but it is not large enough, or they are busy at that hour, or they keep putting it off. But on one day in the year we all go upstairs and show them what we do on Sunday morning in our room. What have we been doing that you want to share with them? What have you enjoyed most?"

If the children themselves plan and work out a special program it will have lasting results for them as well as for their parents. The tendency toward pride and embarrassment will be negligible, for they will become so interested in sharing what has already had meaning for them that they will forget that they are the cynosure of many eyes.

In this type of program little if any outside drill will be needed, because the material is familiar. If part of a couple of Sunday sessions before Children's Day are reserved for going through the program as it will be presented time will not be wasted, for it will be repetition of the most vital things that have been taught. The children will be motivated to practice until they perfect both Scripture and songs.

Building a special program consists of a unified arrangement of regular activities. It can be made a really special day by letting the boys and girls explain objects of interest that have been used previously, as foreign dolls or flags or costumes for missionary themes, film slides or large pictures or models, or a flannelgraph story. Juniors enjoy giving one of the salvation object lessons that especially appealed to them, incorporating Scripture and correlated songs.

It is worth while to make Children's Day one to be long remembered because it is attractive to the children and built on the Word of God that He has promised to bless. It can be a day of special *spiritual* blessing to both children and parents.

After a group of Primaries were reminded by the superintendent of some of their outstanding experiences through the year, they chose to share with their friends for Children's Day their last unit, a missionary theme. Each Sunday for several weeks teachers or pupils had brought to church a foreign doll. They had discussed the distinctive manners and customs of that country, and as a group had composed a short story about each doll, incorporating a pertinent Scripture verse.

Various children practiced these stories in their own words; the stories were never written down, and therefore were not recited parrotlike. Only the week before the special day did the group choose the individuals who would take the parts. When Andy was sick on Children's Day Sunday, George easily took his place, because he too was very familiar with the story.

As the Primaries decided what else they would like to present, the superintendent wrote their ideas on the blackboard. They decided that a Bible story would be too nearly like the missionary stories, but that some Bible verses and songs would go well with the stories. A favorite song was rejected when the children realized that in so short a program everything should be about missions. They chose the last verses of Matthew to say together, with one child holding up at the right time attractive cards saying: ALL POWER, ALL NATIONS, ALL THINGS, and ALWAY.

Next they considered the order of their program. They preferred to sing together a song at the beginning and at the end. The first one urged Christians to "Go, Tell" the people of all lands; the second praised "Jesus, Our Saviour," the Saviour everyone needs.

Once the first week and twice the next the group practiced the program in this order. During the time when some of the children were telling the missionary stories, the others pretended to be the audience of parents and friends. At the end the latter made helpful suggestions as to ways of improving each part.

Before the last practice permanent parts were carefully chosen by the boys and girls themselves. As the stories were told this last time the audience took their chairs a good distance away at the back of the room so that those who spoke would be sure to speak loudly enough for them to hear every word.

Because many adults have seen only the "speaking pieces" type of program and do not understand our motives for the children, it may be wise to inform them of their part by way of announcement, either from the platform or in the printed bulletin. Otherwise, they may laugh and spoil the atmosphere that you have worked hard to create. You may say to the audience in introduction, "We have prepared this program not to entertain our friends, but to share with you the things that we regularly enjoy each Sunday morning in our own rooms. Won't you worship with us?" This announcement will help to put the adults in an attitude receptive to the gospel message which the children will present.

1. Think through how you would lead a group of children to plan and execute a special day program, using a unified arrangement of activities which already they have enjoyed. Anticipate their interest and preferences; be ready to suggest concrete materials. Outline two or three possible procedures and explain how to practice for the presentation to parents.
2. Work out (with a group of boys and girls) a beneficial way of celebrating Mother's Day or Easter in your own department.

OBSERVATION REPORT

One of the best ways to enrich one's teaching is to observe other teachers who are seriously giving themselves to helping children grow spiritually. Observe at least one department of the age you teach, and carefully fill out the following report. What kind of deportment should be expected of a visitor? When should one arrive? Can he take notes inconspicuously? Should he make known his purpose? How can he be one of the group without intruding?

Name of church ....
Address of church ....
Date of visit ....

Department visited ....
Number of pupils present ....
Number of teachers present ....

Answer the questions with specific illustrations.

1. What do you see in the room itself which is conducive to spiritual growth?
2. What features of the room show that it is a children's, not an adults', room?
3. Is there space enough for an activity program and privacy for classes?
4. Are there profitable presession activities from the minute the first child arrives?
5. Do the teachers reflect a warm love for Christ, and deep concern for the salvation and growth of the pupils?
6. Is the atmosphere reverent, expectant, and informal?
7. Do the teachers know and respect each child's personality?

8. Do the teachers stimulate pupil purposes and activity?
9. Is there a good balance between uniformity and variety in procedure?
10. Do the children sing joyously because they know the songs well and enter into the experience of the words?
11. Is prayer genuine communion of the children with God?
12. Is the Bible lesson approached from the children's needs and interests?
13. Does the Bible lesson make a difference in daily life, definitely and personally?
14. Are the pupils challenged to know and love and obey the Word of God?
15. Is the expressional work an integral part of the whole session?
16. Is all the material on the children's level of understanding?
17. Do all the materials and procedures further the aim of the lesson?
18. Is the department well organized, with a place for everyone and everything?
19. Is there enough change of activity for growing muscles?
20. Is preparation adequate, with a feeling of confident leadership?
21. Do you feel that it is the children's rather than the teacher's session?
22. Are there any interruptions which might have been avoided?
23. Is every minute of the session made to count for eternity?

NOTES

1. Andrew Murray, *The Spirit of Christ* (London: Misbet and Co., 1888), pp. 204-206.

2. Frederic Sondern, Jr., "Thousand-Year Reich," *Reader's Digest,* September, 1939, p. 50.

3. Antoinette Lamoreaux, *The Unfolding Life* (Chicago: The Religious Publishing Co., 1907), p. 94.

4. The Interdenominational Bureau of Architecture, *Building and Equipment for Christian Education,* Service Bulletin No. 8 (Revised; New York: The Interdenominational Bureau of Architecture, 1944), p. 18.

5. Emma Mott Whittemore, *Mother Whittemore's Modern Miracles* (Toronto: Missions of Biblical Education, 1931), pp. 139-41.

6. Lamoreaux, *op. cit.,* p. 110.

7. G. F. Barbour, *The Life of Alexander Whyte* (New York: George H. Doran, 1923), p. 272.

8. William J. Johnstone, *How Lincoln Prayed* (New York: The Abingdon Press, 1931), pp. 59-61.

9. Amy Carmichael, *Kohila* (London: Society for the Promotion of Christian Knowledge, 1939), p. 69.

10. Margaret A. Yoder, *A Study of the Nature and Criteria of Regeneration* (Unpublished Master's thesis, Department of Christian Education, Wheaton College, 1939), pp. 69, 79, 142.

11. Lamoreaux, *op. cit.,* p. 83.

12. Carleton Washburne, *A Living Philosophy of Education* (New York: John Day Company, 1940), p. 359.

13. Lamoreaux, *op. cit.,* p. 28.

14. *Ibid.,* p. 30.

15. *Ibid.*, pp. 34, 35.

16. James J. Ellis, *John Wesley* (New York: Fleming H. Revell Co., 1891), pp. 15-18.

17. Carmichael, *op. cit.*, p. 53.

18. Margaret T. Applegarth, *Missionary Stories for Little Folks.* First Series: Primary (New York: Harper & Bros., 1917), pp. 20-26.

19. George Stoddard and Beth Wellman, *Child Psychology* (New York: Macmillan Co., 1938), p. 283.

20. Raymond Frame, "Honan Audiences," *Young China*, February, 1937, pp. 18, 19.

21. From a personal letter written to A. F. Gaylord on February 12, 1941.

22. Raymond H. Huse, *The Soul of a Child* (New York: Eaton and Mains, 1914), p. 121.

23. Adapted from Gipsy Smith, *Gipsy Smith* (New York: Fleming H. Revell, 1902), pp. 27-35.

24. Carmichael, *op. cit.*, p. 28.

25. Ira D. Sankey, *My Life and the Story of the Gospel Hymns* (New York: Harper & Bros., 1906), pp. 199-200.

26. W. R. Siegart, *He Started from Nowhere* (Philadelphia: United Lutheran Publication House, 1940), p. 185.

27. Frances Weld Danielson, *Lessons for Teachers of Beginners* (Boston: Pilgrim Press, 1914), p. 146.

BIBLIOGRAPHY

The following books in 1951 seem to be the most helpful for teachers of children. They include all types of books—inspirational and informational, secular and religious and Christian, books for popular reading as well as texts. It is regretted that not many works in the field may be wholeheartedly recommended. An excellent project for a group of children's workers would be for each of them to take one of these books, to inform the others as to the type of contribution it makes to their teaching, and to read selected excerpts for appreciation or discussion. Alert teachers will keep adding to this list those that they find practical.

The volumes which are starred might be the best for new teachers to read first as general introduction to an area of interest.

SECULAR

Understanding Children

Beverly, Bert I. *In Defense of Children.* New York: John Day Co., 1941.

Dixon, C. Madeleine. *Children Are Like That.* New York: John Day Co., 1930.

Dixon, C. Madeleine. *High, Wide and Deep.* New York: John Day Co., 1938.

Gesell, A. L., *et al. Infant and Child in the Culture of Today.* New York: Harper & Bros., 1943.

Gesell, A. L., and Ilg. *The Child from Five to Ten.* New York: Harper & Bros., 1946.

Hohman, Leslie B. *As the Twig Is Bent*. New York: Macmillan Co., 1940.

Leonard, E., Miles, L., and VanderKar, G. *The Child at Home and School*. New York: American Book Co., 1942.

Reynolds, Martha May. *Children from Seed to Saplings*. New York: McGraw-Hill Book Co., 1939.

Runbeck, Margaret Lee. *Our Miss Boo*. New York: D. Appleton-Century Co., 1942.

*Strang, Ruth. *An Introduction to Child Study*. New York: Macmillan Co., 1937.

U. S. Children's Bureau. *Your Child from One to Six*. Washington: Department of Labor, 1945.

Washburn, Ruth W. *Children Have Their Reasons*. New York: D. Appleton-Century Co., 1942.

Weill, Blanche. *Through Children's Eyes*. New York: Island Workshop Press, 1940.

Woodcock, Louise P. *Life and Ways of the Two-Year-Old*. New York: E. P. Dutton and Co., 1941.

Educational Method

Blatz, William, and Bott, Helen. *The Management of Young Children*. New York: William Morrow and Co., 1930.

Caswell, Hollis L. *Education in the Elementary School*. New York: American Book Co., 1942.

*Saucier, W. A. *Theory and Practice in the Elementary School*. New York: Macmillan Co., 1941.

Westcott (Wieman), Regina. *Does Your Child Obey?* New York: Harper & Bros., 1943.

RELIGIOUS

Teaching Method in General

Benson, C. H. *An Introduction to Child Study*. Chicago: Moody Press, 1927.

BIBLIOGRAPHY

Berkeley, J. P. *You Can Teach*. Philadelphia: American Baptist Publication Society, 1941.

Bowman, Atha S. *You Can Do It*. Philadelphia: Judson Press, 1943.

Caldwell, Irene. *Our Concern Is Children*. Anderson, Ind.: Warner Press, 1948.

Carmichael, Amy Wilson. *Kohila*. London: Society for the Promotion of Christian Knowledge, 1939.

Carmichael, Amy Wilson. *Lotus Buds*. London: Society for the Promotion of Christian Knowledge, 1923.

Conover, E. M. *Church School and Parish House Building*. Chicago: International Council of Religious Education and Interdenominational Bureau of Architecture, 1949.

Jones, Mary Alice. *The Church and the Children*. Nashville: Cokesbury Press, 1935.

Lamoreaux, Antoinette. *The Unfolding Life*. Chicago: Religious Publishing Co., 1907.

Moss, Sallie. *Give Your Child a Chance*. Nashville: Broadman Press, 1938.

Odell, Mary C. *Our Family Grows Toward God*. Nashville: Cokesbury Press, 1949.

Odell, Mary C. *Our Little Child Faces Life*. Nashville: Cokesbury Press, 1939.

Plummer, L. Flora. *The Soul Winning Teacher*. New York: Fleming H. Revell Co., 1934.

Rogers, William L., and Vieth, Paul H. *Visual Aids in the Church*. Philadelphia: Christian Education Press, 1946.

Smith, Irene. *Solving Church School Problems*. Anderson, Ind.: Warner Press, 1944.

Thorburn, Marjorie. *The Spirit of the Child*. London: George Allen and Unwin Limited, 1946.

*Trent, Robbie. *Your Child and God*. New York: Harper & Bros., 1941.

Vieth, Paul H., editor. The Church and Christian Education. St. Louis: Bethany Press, 1945.

Vieth, Paul H. *Improving Your Sunday School*. Philadelphia: Westminster Press, 1938.

Vieth, Paul H. *Teaching for Christian Living*. St. Louis: Bethany Press, 1929.

Whitehouse, E. S. *Opening the Bible to Children*. St. Louis: Bethany Press, 1945.

Storytelling

Association for Childhood Education. *Storytelling*. Washington: Association for Childhood Education, 1942.

Bailey, Carolyn S. *For the Story Teller*. Springfield: Milton Bradley Co., 1913.

Bryant, Sara Cone. *How to Tell Stories to Children*. New York: Houghton, Mifflin and Co., 1905.

Cather, K. D. *Religious Education Through Story-Telling*. New York: Abingdon Press, 1925.

Cather, K. D. *Story-Telling for Teachers of Beginners and Primaries*. New York: Methodist Book Concern, 1921.

*Danielson, Frances W. *The Practice Story-Telling Class*. Boston: Pilgrim Press, 1930.

Sawyer, Ruth. *Way of the Storyteller*. New York: Viking Press, 1942.

Shedlock, Marie. *The Art of the Story Teller*. New York: D. Appleton-Century Co., 1936.

Worship

Baker, Edna Dean. *The Worship of the Little Child*. Nashville: Cokesbury Press, 1927.

Blashfield, Clara. *Worship Training for Primary Children*. New York: Methodist Book Concern, 1929.

Jones, Mary Alice. *Training Juniors in Worship*. Nashville, Cokesbury Press, 1925.

McDormand, T. B. *The Art of Building Worship Services*. Nashville: Broadman Press, 1942.

*Martin, A. W. *Worship in the Sunday School*. Nashville: Cokesbury Press, 1930.

Powell, Marie C. *Guiding the Experience of Worship*. New York: Methodist Book Concern, 1935.

Shield, E. M. *Music in the Religious Growth of Children.* New York: Abingdon-Cokesbury Press, 1943.

Cradle Roll

Groves, E. R. *Christianity and the Family.* New York: Macmillan Co., 1942.

Leavell, Martha. *Building a Christian Home.* Nashville: Broadman Press, 1936.

Lynch, Ella F. *Bookless Lessons for the Teacher Mother.* Philadelphia: Peter Reilly Co., 1931.

*Von Hagen, E. W. *The Cradle Roll Department of the Sunday School.* Nashville: Broadman Press, 1947.

Nursery Class

Carlson, Jessie. *Guiding Children in the Nursery Class.* Philadelphia: American Baptist Publication Society, 1948.

Jones, Orabelle. *The Nursery Department of the Sunday School.* Nashville: Broadman Press, 1946.

*LeBar, Mary E. *Patty Goes to the Nursery Class.* Chicago: Scripture Press, 1945.

Lloyd, Edna Dean. *Religious Nurture in Nursery Class and Home.* Nashville: Methodist Publishing House, 1943.

McCallum, Eva B. *Learning in the Nursery Class.* St. Louis: Bethany Press, 1944.

Beginner Department

*Hargis, Pauline, *et al. Teaching the Beginner Child.* Nashville: Broadman Press, 1948.

Shields, E. M. *Guiding Kindergarten Children in the Church School.* Richmond: Onward Press, 1931.

Strickland, H. N., and Leatherwood, Mattie. *Beginner Sunday School Work.* Nashville: Broadman Press, 1943.

Primary Department

Bryan, Allene. *Primary Sunday School Work.* Nashville: Broadman Press, 1941.

Lewis, Hazel. *The Primary Church School.* St. Louis: Bethany Press, 1932.

*Pettey, Emma. *Guiding the Primary Child in the Sunday School.* Nashville: Broadman Press, 1936.

Smither, Ethel. *Primary Children Learn at Church.* New York: Abingdon-Cokesbury Press, 1944.

Junior Department

Allen, Hattie Bell. *Living for Jesus: Stewardship for Juniors.* Nashville: Broadman Press, 1939.

Creasman, Myrtle. *Working with Juniors.* Nashville: Broadman Press, 1925.

Eakin, Mildred. *Teaching Junior Boys and Girls.* New York: Methodist Book Concern, 1934.

Lambdin, Ina. *The Junior Leadership Manual.* Nashville: Broadman Press, 1923.

Linthicum, Blanche. *Junior Sunday School Work.* Nashville: Broadman Press, 1941.

*Looney, M. O. *Guiding Junior Boys and Girls in the Sunday School.* Nashville: Broadman Press, 1936.

Roop, G. A. *The Junior and His Church.* Nashville: Broadman Press, 1937.

Smith, Una R. *The Junior Department of the Church School.* Nashville: Cokesbury Press, 1934.